SOCIETY, STATE AND SCHOOLING

Readings on the Possibilities for Radical Education

Edited and introduced by
Michael Young
and Geoff Whitty

 The Falmer Press

First published 1977

ISBN 0 905273 02 8   cased

ISBN 0 905273 01 X   paper

Printed by BILLING & SONS LIMITED
Guildford, Surrey
for
THE FALMER PRESS
Broome House
Delves Close
Ringmer
BN8 5JW

Made in England

Contents

Introduction: Perspectives on Education and Society

Michael Young and Geoff Whitty

FROM ACCESS TO IDEOLOGY

One of the most striking features of the world of education in the 1970s, compared with that of only ten years ago, is the sudden disappearance of the overwhelming assumption that schooling is a 'good thing'. Even more striking is the way in which many of those who consider themselves to be on the Left in politics have begun to take seriously - in larger numbers than at any time since the 1870 Education Act - the suggestion that compulsory schooling for all children may not be a 'good thing', and indeed may be counter-productive for the realization of their political ideals. A hundred years ago there were substantial doubts amongst those on the Right about the wisdom of compulsory education, (on the ground that too much knowledge might breed revolution), but most of these doubts were soon allayed by the recognition of the role schooling could play in 'gentling the masses'. In other words, the Right were rather quicker than the Left in realizing that the so-called 'education' which was granted to the working classes could be as much a process of domestication as of liberation. For many years the reformist wing in British politics, whether liberal, socialist or even Marxist in inclination, has tended to blur any distinctions between education and schooling, and treat the extension of compulsory state education as unambiguously offering the potential for a just society.

The prevailing faith in the school system amongst many who would regard themselves as radicals, resulted partly from a failure to analyse critically the concepts of 'education' and 'society' with which they were operating. In a context where there was so much obviously wrong with the educational system in terms of its unfairness to working-class children, there was little

incentive to look beyond the reform of its surface
features for a solution. Thus policy-makers - particularly those in Labour administrations - and their
academic advisers, have been obsessed during the past
thirty years or so with the problem of working-class
failure at school. Deficiencies in the system of education have been seen to lie in its failure to provide
'equality of opportunity' and sufficient paths to upward
social mobility. When, during the fifties and sixties,
a whole variety of statistical studies made it clear
that, in this respect, the 1944 Education Act was not
working as 'fairly' as had been hoped, their main concern was (not unnaturally) to discover ways of enabling
more working-class children to succeed at school, i.e.
to obtain access to grammar school-type education,
institutions of higher education and ultimately high-
status occupations.

The 'functional' necessity of a society stratified
into occupations of different status and rewards was a
subject of considerable debate by sociological
'theorists' in the 1960s, though these debates were
firmly restricted to a highly general and abstract conception of theory. Sociologists of education remained
content to accept the necessity of a hierarchy of occupations, and to concentrate on questions about the extent of social mobility within such stratified societies.
The more conservative features of functional analysis
were alleviated by the conscience of Fabian socialism,
but essentially the quest for 'equality of educational
opportunity' seemed designed not to create a more egalitarian society, merely to facilitate the 'rise of the
meritocracy'. This 'social democratic' view of equality
conceived of the possibility of replacing a society in
which parental occupation played a dominant part in a
child's educational or occupational destiny, with one
in which such destinies were decided on some idea of
individual merit and talent. Halsey (1975), a sociologist most of whose work has been concerned with identifying and overcoming inequalities, put it this way:

> Institutions of scholarly elitism can only be recon-
> ciled to an egalitarian age if teachers and students
> enter exclusively on the test of academic merit ...
> selection of the elite would ... be substantively as
> well as formally open to all the classes, all the
> races and all the sexes.

It is not, in this view, a question of abolishing classes,
but of making access to classes more genuinely 'open' to
each generation of competitors.

Few social scientists seem to have considered the suggestion that prevailing definitions of 'merit' were sufficiently class-biased to ensure that 'equality of opportunity' would remain a sham, while even fewer were prepared to entertain any more radical concept of equality. Existing definitions of education were treated equally uncritically - it was both a 'good' in itself, and a means towards that other unquestioned 'good', social mobility. The predominantly Fabian outlook of the researchers found a receptive audience amongst politicians concerned to feed our ailing economy with more skilled manpower. Thus, the primary obsession of educational policy for over twenty years was with finding ways of reorganizing the system in such a way as to provide access and opportunity for upward social mobility for those denied it hitherto. Though it was never expressed as crudely as by the American educationists described by Callahan (1962), talent, from the Crowther Report of 1959 onwards, was viewed as an untapped natural resource to be exploited and converted into a productive force of skilled labour. Social justice and economic growth were seen as inseparable, and education was regarded, by sociologists and politicians alike, as the major route to personal and national salvation.

It nevertheless became increasingly clear that the number of upwardly mobile working-class children remained small, and that the educational success rates of working-class children were not rising significantly. Beginning with Early Leaving (C.A.C.E., 1954), report after report documented the failure of educational reforms to have more than a marginal effect on the distribution of educational success between different social class groups. Not surprisingly, sociologists focused their attention on social class, and it became almost the hallmark of sociology of education in both teaching and research, that social class was treated as the crucial explanatory category. However, class was not seen as a relation, pointing to conflicts and contradictions between classes, which might be expressed, in the context of education, in the varieties of resistance to school by working-class children (non-cooperation, truancy and destruction of material goods). Certainly 'low' social class was rarely treated as a source of desirable cultural identity. Rather, class was seen as a position on a hierarchical scale of attributes, measured in terms of parental occupation, usually simplified into a distinction between manual and non-manual work. The researchers then set out to show which measurable attributes of those lowest on the scale, the children of unskilled manual workers, had a 'detrimental' effect on school

performance. The problem became to identify correlations between cultural features of working-class life
and failure at school - factors which then became
'deficiencies' for which educational policy-makers
attempted to devise programmes of compensation. Nursery
education, language enrichment programmes, comprehensive
schooling, ROSLA and non-streaming can all be seen as
policies which attempt to remedy deficiencies in home
background by exposing children to more education and
more 'desirable' influences. The organizational structure of education has been changed in successive attempts
to provide more people with the education which reformist researchers and politicians regarded as, without
question, a 'good thing'. The weakness of this position
has only slowly become apparent as one organizational
innovation, along with its inevitable sloganizing, has
swiftly followed another. Neither the American experience, nor our own, has so far suggested that any of
these innovations have made much impact on the figures
which relate school achievement to social class background. The correlations have remained remarkably
consistent over time.

The failures of these policies have provided a golden
opportunity for the political Right to return to their
beloved themes of elitism, standards and tradition. In
the USA, the crude and ethnocentric explanations of the
failure of educational reform expressed in the work of
Jensen, Herrnstein and Shockley (see Kamin, 1974), and
paralleled to some extent in Eysenck's work here, have
generated renewed support for racist educational policies. Of more significance in this country has been
the call for a return to traditional standards of morality and excellence, an emphasis on didactic teaching
and public accountability of schools and the preservation of selective and independent schools. This view
is best articulated in the Black Paper critiques of contemporary educational trends (e.g. Cox and Dyson, 1971).
These arguments are presented, plausibly enough, not as
the protecting of the interests of the few (which they
are), but as the only basis of a just society for all.
Their appeal has a far deeper significance than as an
expression of the political rhetoric of the far-Right
which has been largely missed by those unable to stand
outside the increasingly unreal liberal consensus that
characterizes most academic theorizing about education.
The plausibility of the 'return to old standards' is
easy enough for educational 'theorists' to dismiss with
their well intentioned progressiveness. But to teachers
and parents confronted with little understood 'new
methods' and secondary reorganization, often imposed

without their active cooperation, and without the resources that might make the new arrangements viable,
such pleas have the merit of appearing to offer a solution to the gradual breakdown of what they had generally
recognized school to be about. Yet, what is surprising,
in a way that points to the failure of the Left to
develop any coherent critique of education in contemporary capitalist society, is that a number of these
views are espoused and defended by those with radically
different political commitments. Even for the Marxists
of the British Communist Party the problem, as with
Halsey's 'egalitarian elitism', is one of access, not
ideology. The problem of class in British education is
for them that working-class children are denied what
'our best schools offer'. In other words, like the
'social democratic' ideology that goes back to Tawney,
class injustice is seen purely in terms of unequal
opportunities, and the practical problem of how you abstract out socialist 'elements' from what have historically been created as bourgeois institutions is hardly
considered. This view is optimistic about what 'good
teaching' (conventionally conceived) can do, and it
presents an emphasis on standards, hierarchies and established procedures as politically 'radical' in that it
is seen as enhancing the opportunities of working-class
children to succeed. Thus, the superficially unlikely
alignments between conservative educationalists, such as
Rhodes Boyson, and the Communist leadership within the
National Union of Teachers become less surprising. For
those on the Right, the potential embarrassment of having
such allies in their assault on alternative conceptions
of education must be far outweighed by their recognition
of who will benefit if their campaign succeeds.

It is clear from what has been said so far, that many
of those committed to some form of social change, as
well as those consciously committed to preserving the
status quo, have adopted modes of social analysis and
social policy which, by their narrowness of vision, have
concentrated on tinkering with what 'is'. The social
democratic policy of increasing 'equality of opportunity'
by changing the organizational structures of education
has, we have suggested, had the support of old-Left
communists who envisage that a better 'educated' proletariat would have a better chance of transforming the
nature of society. In practice, however, the few
working-class pupils who succeed in schools are put
under considerable pressure to embrace the cultural and
political values of existing elites, while organizational
changes, designed to promote more efficient 'schooling',
sometimes seem more likely to educate the population

into accepting a class society than to enable the working-class to transform it.   Neither the old-Left, nor
the Fabian social democrats, seem to take seriously the
suggestion that the educational policies they support
merely provide more efficient means of maintaining the
status quo.   Certainly neither group seems to have recognized that we need to examine 'what counts as education', and thus the way in which prevailing definitions
of it sustain just that form of society which those on
the Left, albeit in varying degrees, wish to change.

This is not just a problem for radical or socialist
theorizing about education;   it raises, we think, more
fundamental questions about the ways in which Marxist
and social democratic traditions of theorizing have
developed.   The adherence of both groups to positivistic
modes of analysis has, as Arblaster (1975) has suggested,
limited the possibilities for both envisaging and realizing alternatives.   He argues that:

> It is necessary that ... criticism should be extended
> even to such apparently neutral, common ground as the
> concepts of science, fact, objectivity and rational-
> ity.   The willingness of both revolutionary Marxists
> and social democrats simply to inherit the bourgeois
> forms of these concepts and incorporate them into
> their own thinking has done great damage to socialism.
> Hence the effort to develop new and radical ways of
> thought in this area is a political as well as a
> philosophical necessity.

What is equally urgent is that such criticism should be
extended to the concept of 'education', and what is surprising is the extent to which the Left has been
uncritical of the ideological import of the schooling to
which they have looked for major contributions to social
change.

Outside the mainstream organizations of the political
Left, this tendency to accept the institutionalized
categories of education and science has come in for considerable criticism in recent years.   The new-Left and
the student movements of the sixties re-emphasized the
importance of criticizing the ideological dimensions of
education, though their hopes of transforming the cultural climate of the universities and of society at
large proved premature.   Their ideas and their example
nevertheless have had a considerable influence upon the
way in which relationships between school and society
have been conceptualized, and many theorists, including
some whose work is considered in this volume, have come

to look for obstacles to social change not so much in
terms of the extent of 'access' to schooling, as in
terms of its ideological dimensions. This is not to
deny that the inequalities and injustices that the emphasis on 'access' highlight do not persist and remain
important. The recent attempts to explore regional
differences in the allocation of resources (Byrne and
Williamson, 1975) are likely to be more rather than
less significant as overall resources are reduced.
What we would argue is that to separate out questions
of access and distribution from consideration of what
access is to, what is distributed, and who are involved
in these processes, is to limit both sociological analysis and possible alternative practices to questions of
administration. In neglecting the cultural significance of the content of education, such studies lay
themselves open to the criticism that there is a sense
in which they are not about education at all.

It is interesting that theorists of the political
Right in this country have recognized the importance of
the cultural content of education for much longer than
those of the Left, with the notable exception of Raymond
Williams (1961). Thus, in an article otherwise critical
of recent work in the sociology of education, Bantock
(1973) writes that 'after so much of the organizational
nonsense which has been preached during the last fifteen
years' it is a relief 'that at long last there seems to
be a chance we shall come to see that the basic educational dilemma of our time is a cultural one and affects
the nature of the meanings to be transmitted by the
school'. Here Bantock is referring to developments
within the sociology of education in which the tendency
to attribute the class differentials in educational
achievement to the 'detrimental' effects of working-class
culture has come in for some critical scrutiny. Analysis has shifted away from the supposed deficiencies in
children's home backgrounds to a consideration of the
very nature of the 'education' as carried out in schools
(Keddie, 1973). Studies of what happens to pupils in
school and the nature of the curriculum to which they
are exposed are beginning to be given more significance
than the sort of input-output analyses which until recently constituted the bulk of work within this field.
Unfortunately, however, many of these studies about the
minutiae of classroom interaction, or analyses of the
assumptions underlying prevailing definitions of curricular knowledge, seem to present education as being
carried on in a social vacuum, and whilst they often
tell us a great deal about 'how' schools perpetuate

social inequalities, their failure to discuss 'why' this
may be so helps to obscure the difficulties of change.
In other words, while the sociology of education has
increasingly focused upon 'cultural' aspects of schooling, it has failed to locate them in their broader
historical and political contexts. Thus we can see
certain parallels between the theoretical and political
'radicalism' of the 'new' sociologists, and the theoretical and political conservatism of Bantock. Both
display the typically 'idealist' educationist's tendency
to separate out cultural meanings from their material
base, and thereby give them some kind of autonomous life
of their own. Whilst agreeing that our educational dilemmas are about culture and meanings, we would argue
that these dilemmas are not separable from the political
and economic struggles of which such meanings are an
expression. It is the failure to recognize this that
makes the recent debate concerning cultural 'deficit'
and cultural 'difference' theories of educational failure little more than a scholastic exercise - for
'differences' only take on their hierarchical significance in specific historical and political contexts.
Nevertheless, this focus on the cultural content of
education as part of a more adequate theory of ideology
will be a crucial element in any understanding of the
relationship between school and society.

EDUCATION AS DETERMINED OR DETERMINING?

The recognition that there is an ideological dimension to the way in which schooling helps to reproduce
society, important as it is, does not necessarily help
us to clarify the nature of the relationship between
school and society, or to decide upon strategically
appropriate contexts for action. The traditions of radical theorizing discussed in the papers of section one
of this book - which (with inevitable over-simplifica-
tions) we shall call the 'new' sociology of education,
'deschooling' and Althusserian Marxism - illustrate this
clearly. All point valuably to some of the basic weaknesses in the social-democratic or Fabian model of
'access' to which we referred earlier, and all are
critical of most contemporary educational theory and
practice as, in different ways, ideological and mystifying. At the same time, each of them by emphasizing a
particular aspect of the relationship between schooling
and society ends up either by obscuring any possibility
of alternative educational practice, or by seeming to
elevate a particular strategy of change to an absolute.

Thus, Althusser's characterization of schools as part
of the Ideological State Apparatus is often taken to
suggest that any teacher working for radical change
within the school system faces overwhelming odds, whilst
a number of exponents of the so-called 'new' sociology
of education have argued that a recognition that the
curriculum is a social construction could initiate
change in schools with wide-ranging social consequences.
Illich seems to share some of Althusser's pessimism about the possibilities for change within schools whilst
being optimistic about the possibility that education
can be deschooled and a non-elitist form of social organization developed. The readings in this volume
have been selected for the contribution they make to a
critical examination of the common ground between these
various perspectives and to the development of theories
on which more realistic strategies of educational and
social change might be based.

Educational theories of the kind considered in section one have gained considerable influence within the
sociology of education as the limitations of earlier
traditions of theorizing have been exposed. However,
if, as is often argued, the mainstream or traditional
sociology of education which we discussed earlier in
this introduction bore a close affinity to the concerns
of administrators and policy-makers, these more recent
developments have remained largely within the confines of
the academy. Although 'in theory' often challenging the
ideas of policy-makers and classroom teachers (and, in
the case of the 'new' sociology, claiming 'relevance'
to teachers), these theories have probably been most
influential amongst academic sociologists or educationists and their students. It is therefore scarcely surprising that these sociological accounts of the relationship between school and society are often attacked by
others as simplistic and irrelevant to the 'real'
world of education. Thus, for instance, Max Morris
(1975), the Communist ex-President of the NUT, recently
attacked 'trendy sociologists' for taking up one of two
diametrically opposed positions - either that 'education
reflects society' and schools are 'cogs in a capitalist
machine' simply confirming the status quo; or, alternatively, that schools could be revolutionary agents,
'main media for changing society'. While it is difficult to agree that sociological theories are quite as
simplistic as that, the criticism is a telling one and
one which is echoed in the contributions to section one.
At the same time, we would argue that, however misconceived, the dichotomous views of the school determined

by society and schools determining society are not just aberrations of sociologists but a pervasive force throughout educational theory and practice.

Discussions of the relationship between schooling and the wider society seem to oscillate violently between positions which characterize education as either 'determined' or 'determining'. In the first of these models, schools are presented as nothing but the reflection of the wider society, responding to the demands of social structure, the economy and its associated technology. Education is the dependent variable and teachers but puppets of the social system. The function of the school is to reproduce individuals in the form most suited to the wider demands of society, and the determining forces in such a model imply that any attempt to deviate from such demands is virtually impossible and certainly bound to be short lived. Though somewhat of an oversimplification this is, in essence, the account of Althusser's theory presented in the paper by Erben and Gleeson.

In the opposite model, in which education is viewed as 'determining', it is suggested that social structure, being made up of people, can only be sustained in a particular form as long as people continue to act in a manner which gives it that form. Social structure is changed by those who make it up, and hence education and the curriculum, as powerful socializing influences on the young, can change the wider society. Rather than educational change being seen as the mere product of wider social changes, changes in school practice, e.g. the introduction of non-competitive modes of working, produce changes of consciousness in the young which ultimately have wider social consequences.

Certainly, these dichotomous modes of theorizing have been significant features of recent work in the sociology of education, but they are also a common feature of the way teachers and others think about education. The tendency to theorize in a non-dialectical manner, and the problems of specifying the nature of the linkages between school and society, is perhaps a feature of the non-relational mode of thinking which Hextall and Sarup discuss in their paper, and which Ollman (1971) has identified as a prevailing feature of modern western thought. Thus, although Morris makes an important criticism, his attempt to dismiss the problem as the creation of 'trendy sociologists', which would disappear if teachers were left to get on with their job, is equally simplistic.

An unquestioning faith in the power of education to
change society has over many years motivated radicals
to enter teaching. On the other hand, few large comprehensive schools can be without their staffroom
equivalent of Skates in James Herndon's The Way It
Spozed To Be who tells Herndon:

> You've got to wait, Jim! You got to wait for the
> revolution! Socialism! This isn't a school! It's
> a place where those kids can find out once and for
> all what they're up against, where the ruling class
> says in no uncertain terms to them, 'Forget you!
> You ain't going nowhere! Go on and learn to tap-
> dance or be a jitney girl, because you ain't going
> nowhere!'
> But you, Jim, you got to live. You got your wife -
> your wife, Jim, who makes that soup on those cold
> evenings, that beautiful kid. You got to put those
> paragraphs on the board for them to copy as long as
> they'll still do it. You've got no real union here,
> you're alone in there, between the victims and the
> exploiters ...

While this position - that schools will only be different after the Revolution has wrought changes in the
reorganization of society - has an academic equivalent
in a crude mechanistic Marxism, it is probably a stance
which emerged from the situation in which Skates found
himself:

> I could never tell if Skates was serious about the
> revolution or not. In the end I thought he had
> believed in it once, didn't see any chance for it
> now, but continued talking in terms of it anyway.
> It was, in a sense, a useful way of interpreting
> things...

It seems likely, then, that rather than being merely
'webs' spun by educational theorists, these dichotomous
theories are different responses to the contradictions
which constitute the social context of schooling. Like
other dichotomies, such as that between individual and
society, this is not just a feature of academic social
theorizing but of the theorizing of teachers and educational policy-makers as well, and therefore of the
circumstances those concerned with change must confront.
What is needed is an attempt to locate this dichotomous
thinking as a form of consciousness which is an expression of particular historical sets of social relations. In the specific case of school and society, we

can view their separation as based in the institutional
separation of work from education, a separation the
interdependence of which we can only understand in terms
of the historical development of monopoly capitalism.
Only in society in which 'theory' is institutionalized
as separate from practice, and in which thought itself
is separated from action, can abstract categories such
as 'determined' and 'determining' counterpose each other
as opposites. In accepting them as such, rather than
trying to formulate them relationally, we accept an
ideology, in the sense that they present an appearance
`(or a particular experience of educationists) as reality.
A relational approach would involve seeking the conditions in which such abstract opposites can be transcended as the real separations of the material world are
transcended.

Equally, it is in the attempt to analyse and transform the contradictory character of educational practice
that we discover both the possibilities of change in
schools and the limits to them. As the contributors to
section two make clear, the many contradictions which
confront teachers and pupils can also provide the
'space' for practical action for change. But change does
not just happen as evolutionary (and many revolutionary)
theorists suppose, it is made by people and, in relation
to the concerns of this book, by teachers and pupils
who recognize that their actions can only become radical
when they realize the interrelations of what they do
with wider political and economic struggles. However,
to recognize the dual character of the relationship between school and society is only an advance if it can
be exposed in the context of particular concrete struggles. It does not necessarily take us very far to argue
that the relationship is a dialectical one unless we
explore further the nature of that dialectic. Morris
(1975) himself argued that the true relationship was one
in which education had to reflect in its structure and
content the society of which it was a part. The key
point, for Morris, was that social needs were never
static and so new demands were constantly being placed
by society on the schools. 'There is a constant process
of interaction between schools and people in the social
context' and 'to deny totally the effect of schooling is
to know little about either children or society'. The
problem with arguments like Morris's is that beyond a
superficial reasonableness, they are little more than
a rather naive kind of social Darwinism or evolutionism,
in which 'society', which is never specified, has needs
which are constantly changing, for no apparent reason,
and to which schools harmoniously 'adapt' (though we

never know how or why). In Morris's case this evolutionary model, which is made much more explicit by
Levitas (1974), associates changing needs somehow with
the rising demands of the proletariat which sooner or
later will achieve state power. Then, for these writers,
history or evolution appears to end, except as a kind
of metaphysic, as in the Soviet Union, where, it would
be argued, society's needs are the proletariat's needs
and the struggle is over. Leaving aside the question of
their inadequacy as accounts of Soviet society, versions
of Marxism such as those espoused by Morris and Levitas
seem peculiarly inappropriate for describing the conflicts and struggles over popular demands for education
in the last century, and the struggles within education
and outside it which must take place if they are to be
realized.

The attempt to overcome simplistic dichotomies, and
in particular to resolve the determining/determined
alternatives by equally simplistic combinations of the
two, as in Morris's example, are paralleled by recent
functionalist and phenomenological formulations of the
dialectic process. In these, as Swingewood (1975)
points out, the dialectic is equated with reciprocity
and interdependence, losing the historical and practical
characteristics that were the particular features of
Marx's own writing. In relation to the specific problems of those working for change in education, it is our
intention in this book to bring out the crucial importance of these elements in any critical theory. In
section one we seek to show how such elements are obscured in theories which through other weaknesses become
justifications for, at best, irrelevant or impractical
strategies, and, at worst, the kind of idealism which
can only lead to pessimism and inaction. From this
analysis, we take up in section two the themes of histor-
icity, contradiction and interrelatedness of educational
and other practices, and point to the kind of critical
theory which might develop from such themes. None of
the pieces in this section successfully embraces all
these themes, but together they serve to indicate
something of the scope which a critical theory would
entail. Finally, in section three, we take up the
fundamental point made by Brian Fay (1975) in distinguishing critical from traditional theory, that:

> the translation of social science into practice would
> necessarily require the participation of and active
> involvement of the social actors themselves ... (as)
> its theories can only be validated in the self

understandings of the actors involved.

Thus, in this last section we introduce readings that
begin to explore, in the context of radical educational
change, the nature of such involvement and who concretely
the social actors might be.

REFERENCES

ARBLASTER, A. (1975) Socialism and the idea of science,
in B. Parekh The Concept of Socialism London: Croom
Helm.

BANTOCK, G. H. (1973) Are we in the wrong struggle?
The Times Educational Supplement 5th October 1973.

BYRNE, D. and WILLIAMSON, B. (1975) The Poverty of
Education London: Martin Robertson.

C.A.C.E. (1954) Early Leaving Report of the Central
Advisory Council for Education (England), London: HMSO.

CALLAHAN, R. (1962) Education and the Cult of Efficiency
Chicago: University of Chicago Press.

COX, C. B. and DYSON, A.E. (1971) Black Papers on
Education London: Davis - Poynter.

FAY, B. (1975) Social Theory and Political Practice
London: Allen and Unwin.

HALSEY, A. H. (1975) The real enemies: class, status
and power, The Times Higher Educational Supplement
24th November, 1975.

HERNDON, J. (1970) The Way It Spozed To Be London:
Pitman.

KAMIN, L. J. (1974) The Science and Politics of I.Q.
New York: John Wiley.

KEDDIE, N. (1973) Tinker, Tailor ... The Myth of
Cultural Deprivation Harmondsworth: Penguin Books.

LEVITAS, M. (1974) Marxist Perspectives in the Sociology of Education London: Routledge and Kegan Paul.

MORRIS, M. (1975) Speech reported in The Guardian 25th
July 1975.

OLLMAN, B. (1971) Alienation - Marx's Conception of Man
in Capitalist Society London: Cambridge University
Press.

SWINGEWOOD, A. (1975) Marx and Modern Social Theory
London: Macmillan.

WILLIAMS, R. (1961) The Long Revolution London: Chatto
and Windus.

1.0
Locating the Problem

Introduction

The failure of well-worn liberal educational policies
to create a significantly 'fairer' society, even within
the limited frame of reference of their supporters, has
helped to create a pervasive sense of crisis within the
world of education. As we argued in our introductory
paper, the failure of efforts to provide 'equality of
opportunity' or of 'compensatory education' to make a
major impact on the statistics of working-class failure,
has allowed the political Right to conclude with satisfaction that the vision of a different type of society
(whether meritocratic or egalitarian) was a chimera all
along. For those who desire change, however, the failure of such policies to be 'progressive', even in the
most limited sense of that term, has created an opportunity to reassess the validity of the analysis upon
which the earlier optimism was founded, without, at the
same time, abandoning their hopes for a different future.

The theories of liberals and social democrats proved
inadequate, we suggested, because they could not comprehend that the education to which they sought to widen
access might itself be involved in perpetuating the
inequalities they were concerned to overcome. Social
democratic writers in a variety of fields tended to obscure the nature of class, as an expression of a
relationship to the means of production, by their obsession with documenting the unequal distribution of
wealth in society, and by ranking groups in terms of
various measures of poverty. Likewise, education became
viewed as a quantifiable resource unequally distributed,
rather than a relation between people, their history,
and their environment. Such views of class and education did involve a theory of society as a totality, but
it was a totality in some sense given and external to
people, an instrument through which it would be possible,
in time, to realize what were seen as universal needs

and desires for justice and equality. Thus society was
separate from men and women's actions, who were limited
to responding to injustices with piecemeal adaptations.

The failure of social democratic policies to fulfil
their promises, and the theoretical inadequacy of the
theories underlying them, have not passed without comment from educational theorists. It is perhaps not
surprising that the early 1970s, a period of expansion
of investment in education, should have provided the
necessary 'autonomy' for the development of what on the
surface appeared to be potentially radical styles of
theorizing. The contention of the papers in this section is that in very different ways, each of these
styles of theorizing, despite pointing to a fundamental
weakness in the social democratic tradition, was itself
unable to transcend the particular problems that it had
identified. Just as social democratic theory focused
on inequality of access to education, so each 'new'
theory took a particular problem that had previously
been neglected. However, in treating their particular
critique as in some sense separable from the totality
of social relations in capitalist society, they fell
into the same trap as the traditions which they crit-
iqued. Through an examination of the partial character
of these 'radical' theories we attempt, in this section,
not just to identify problems in theories of education,
but to see these problems in relation to a need to grasp
the complex dynamics of capitalist society itself. A
major ideological force faced by those concerned with
radical change is the appearance of separateness, and
the emphasis on the particular or the general. Such
an ideology separates and reifies schooling, society,
the State and teachers, and precludes an understanding
of the relations between them which, if expressed concretely, might form the basis of strategies for change
within education and beyond.

Our contributors focus critically on three styles of
radical theorizing about education which all to some
extent owe their origins or their popularity to the
crisis of liberal thought and liberal policy. Each has
seemed on occasions to offer the sort of analysis which
could lead the sociology of education out of the cul-de-
sac into which the dominant traditions of educability
studies and organizational analyses have led it. Each
recognizes the weaknesses of those earlier traditions,
but each, we shall argue, is itself in danger of denying
the subtleties of the dialectical relationship between
school and society by concentrating attention on a
particular feature of that relationship. Each thus

provides an inadequate account of the current crisis,
and points towards an inadequate strategy for attaining
that egalitarian and liberated society which each in
its own way envisages.

The first of the approaches, discussed in the papers
by Whitty and Ahier, has come to be known as the 'new'
or 'new direction' sociology of education. It is
usually associated with the book Knowledge and Control
(Young, 1971) which was subtitled New Directions for the
Sociology of Education. It is often characterized as
a phenomenological or interpretive sociology of education, and most discussion of its strengths and weaknesses has centred around the papers by Young, Esland
and Keddie. These papers, and much of the subsequent
work in this genre, have made an important contribution
to our understanding of the process of education in
terms of the definitions of knowledge, ability, etc. with
which teachers and pupils operate in the school context.
The recognition that it is these taken-for-granted practices, and the hierarchical assumptions upon which they
are based, that in an important sense sustain social
order and reproduce the statistics of success and failure with which earlier studies were concerned, has stimulated a radical redirection of research towards (a)
classroom interaction studies and (b) studies of the
cultural assumptions underlying prevailing definitions
of school knowledge. Earlier work has thus often been
rejected by the new direction sociology as glossing the
educational process - interaction between teachers and
their pupils.

This stress on the importance of teachers' practices
and teachers' consciousness has sometimes led critics
(e.g. Simon, 1974) to term the new approach the 'blame
the teacher' school of sociology. At the same time,
it has led its more enthusiastic advocates (e.g. Gorbutt,
1972) to locate hopes for educational change with teachers reflecting upon the assumptions which underlie
their everyday practices and thus recognizing the
possibility of changing them. There is something of a
parallel within the field of curriculum studies, where
the realization that teachers have the power to resist
innovations in the classic Research, Development and
Dissemination mode has led to a celebration of the self-
critical researching teacher as a primary agent of
change (see Stenhouse, 1975). The paper by Whitty included here argues that the recognition that definitions
of knowledge, ability etc. are potentially changeable
must now be linked to an understanding of why and how
particular definitions do in fact prevail in the current

context of schooling. Whilst the 'new direction' sociology has generated a powerful critique of prevailing
educational assumptions and a reassertion of the significance of teachers' everyday practices, it has tended
to abstract schools and school knowledge from their
historical, political and economic contexts, and thus
to locate the current crisis and its solution within the
schools.

Ahier is even more severe on the work of the 'new
direction' sociologists. After welcoming the new-found
sociological interest in the curriculum for 'bringing
to the forefront ... the problem of ideology and the
functioning of the State in this respect', he argues
that their activities are likely to be 'of limited
value, at least for the development of a theorized
understanding of education in society'. Whilst the 'new'
sociology sees radical implications in a view of school
knowledge as constituted in sets of potentially changeable social relations, rather than expressions of agreed
truths, Ahier regards the debate with philosophers on
this issue as myopic and 'education-bound'. Esland's
analysis is thus seen to locate possibilities for action
'only within certain educational or professional confines', whilst Young (1971) is forced into believing
that if the prevailing social organization of knowledge
were upset 'there would be a massive redistribution of
the labels "education", "success", and "failure", and
thus also a parallel redistribution in terms of wealth,
prestige and power'. For Ahier, this suggests a too
direct and 'idealist' connection between what goes on
in the ideological apparatus of the State and the economic and political, and he argues that changes in
educational conceptions create 'no necessity for the
social distribution of new kinds of rewards to be
different'. However, whilst this is again an important
warning against the over-optimism of 'new direction'
sociology, it would be unfortunate (and indeed misguided)
if the argument that there is no necessity for this to
happen were taken to imply that activity within the ideological state apparatus of the school had no possible
relevance to broader struggles for social and political
change. There is a danger that the strength of the
'new' sociology's stress upon teachers as active agents
in the process of education will be lost in the discussion of its weaknesses. We, therefore, maintain

considerable reservations about the style of theorizing
advocated by Ahier whilst accepting the importance of
his critique. It is particularly important that sociologists and teachers theorize rather than ignore their
own historical circumstances as employees of the State,
and that, in doing so, they recognize that the crisis
they experience is not to be resolved merely by the
idealist solution of redefining and restructuring knowledge.

The limitations of the alternative form of theorizing
towards which Ahier's analysis points are discussed in
the third paper in this section, Erben and Gleeson's
critique of Althusser's (1971) view of the school as an
Ideological State Apparatus. Ironically, in view of
Ahier's comments on the 'new' sociology, and in view of
the capacity of other aspects of Althusserian theory to
account for disjunctures, Erben and Gleeson charge
Althusser with over-emphasizing the intimate connection
between schools and the purposes of the State. From a
Marxist view of the State, as a 'machine of repression
which enables the ruling class to ensure their domination', the school is seen as part (and in capitalist
society the dominant part) of the Ideological State
Apparatus which sustains this domination while invoking
a minimum of explicit force. For Erben and Gleeson,
Althusser's analysis stresses 'the "crushing" influences
of apparatuses in dominance which condition man in his
pursuit of the maintenance and reproduction of production'. His passive view of man operating within such a
system 'inhibits teachers and students from considering
the possibility that they may be concerned with struggle
and change'. Both the analysis within the paper under
discussion, and Althusser's response to the students'
struggle in Paris in May 1968, are shown to undervalue
the contribution which work within the educational
Ideological State Apparatus can make to revolutionary
change. Such a view stimulates an unfortunate form of
quietism amongst socialist teachers who must await the
'correct' situation for revolutionary struggle, and it
is thus a mirror image of the equally naive view of the
'new direction' sociologists that teachers' practices
can transform society. For Althusser there are few
weapons for the radical teacher to turn against 'the
ideology, the system and the practices in which they are
trapped', and his jibe at the 'famous new methods' seems
to suggest that whatever teachers do, and whatever they
think they do, they merely carry out 'the "work" the
system (which is bigger than they are and crushes them)
forces them to do'.

We recognize, as to some extent do Erben and Gleeson, that it is somewhat over-simplistic to characterize Althusser as a quasi-functionalist. The key notions in a functionalist theory of system maintenance and inter-dependence of parts cannot be equated with Althusser's concepts of relative autonomy of the superstructure and over-determination. Nor does drawing a parallel between Parsons and Althusser display the fundamentally differ-ent problematics of the two theorists. Parsons (1959), like other functionalists, is concerned with the general problem of how social order is possible in any society. Althusser, however, as Stevenson and Matthews (1976) argue, is explicitly attempting 'to relate change in all parts of the social formation to a revolutionary conjuncture'. Despite this, his work can, as Erben and Gleeson's paper shows, be read as a functionalist ac-count and can end up as lending theoretical support to just those institutions of capitalist society that he is politically committed to oppose. In Althusser's work, we have an abstract and general theory of the State which lacks any attempt to grasp the complex var-iety of processes of state intervention in capitalist societies, together with a view of the agents of produc-tion (and reproduction), workers and teachers as 'never more than the occupants of ... places'. This leaves us with a merely formal theory of the position of tea-chers in an abstract concept of the state, rather than a theory of the practice of teachers in relation to the wider processes of state intervention, that might give teachers and others involved in education, some way of relating the possibilities and constraints they exper-ience in the classroom to their ambiguous position as employees of the state.

On the other hand, it must also be noted that Althusser does recognize the possibility that the Ideological State Apparatuses can be the site of bitter forms of class struggle 'not only because the former ruling classes are able to retain strong positions there for a long time, but also because the resistance of the exploited classes is able to find means and occasions to express itself there, either by the utilisation of their contradictions or by conquering combat positions in them in struggle'. If Althusser is merely saying that the struggle for change within schools must, if it is to have any significance for a transformation of society, extend beyond them, then his analysis is a useful corrective to the over-optimism of the 'new' sociology of education. His recognition that the class struggle is 'rooted elsewhere than in ideology, in the infra-structure, in the relations of production, which

are relations of exploitation and constitute the base
for class relations' resonates closely with the critique
of the idealism of 'new direction' sociology in the
papers by Whitty and Ahier. Unfortunately, however, the
particular form of structural analysis which Althusser
adopts does resemble just that which Bourdieu (1973)
criticizes for 'seeing agents as the simple "supports"
of structures invested with the mysterious power of
determining other structures', and it thus produces a
caricature of the concrete historical situation in which
educators find themselves. It therefore becomes difficult, as it was with Ahier's paper, to see in concrete
terms what sort of struggles socialist teachers might
actively engage in, and the general tenor of Althusser's
argument is indeed (as Erben and Gleeson suggest) that,
whilst schools are highly significant as institutions
for the reproduction of capitalist society, they cannot
be considered a serious arena in the struggle for social
transformation. Those who work in schools can have
little part in making history and changing the world.

The third form of theorizing, discussed here in
Apple's paper, is the deschooling thesis of Ivan Illich
(1971). It has some superficial similarities with
Althusser's analysis of the role of the school, but its
proposed solutions to the current crisis share something
of the simplicity of those favoured by the 'new direction' sociologists. Schools are seen as instruments of
social control which reproduce the relations of the
wider society, but, contrary to Althusser's analysis, the
institutions of schooling are themselves identified as
the problem. All the dehumanizing aspects of schooling
- grades, compulsory attendance, packaged knowledge,
professional authority and monopoly, etc - are seen as
intrinsic to schooling itself, and it therefore follows
that schools, together with other institutions which
encourage passive consumer demand for professional services, must be abolished. The abolition of the
'manipulative' institution of school would thus, it is
argued, open up radical possibilities for education as
self-realization and herald the end of elitism and
repression. Illich's description of schooling implies
that it can be nothing but a process of domestication
and that there is no possibility for transforming
schools from within. The picture of schools which
Illich paints does not, however, lead him to the same
conclusions as Althusser about the possibilities for
change because, by placing school at the heart of the
crisis, he is able to propose the stunningly simple solution of 'deschooling society'.

The alienative characteristics of schooling seem so
pervasive that Illich's views seem even more open to
the criticisms that Erben and Gleeson made of Althusser's
theory than that theory itself, i.e. they over-emphasize
the consumption of knowledge at the expense of its production, they advance a passive model of socialization,
and they fail to explain how radicals can possibly
emerge from the 'crushing' influences of such total
institutions. It therefore seems all the more extra-
ordinary that his apparent strategy for deschooling
society is an individualistic one in which 'each of us
is personally responsible for his deschooling'. There
is, as Apple points out, no recognition of the necessity
for collective action to transform society, and one is
left wondering how men with such a facility to volun-
taristically liberate themselves ever fell victim to
such manipulative institutions as schools. At the root
of these apparent contradictions is Illich's essentially
ahistorical and undialectical mode of theorizing. Man
as a potentially autonomous actor is separated from the
institutions which he created. The relations between
schooling and its social, economic and political context
are described in a superficial manner. The concept of
collective struggle is missing even from Illich's more
recent work (Illich, 1974) because the issue of why
education is schooled is consistently avoided and the
difficulties of transforming it thus obscured.

Apple's critique of Illich echoes many of the criticisms which Whitty's paper makes of the 'new' sociology
of education. Both point to the limitations of those
modes of theorizing which imply that a recognition of
the phenomenon of alienation in contemporary schooling
will enable us to transcend it. Illich shares with the
more optimistic 'new direction' sociologists the tendency to operate at a level of description rather than
analysis and to ignore, or offer simplistic answers to,
questions about why the world appears as it does. This
in turn has led them both to propose 'education-bound'
strategies of change (whether within the institutions of
schooling or outside them) and thus to avoid confronting
questions about the wider political struggle which the
transformation they envisage would in reality entail.
It is thus scarcely surprising that Illich's work has
been described by Gintis (1972), as a diversion from the
'immensely complex and demanding political, organizational,
intellectual and personal demands of revolutionary reconstruction in the coming decades'. Best (1976) makes
a similar judgment on the 'new' sociology of education,
and argues that most work in this field, including our

own, is not particularly significant in relation to the
'major problems of education from a socialist point of
view'. All these commentators are agreed, despite their
many differences, that realistic strategies of change
can only emerge from a more profound analysis of the
problems to which both the deschoolers and the 'new'
sociologists point, and thus of the nature of the relationship between the economic roots of social order and
the institutions of cultural production and reproduction.

Apple and Whitty both comment on the tendency of the
writers whose work they are discussing to eschew, or
utilize superficially, the various Marxist or neo-
Marxist perspectives which could help in the exploration of these issues. This does not, however, for the
reasons advanced by Erben and Gleeson, necessitate the
adoption of the sort of Marxist perspective which would
involve the denial of the strengths of these other modes
of theorizing. Apple argues in this paper that once the
larger political and economic context of schooling is
revealed, the task of the educator committed to change
is twofold. Part of his task is 'to engage in the rigorous historical, analytic and empirical scholarship
necessary to show how many of the tools, categories,
perspectives and ideologies of education provide unquestioned support for this socio-political framework',
and how 'support for existing and often problematic
institutional structures is marshalled in education'.
His second task, Apple argues, lies in 'concrete and
practical arenas of action', such as the struggle for
student rights, and ultimately in affiliation to political movements and involvement in the broader political
struggle for change. Whilst it would be theoretically
and practically impossible, and, indeed undesirable, to
draw a clear distinction between these two tasks, the
papers in the second section are attempts to develop
what Apple might call 'critical scholarship', whilst
those in the final section discuss some of the concrete
and practical arenas of action in which politically-
oriented educators might become involved. The contributors to both indicate that the sort of quietism which
Erben and Gleeson fear might stem from an Althusserian
analysis of education in capitalist societies, would be
as inadequate a response as the individualistic strategies of change for which Whitty and Apple criticize
the 'new direction' sociologists and the deschoolers.

REFERENCES

ALTHUSSER, L. (1971) 'Ideology and Ideological State
Apparatuses' in Lenin and Philosophy and Other Essays
London: New Left Books.

BEST, R. (1976) New directions? Some comments on the
'new' sociology of education, Radical Education No. 5.

BOURDIEU, P. (1973) 'Cultural reproduction and social
reproduction', in Brown, R. (Ed), Knowledge, Education
and Cultural Change, London: Tavistock Publications.

GINTIS, H. (1972) Towards a political economy of education: a radical critique of Ivan Illich's Deschooling
Society, Harvard Educational Review, 42(1).

GORBUTT, D. (1972) The 'new' sociology of education,
Education for Teaching.

ILLICH, I. (1971) Deschooling Society, London: Calder
and Boyars.

ILLICH, I. (1974) After Deschooling, What? London:
Writers and Readers Publishing Co-operative.

SIMON, J. (1974) 'New direction' sociology and comprehensive schooling, Forum 17(1).

STENHOUSE, L. (1975) An Introduction to Curriculum
Research and Development, London: Heinemann.

STEVENSON, J. and MATTHEWS, P. (1976) Locating
Althusser, mimeo, University of London Institute of
Education Library.

YOUNG, M. F. D. (Ed) (1971) Knowledge and Control
London: Collier-Macmillan.

1.1
Sociology and the Problem of Radical Educational Change:

Notes towards a reconceptualization of the 'new' sociology of education

Geoff Whitty

I want to consider in the course of this paper some
of the problems which seem to me implicit in various
manifestations of the 'new' sociology of education -
a term applied by Gorbutt (1972) to those approaches to
the sociology of education which are, in one way or
another, informed by recent 'new directions' in sociology. In the course of this discussion, I shall concentrate attention on that work within this emergent
tradition which is concerned with school knowledge and,
in particular, upon work which claims, explicitly or
implicitly, to have some relevance to the problems and
possibilities of change in the school curriculum. I
do this, not because such work constitutes the whole
of this 'new' sociology of education, but because it
has been in the course of my own work in this field
that I have begun to develop the critique which I shall
attempt to articulate here.

SOCIOLOGY AND THE CURRICULUM: CHANGING EMPHASES

The focus of interest amongst sociologists of education has shifted markedly in recent years and the
sociology of school knowledge can no longer be regarded as a marginal concern. It is, however, less than a
decade since Musgrove (1968) put forward the seemingly
novel suggestion that sociologists should:

... examine subjects both within the school and the
nation at large as social systems sustained by communication networks, material endowments and

---

* A modified version of this paper appeared in
FLUDE, M. and AHIER, J. (eds) (1974) Educability,
Schools and Ideology, London: Croom Helm.

ideologies. Within a school and within the wider
society subjects are communities of people, competing and collaborating with one another, defining
and defending their boundaries, demanding allegiance
from their members and conferring a sense of identity upon them ... Even innovation which appears to
be essentially intellectual in character can usefully be examined as the outcome of social interaction...

While today there is nothing exceptional about this
proposal for the sociological study of the school curriculum, at the time such a perspective - together with
that being developed by Bernstein (1969) during the
same period - marked a refreshingly new approach within
the sociology of education. Musgrove remarked that
'studies of subjects in these terms have scarcely
begun, at least at school level' and, even in 1971,
Banks could suggest that sociological studies of the
school curriculum had been rare. It can, however, no
longer be convincingly argued that sociologists have
ignored the curriculum as a potential field of study,
even if their exploratory writings have sometimes led
them into philosophical speculation about the nature of
knowledge rather than to the style of empirical work
proposed by Musgrove. Some of the more illuminating
questions have derived from the shift of interest indicated by Young (1971) when he writes that 'sociology
of education is no longer conceived as an area of enquiry distinct from the sociology of knowledge'.
Although Young also notes the lack of empirical work
in this area, his book Knowledge and Control contains
a variety of papers pertinent to the asking of sociological questions about 'educational knowledge', many
of which may be regarded as central to the development
of the 'new' sociology of education.

    Even before this, there had of course been a number
of studies from within a variety of traditions which
attempted to relate educational ideas and social circumstances. Most of these have, however, been concerned with aspects of knowledge in Higher Education
rather than the schools - one of the most impressive
being the study by Davie (1961) of the way in which
prevailing conceptions of knowledge and styles of
pedagogy in the Scottish universities were destroyed
by the triumph of English intellectual imperialism.
Similarly, most of the critiques of what counts as
educational knowledge today have been directed at the
curricula of Higher Education, for example Roszak (1969)
and Pateman (1972), although the arguments of the

deschoolers and the activities of the Free School movement have helped to stimulate a widening of the debate.
There is, however, in some accounts of the development
of subject disciplines and the critiques of their
ideological assumptions, a tendency to discuss objectified subject categories and to devote little attention
to members' practices for the maintenance of such
categories as non-problematic. These accounts - since
they do not attend to the processes whereby such
definitions are legitimated and sustained - may be
assigned to the broad category of 'structural' explanations. Even where the processual aspects of subjects
are specifically addressed, the linkages between structure and process often tend to be conceived in terms of
a relatively unexplicated notion of a 'dialectical
relationship'.

It is for these sorts of reasons that representatives
of the recent reorientation in the sociology of education have tended to attack the 'reification'[1] of the
content of the curriculum in the work of other writers,
to eschew structural concerns, and to concentrate upon
the social processes whereby particular conceptions of
school knowledge are legitimated and sustained. This
shift of emphasis has been accompanied by a tendency
to regard problems of the relative validity of knowledge as misconceived and by a concern to explore, without pre-defined limits, the nature of the relationship
between the cognitive aspects of knowledge and social
organization. Such reorientations have certainly provided us with valuable insights which were missing
from most earlier studies and, in particular, the emphasis on the process of legitimation has led to a more
critical approach to theories of structural causation
of both Marxist and functionalist varieties. Instead
of regarding definitions of knowledge as absolute or
outside the influence of the classroom teacher, his
assumptions and his everyday activities are shown to
be crucial to the process whereby particular conceptions of knowledge are sustained. Recent studies of
such assumptions and activities at school level have
made an important contribution to the sociology of
education, and have often benefited from insights
from other fields, such as anthropology and linguistics.
Most of the studies associated with the 'new' sociology
of education are necessarily limited in scope and make
little claim to offer a thorough-going sociological
approach to the study of school knowledge. Thus, for
example, Keddie (1971) is quite explicit about the

limitations of her study of 'classroom knowledge' and
remarks that:

> Clearly there is also a need to examine the linkages
> between schools and other institutions, and attempt
> to understand the nature of the relationship between
> what counts as knowledge in schools and what counts
> as knowledge in other societal areas ... The origins
> of these categories are likely to lie outside the
> school and within the structures of society itself
> and the wider distribution of power.

However, there are writers who make considerably
greater claims about the significance of the 'new directions' in the sociology of education to which I have
referred. In this respect, a paper by Esland (1971)
is the most ambitious attempt to date to develop a
perspective on teaching and learning out of an 'all-
embracing conception of the sociology of knowledge' in
order to 'understand the complex relationship between
school and society as being more than a system within
a system'.

In this paper, I want to suggest that, despite the
strengths of the 'new' sociology of education, there
are certain dangers in such a reorientation of sociological studies. These lie particularly in the too
ready acceptance of the suggestion that there is a
community of interest between sociologists engaged in
such studies and those radical teachers who wish to
mount a challenge against prevailing definitions of
schooling - a view implied in the following comments
by Esland:

> It is arguable that the dereification of much that
> is taken for granted in educational culture will
> sensitize to the open human possibilities of creat-
> ing new knowledge structures and their modes of
> transmission. For teachers, as for Berger and
> Pullberg, 'Sociology will only accomplish its task
> if it studies not merely giveness, but the various
> processes of becoming giveness'.

I have discussed elsewhere (1973), the strengths and
weaknesses of Esland's paper, but here I merely wish
to make two points pertinent to my present concerns.
The first is that his very use of the term 'paradigm'
to characterize supposed changes in teachers' pedagogical and subject perspectives may, in effect, blind
us to essential continuities in these perspectives,
and thus enable us to present minor modifications in

the school curriculum as evidence of the 'open human
possibilities' of change. The second and related
point is that his stress upon the day-to-day activities
of epistemic communities in developing and sustaining
particular conceptions of knowledge may obscure the
significance of parameters - whether logical, material
or social - within which adjustments to subject knowledge or teacher perspectives may conceivably take
place.

There is a danger that too narrow a concentration on
the processes of change in the terms suggested by
Esland, will permit us to perpetuate an ambiguity in
the thesis of the social construction of knowledge, and
to imply that any educational alternative or redefinition of legitimate knowledge is possible so long
as its adherents are properly organized within the institutional arena of change. I want to suggest that
a similar ambiguity is to be found in other manifestations of the 'new' sociology of education and to argue
that, until we have faced up to questions about what
constitutes the appropriate arena of change, and what
comprise the parameters within which alternative
notions of knowledge are possible, the sort of study
of the 'various processes of becoming giveness' which
Esland proposes may accomplish a somewhat more limited
task than he appears to suppose.

SOCIOLOGY AS A CRITIQUE OF SCHOOL KNOWLEDGE

(a) Derivations - Analytic and Possibilitarian

In his discussion of the 'new' sociology of education, Gorbutt (1972) tells us that its roots lie in the
'interpretive' rather than the 'normative' tradition in
sociology[2] and that it draws its intellectual stimula-
tion from, inter alia, Marx, Mead, Mills, Schutz,
Berger, Blumer, Cicourel, Garfinkel and Becker. It is
therefore clear that, insofar as it is possible to
assign sociologists to competing camps in the manner of
the 'crisis sociologists'[3], the 'new' sociology of
education draws its inspiration from what Bandyopadhyay
(1971) characterizes as a 'radical tradition' confronting the 'institutionalized orthodoxy' of academic
sociology. While, however, this radical tradition is
in some senses agreed in its critique of a prevailing
'positivist' orthodoxy, there remains considerable
controversy about the nature of the 'new directions'
which sociology might take in the future.
Bandyopadhyay, for instance, suggests that there is a

sharp distinction between the work of adherents to the
neo-Marxist school of Critical Theory and that of the
'ex-liberals' amongst the fraternity of sociologists,
who have been variously influenced by Kuhn's paradig-
matic view of science, Winch's linguistic and cultural
relativism, the sociology of knowledge, and a 'humanistic perspective often associated with phenomenology'.

That there is a similarly eclectic foundation to the
'new' sociology of education is evident from a glance
at the recent literature which may be taken as representative of this emergent tradition[4]. It is, therefore,
not difficult to understand why there are numerous
points of ambiguity in the work which it has so far
generated. These ambiguities are nowhere more in evidence than in work related to the possibilities of
cultural change, and they are further exacerbated by a
certain amount of confusion amongst the wide variety
of stances which may be detected even within the
'humanistic perspective often associated with phenomenology'. There is considerable variation in the extent
to which the work of sociologists often assigned to
this category may be regarded as 'humanistic' -
Berger (1966), for instance, suggests that the 'humanistic discipline of sociology' may be a 'first step
towards freedom', while others seem attracted to phenomenology in the course of a dispassionate search for
an appropriate methodology for the human sciences.
Advocates of the former position, which I shall term
'possibilitarian'[5] see, in the activity of doing sociology, a possibility of transcending the experienced
realities of everyday life, while the advocates of the
latter 'analytic' stance do not seek, in exposing the
constitutive features of lived reality, to actually
challenge the mundane experience of that everyday
world. Within this 'analytic' tradition, I would be
inclined to include most ethnomethodologists[6]and, in a
rather different sense, exponents of the emerging tradition of 'analysis'[7]. Within the 'new' sociology of
education there is some ambiguity on the issue of the
potential purchase of a phenomenological sociology,
but generally, although ethnomethodological
studies have had their influence[8], it would be fair to
claim that it is the 'possibilitarian' position which
has caught the imagination of sociologists working
within the field of education. It is this which has
contributed to the possibly premature tendency to
celebrate the ecstatic possibilities for 'freedom'
which stem from analysing the 'various processes of
becoming giveness'.

A central feature of the 'radical tradition' in
sociology is, of course, its stress on intentionality
and the meaningful nature of social action. Sociologists concerned to analyse the process of learning have
therefore been attracted by parallel work being carried
out by those writers in the field of curriculum theory
who have been influenced by the philosophical tradition
of existential phenomenology. They seem to have been
particularly attracted by the attack by Greene (1971)
on the prevailing tradition within the philosophy of
education which, she suggests, presents '"disciplines"
or "public traditions" or "accumulated wisdom" or
"common culture" ... as objectively existent, external
to the knower - there to be discovered, mastered,
learnt'. Writers in such a tradition forget, it is
argued, that the learner is actively engaged in what
Postman and Weingartner (1971) have termed 'meaning
making'. There is, however, some ambiguity between
the claim that knowledge is not ultimately independent
of the knower so the matter can be disposed of by
suggesting that the traditional philosophers are wrong,
and the alternative argument that knowledge ought not
to be independent of the knower, but is often experienced as such. Popkewitz (1972), for instance, suggests that forms of knowing are often reified in such
a way as to produce a 'view of social reality that is
mechanistic and predeterministic', but he does not
appear to foresee major difficulties in modifying such
a perception of knowledge once this point has been
recognized. Vandenburg (1971), on the other hand,
presents an analysis which suggests that the prevailing
'forgetfulness of being' is related to the world-wide
dominance of 'manipulative, technological thinking'.

It seems to me, however, that much of the work in
this tradition takes possibilitarianism to such lengths
that its appeals for the 'recovery of being' sometimes
have little to say about lived experience and the real
possibilities of transcending it. In a typical example, Greene (1972) appeals to the individual to recognize in experience that he is free and not ultimately
constrained:

> To defy determinism, then, is to become fully con-
> scious of one's freedom - with all its risks, with
> all its dread responsibilities. It is to break with
> the crowd, to know one's own inwardness, to be wide-
> awake with respect to the world around and its
> 'iron laws', its limitations, its causes which need
> not compel.

I want to suggest that a sociology of education which
has so rightly swung away from a tradition which seemed
to put the responsibility for educational shortcomings
in the hands of external and constraining forces,
should also beware of treading too far along the path
of the sort of possibilitarianism which verges on a
romantic individualism. Otherwise, its proponents may
forego the right to speak meaningfully to teachers who
experience constraint in their everyday lives and for
whom, if not taken to extremes, the 'new' sociology of
education could suggest real and constructive possibilities for involvement in radical change. I shall,
therefore, consider some examples of work influenced by
'new directions' in sociology in order to expose and
explore certain critical ambiguities which make it
problematic whether, in the actual context of change,
they will be dismissed as naive and utopian, or seen
to offer the very real hope for the future which is
undoubtedly implicit in them.

(b)   Sociology as Liberation?

There can be no doubt that the exponents of the
'new' sociology of education are concerned to question
prevailing taken-for-granted assumptions in the world
of education. Young (1973a) has summarized its stance
towards our central concern in this paper - the nature
of curricular knowledge. He suggests that it starts
by:

       ... rejecting the assumptions of any superiority of
       educational or 'academic' knowledge over the every-
       day commonsense knowledge available to people as
       being in the world. There is no doubt that teachers'
       practices ... are predicated on just the assumption
       of the superiority of academic knowledge that is
       being called into question.

Clearly, this questioning may be viewed either in terms
of what I have characterized as the 'possibilitarian'
position in sociology or those of the 'analytic'
stance. I want, however, to consider here those strands
of thought which regard such questioning of the constitution of 'educational' knowledge not merely in an
analytic manner, but as a direct challenge to prevailing conceptions of school knowledge with a power to
contribute significantly to the transformation of the
lived realities of school and society. For those who
hold the views which I am about to consider, the world
of education does not merely provide an occasion for

'doing analysis', rather, the very activity of questioning assumptions reveals and contributes to the 'open
human possibilities' of changing our ways of seeing and
experiencing that world.

I have already indicated that, in the work of Esland,
there is a strong suggestion that the study of the process of 'becoming giveness' may make a significant
contribution to the abandonment of 'reified and dehumanising' views of knowledge. In Gorbutt's work[9] there is
an even more explicit and optimistic account of the
contribution which a sociology of education based on
the 'interpretive' paradigm can make to the transformation of our educational system. A sociology which
views society as 'socially constructed, sustained and
changed through the ongoing interaction of men', in
which truth and objectivity are viewed as human products, and in which there is no 'reality' independent
of the meaning and interpretation which men place on
events, is seen to have far reaching implications.
Such a sociology could question the assumptions which
underlie conventional approaches to educational theory
and the prevailing educational practices which they
support. Of particular importance would be its exposure of the supposedly 'self-evident' justification for
education into particular forms of knowledge as merely
the ideological position of particular interest groups.
Although he recognizes that such analyses tend to be
made in 'educationist' rather than 'teacher' contexts[10],
Gorbutt believes that the micro-analysis of classroom
interaction from such a perspective can, by laying bare
teachers' assumptions and their own part in creating
'problems', overcome the discrepancy between words and
deeds which generally pervades teacher education. The
'self-critical researching teacher' would, he argues,
'constantly monitor the effectiveness of his own and
his colleagues' activities and modify his behaviour
accordingly'. Such activities would, he says, 'revit-
alize schools and colleges and possibly fulfil the
promise of education for all'. It seems to me, however,
that this ecstatic celebration of the power of the
'new' sociology of education to transform the lived
reality of school is not merely (as Gorbutt himself
suggests) 'optimistic' but, in some respects, danger-
ously over-optimistic in its view of the power of
analytic activity to transcend experience.

A number of sociologists, attracted by the possibilitarian strands within 'new directions', have been
quick to perceive a link between their own work and
the more overtly political stance of such radical

educators as Paulo Freire[11]. Freire's critique of prevailing modes of education in the third world - as a
denial of man's subjectivity through the cultural in-
vasion of his being with pre-packaged curricula, has
been tellingly applied to the process of education and
the concept of 'educational' knowledge in the capitalist
world generally. Freire's own programme, developed in
the context of adult literacy schemes in Latin America,
involves a notion of 'dialogic education' in which teacher and student engage together in a critical approach
to 'reality' - a process in which the ideological significance of the prevailing 'banking concept of education' is laid bare, so that the once-oppressed classes
can experience a liberation of consciousness, and regain
an awareness of man's role as 'subject' in the world.
The ecstatic possibilities inherent in such a notion of
education have been recognized and, in terms of Freire's
own position, probably exaggerated by teachers sympathetic to the phenomenological critique of the view of
knowledge espoused by conventional sociology. The
parallels with Gorbutt's position will be clear, while
Vulliamy (1973) has suggested that social studies
lessons in schools should similarly involve teachers and
pupils 'doing sociology together' in such a way that
their critical questioning of the prevailing assumptions
will create the 'potential for what Freire calls "education as the practice of freedom"'. The recognition that
there is no one 'reality' will enable pupils to develop
a 'permanently critical approach to "reality"'. What
is, however, absent from Vulliamy's stance is the
recognition that even when pupils are aware that
'alternative structures are possible', they may not
experience the transcendence of existent realities as
a living possibility. He suggests no strategy which is
likely to prove meaningful to the teacher or pupil who,
while aware of the theoretical possibility of actually
shaping his world, still feels shaped and oppressed by
it. There is, then, in the work of both Gorbutt and
Vulliamy a degree of ambiguity about the manner in
which 'criticism' and the questioning of assumptions
can transform lived reality. In particular, they tend
to exaggerate the power of a theory of 'multiple accounts' of the world to subvert, for all practical
purposes, conventional notions of 'reality' and their
associated hierarchical theories of knowledge and education. Others have seen the implications of questioning the prevailing assumptions about knowledge rather
differently. For them, the suggestion that an
'objectivistic' view of knowledge is fundamentally
dehumanising has involved the abandonment of any notion
of a 'third world'[12] of objective - or even objectified

- knowledge on the grounds that it is an unwarranted
mystification. The stress on man being active in giving
meaning to his world and on the reclamation of knowledge as a human production has led, in its more
extreme interpretations, to a celebration of the activity of 'doing knowledge' and to the abandonment of a
concern for the nature and status of the knowledge
produced. Knowledge, as generally conceived in the
curriculum, is dismissed as 'commodity knowledge', and
the only justifiable activity in schools becomes 'doing
one's own knowledge' regardless. In some respects,
this stance is encouraged by the rhetoric of the
deschoolers who so tellingly point to the way in which
'learning', a term which originally designated an activity, has now come to be regarded as a commodity to be
consumed (see Illich, 1971), but neither they, nor the
pragmatist philosophers also quoted in support of such
a stance, would generally wish to be associated with
its more extreme manifestations. It is, however, a
view which seems to have gained some impact amongst
recent graduates in sociology, for whom a relativistic
view of knowledge and the rejection of the superiority
of an academic curriculum has led to fear of imposing
any mode of thinking upon pupils and hence to a teaching strategy of 'having a chat'. While such a stance
is often seen as liberating from prevailing notions of
'school' and 'knowledge', I am inclined to argue that
it is liable to be profoundly conservative since such
notions are sustained by a whole variety of more or
less subtle means. Indeed, this position seems even
less likely than the 'critical' stance of Gorbutt and
Vulliamy to transform consciousness and subvert the
prevailing hierarchy in ways of seeing knowledge.

I want, then, to suggest that the possibilities of
realizing in practice the supposedly liberating potential of any of these strategies are likely to be sev-
erely limited. Rather than abandoning all concern with
the status of knowledge objectified in the process of
coming to know, I suggest that we might fruitfully
examine the complex of social relations within which
objectified knowledge becomes reified or experienced
as oppressive and constraining - that is, the circumstances in which its manifestations have justly earned
it the label 'commodity knowledge'. Such considerations
are, I am inclined to think, a necessary complement to
an otherwise premature celebration of the potential
purchase of a possibilitarian sociology in achieving a
dereification of experience and the recovery of our
human being within the contexts of schools and colleges.
Before suggesting a way of approaching such problems,

I want to make a brief comment upon the prevailing
culture of these educational arenas.

(c) The Problem of a 'Culture of Positivism'

Part of the liberating potential of the 'new' sociology of education is seen to lie in its stress on the
social construction of knowledge thesis, and its rejection of a prevailing 'positivist' and 'objectivist'
epistemology. In the alternative epistemology, truth
and objectivity are seen as nothing but human products
and man rather than Nature is seen as the ultimate
author of 'knowledge' and 'reality'. Any attempt to
appeal to an external 'reality' in order to support
claims for the superiority of one way of seeing over
another is dismissed as ideological. Knowledge is
seen as inextricably linked to methods of coming to
know and any supposed dichotomy between them is therefore false. Esland (1972) suggests that the new
'phenomenological' perspective challenges the 'widely
prevailing objective emphasis and understanding of
knowledge' and, in the process of returning primacy to
the individual's own mental ordering processes, it may
'necessitate dismantling the objective structures of
knowledge', thus threatening the cultures and institutions within which they have developed.

A particular target of the phenomenological paradigm
has been, as I have already suggested, the prevailing
tradition within the philosophy of education - the
tradition represented in the work of such writers as
Hirst (1971), Phenix (1962) and Hirst and Peters (1970).
It will be clear already that exponents of the phenomenological perspective want to challenge the model of
teaching and learning (implied by Hirst) in which knowledge (X) is transmitted from the teacher (A) to the
pupil (B), and the notion that education can be adequately defined as the 'acquisition of certain fundamental ... public modes of experience, understanding
and knowledge'. In addition, they would have considerable reservations about Phenix's statement that 'the
structure of things is revealed, not invented ... the
nature of things is given, not chosen, and if man is to
gain insight he must employ the right concepts and
methods. Only by obedience to the truth thus discovered can he learn or teach'. In many instances, the
phenomenological position would seem to have rather
more in common with the alternative stance which suggests that 'experience can be categorized and concepts
organized in endless ways, according to the inclination
and decision of individuals and societies' - a stance

which Phenix sees as 'epistemologically impious and
pedagogically disastrous'. Certainly, its supporters
would want to say, with Popkewitz (1972), that each
discipline provides entry to a different meaning system
for interpreting the world, a different human product
which can provide a new viewpoint from which to scrut-
inise and '"see through" the facades of our world-
taken-for-granted and its system of apparently self-
evident and self-validating assumptions.'

It can, of course, be argued that the mainstream
philosophers of education have not erred in the ways
their accusers suggest, but there can be little doubt
that their work has often been interpreted by teachers
in a thoroughly 'objectivist' and 'positivist' manner.
What seems to me more crucial, however, is that the
phenomenological perspective provides a justifiable
critique of the way in which school knowledge is generally perceived by teachers and pupils in schools. It
seems to me, that the way of seeing knowledge which is
under criticism, and which it is hoped will be super-
seded by an alternative notion of consciousness, is
considerably more pervasive than its critics tend to
suppose, and the problems of transcending this 'false'
consciousness considerably more complex than they
suggest. My own account of competing definitions of
social studies in schools (1973) tends to suggest that,
even when teachers attempt to take seriously Hirst's
(1965) claim that forms of knowledge are not 'collec-
tions of information but complex ways of understanding
experience', or Cotgrove's (1967) contention that the
emphasis of his approach is on 'getting across the
sociological perspective rather than conveying a mass
of factual information', the prevailing perception of
school sociology is the one which Vulliamy (1973)
describes as the 'uncritical dissemination by the
teacher of "information" about society' to the student.
More crucially, a similar fate appears to have been met
by those attempts to operate in the classroom with
notions of social studies teaching explicitly informed
by a phenomenological perspective. Certainly, as
Horton(1971) implies, there is no threat to the cultural establishment in a sociology which teaches its
students that 'reality' is socially constructed and
knowledge perspectival, if such insights can themselves
attain the status of 'commodity knowledge', the students' grasp of which can be 'objectively' assessed.
Further, however, it seems to me that even the more
radical alternative conceptions of teaching - where
teachers' intentions have been explicitly concerned
with the 'practice' of freedom - have tended to founder

in the context of their interpretation in schools.

I am suggesting, then, that there is a wider 'culture of positivism'[13], whose embeddedness in the culture of the school creates considerable difficulties for those who want to 'see' the world differently and transcend prevailing conceptions of knowledge. This culture is 'positivist' in that it displays no interest in the grounds of knowledge and assumes that Nature, or an external reality, is the author of 'truth'. Such a culture operates with a notion of valid knowledge detached from particular knowing subjects, and views school knowledge as (at least potentially) verifiable 'knowledge' about a 'real world', rather than arbitrarily legitimated ways of seeing[14]. In making such distinctions, it recognizes a hierarchy between those who possess such knowledge or the means to it (and thus may teach), and those who lack it (and must learn). Within schools, as within scientific communities[15], epistemological problems are rarely regarded as more significant than they are within the pre-scientific world of 'commonsense' - and school knowledge is therefore seen merely as an attempt to remedy the inexactitudes and subjective aspects of commonsense representations of 'objective reality'. We tend, as Popkewitz (1972) suggests, to ignore the 'metaphysical' aspects of the disciplines, and to 'produce a hollowness of thought in which one sort of comforting mystification is replaced with another'. I am suggesting, however, that it may prove less easy than he implies to do otherwise.

The challenge mounted by the 'new' sociology of education against such a way of seeing knowledge has certainly led to attempts to conceptualize the curriculum differently, and to take seriously the implications of the critique of school knowledge for the classroom practice of teachers. I am, however, inclined to suggest that it has, in general, proved impracticable to successfully challenge the embeddedness of the assumptions of the 'culture of positivism' within the culture of the school. To conceptualize this problem more adequately will involve, then, some revision of the stance adopted in the 'new' sociology of education.

TOWARDS RECONCEPTUALIZATION

I have resisted Esland's (1972) claim that a substantially different paradigm of teaching is achieving legitimation in schools, and suggested that his new

'phenomenological' or 'epistemological' paradigm is
likely to attain widespread acceptance only to the extent to which it retains the underlying assumptions of
a prevailing 'culture of positivism'. I have also
suggested that we should not overestimate the extent to
which the sociological study of the constitution of
particular ways of viewing knowledge will assist in a
radical redefinition of the nature of knowledge in
school and society. It may therefore prove valuable
for sociologists, and for those concerned to challenge
prevailing notions of education, to consider more
thoroughly the nature of the parameters within which
redefinitions of knowledge may or may not be feasible.
It may, for instance, be important to make distinctions
between (a) those features of knowledge which may not
be subject to relativization in any conceivable circumstances; (b) those features which conceivably
might be different in substantially different historical circumstances; and (c) those features which might
be altered by the legitimating activities of the type of
epistemic community or interest group with which Esland
seems to be concerned. I am suggesting that more careful attention to such distinctions might permit us to
be less ambiguous about what are and what are not 'open
human possibilities' for teachers surveying the school
curriculum and desiring change. It is, of course, part
of the argument of the more extreme relativizers of
knowledge that there are no features of knowledge which
may be assigned to category (a), and that all such
features may ultimately be subsumed within the remaining categories. There are considerable problems about
the arguments on both sides of this controversy, and
I propose, in the context of this paper, to remain
agnostic on the issue. I do this, not because I believe such issues to be irrelevant, but because it
seems to me even more important to maintain a distinction between categories (b) and (c) - a distinction
too often blurred in the recent debates between sociologists and philosophers[16]. I want to suggest that
recent approaches to the study of school knowledge,
particularly those informed by the possibilitarian
stance in sociology, lay too little stress on the parameters within which redefinitions of education might
prove possible and, that in doing so, they may unwittingly imply that the failure to redefine situations
is a purely personal one.

In proposing alternative ways of approaching these
issues, I do not in any sense claim to have resolved
them. My own consideration of such issues has been an
on-going concern over a number of years with friends

and colleagues in a variety of contexts, and it would
be a denial of the essential nature of those debates to
present a false coherence of thought and an apparent
resolution of issues within an exploratory paper of
this kind. I shall, therefore, confine myself to a
discussion of those issues which have been brought into
focus by my involvement in various attempts to operate
with alternative definitions of knowledge, and attempt
to suggest, on the basis of these experiences, possible
lines of enquiry which we might fruitfully undertake in
the future. If what I suggest constitutes a somewhat
different theoretical perspective from that adopted by
others I have worked with, it is not because I have
rejected a commitment to that humanistic project of
change to which we have adhered, but because I believe
it will suggest an alternative (and only partially
less optimistic) formulation of the problem of change
in schools. I want to suggest that a more thorough
consideration of the perspectives on change offered by
Marx and a number of latter-day Marxist or neo-Marxist
theorists, would be pertinent to the issues raised by
the 'new' sociology of education. I believe such perspectives may enable us to be more precise about those
aspects of knowledge which we wish to criticize, without retreating into a relativism which is purely academic and which gives us little indication of a position
from which we might mount the sort of critique which
could be realized in practice. Such analyses may offer
not merely a 'faith' that things might be different,
but also an indication of the nature of a possible
strategy for change. We may then avoid what I have
characterized as the overconfidence of the 'possibilitarian' position as well as the frequent fatalism of the
'analytic' stance. In doing so, we should be able to
develop a more satisfactory characterization of the
relationship between sociological theorizing and a
political commitment to change. I can here, of course,
only briefly sketch some of the directions in which such
a reconceptualization of the problem of radical change
in education might lead us.

One of the most difficult aspects to grasp in 'new
directions' in sociology is the status of the attempt
to relativize knowledge[17]. It is, for instance,
difficult to be quite clear what Esland is arguing when
he says that an 'objectivistic' epistemology - the
stance of commonsense and of analytic philosophy - is
'fundamentally dehumanizing'. This seems to suggest
that there are epistemologies which are more fully
'human', yet the implications of such epistemologies
are somewhat obscured when he appears to suggest that

'openness' and the awareness of 'open human possibilities' are but temporary features of a period of paradigm crisis before a renewed period of 'closure'. This
pessimistic reading is also to be drawn from Esland's
claim that he uses the concept of 'alienation' devoid
of the utopian assumptions of Marx, a usage which, as
Shroyer (1972) says of such a stance in the work of
Berger and Luckmann, justifies false consciousness as
a human 'need', and denies the terms 'alienation' and
'reification' their critical significance. It is
similarly difficult to understand the grounds of the
argument that one epistemology is more 'human' than
others when, as Esland argues (after Mills), epistemologies and 'criteria of validity and truth ... are ...
open to socio-historical relativization'. Implicitly
such a stance suggests that there is no necessary limit
to the number of potential epistemologies, and no clear
grounds upon which to choose between them, their ac-
ceptability being based solely upon the legitimating
power of organized epistemic communities.

Yet, if I read the ambiguities correctly, this is
not what is in many cases being claimed. Rather, such
stances rest upon an implicit philosophical anthropology which is utilized as a measure of the 'humanity'
or otherwise of particular epistemologies. The relevant criteria appear to involve an assessment of the
extent to which epistemologies stress the thesis of the
social construction of concepts, the notion that man
makes his world. Thus a radical sociology, and a
radical approach to teaching, strive to recover the
memory of man's 'human being' and his 'authorship' of
his world. The problem about practical attempts to
realize man's human being is, however, neatly pointed
up in Geras's (1971) criticism of Berger and Pullberg's
definition of alienation as the 'process by which man
forgets the world he lives in has been produced by
himself'. The idealism and subjectivism in a view
which regards theoretical dereification of an objectivistic view of knowledge as a substantial humanizing
influence is exposed in this comment by Geras:

> But what they themselves 'forget' is that, if for-
> getfulness were all that were involved, a reminder
> should be sufficient to deal with the constituent
> problems of alienation.

There seems to be a similar problem about some of the
proposals for developing a less dehumanizing epistemology which I have considered above - in Esland's
stress on the contribution which the study of 'becoming

giveness' can make to the opening up of possibilities
for change, in Gorbutt's optimism in the power of the
'new' sociology of education to transform the lived
realities of schools, and in the potential of 'doing
sociology together' in the manner proposed by Vulliamy.
Within such formulations there seem to lie shades of
the young Hegel's remark, as quoted in McLellan (1969),
that 'once the kingdom of ideas is revolutionized,
reality cannot hold out'. The overemphasis on the
notion that reality is socially constructed seems to
have led to a neglect of the consideration of how and
why reality comes to be constructed in particular ways,
and how and why particular constructions of reality
seem to have the power to resist subversion. Further,
the problem of how to transcend a particular perception
of the world remains even when the constitutive features
of the way of seeing in which it is grounded have been
unravelled. We may, for instance, imagine that there
are places of work in which Marx's theory of the
fetishized nature of social relationships in capitalist
societies has been accepted by workers, even while they
continue to experience such relations as oppressive
and, for all practical purposes, inevitable.

In order to avoid the idealism implicit in some
recent approaches to sociology, it may then be helpful
to maintain more clearly a distinction between the
activity of 'demystification' and the experience of
'dereification' - a distinction which permits the consideration of the continuing power of constructs to
oppress even after they have been revealed as human
in origin. Epistemologies and their resistance to subversion may then be considered as predicated upon
social relations and the relations of production, and
a theory as well as a description of alienation offered. Otherwise, there is a possibility that the work
of phenomenological sociologists may be exposed to the
same criticism as that mounted against the earlier
works of Sartre - a criticism which, as Gorz (1966)
indicates, Sartre himself was later to accept:

> In Being and Nothingness Sartre ... did not ... make
> real existence intelligible: the reasons why bad
> faith is infinitely more widespread than authen-
> ticity were a matter ... of pure contingency. That
> work only indicated the ontological reasons why
> human reality may - or is given to - be misled about
> itself. If you prefer, Being and Nothingness allows
> one to understand how it is possible that a being
> who is free praxis may take himself for a statue, a
> machine, or a thing ... In the Critique Sartre is

concerned, on the contrary, to analyse the reality
of alienation as necessity - practical necessity in
this world, which cannot be transcended by a simple
subjective conversion ...

In discussing the development of his thought and the
realities of 'Being-in-the-world', Sartre (1974) himself has told us how life taught him 'la force des
choses - the power of circumstances', and led him to
reflect with horror on his earlier view that 'whatever
the circumstances, and whatever the site, a man is always
free to be a traitor or not ...'

Marx and Engels themselves also offered[18], at a time
when they were struggling with their former philosophic
consciences through a critique of the work of the Young
Hegelians, what may well stand as a pertinent comment
on the possibilitarian stance in sociology today:

In the Young Hegelians' fantasies the relationships
of men, all their actions, their chains, and their
limitations are the products of their consciousness.
Consequently, they give men the moral postulate of
changing their present consciousness for human,
critical or egoistic consciousness to remove their
limitations. This amounts to a demand to interpret
what exists in a different way, that is to recognize
it by means of a different interpretation.

Such a criticism does not reject the notion that there
are different ways of seeing, but Marx goes on to
provide us with a way of formulating the problem of the
embeddedness of particular ways of seeing in our
society. Although he does this in such a way as to
resist the idealism implicit in the view that the solution to the dehumanization of knowledge lies merely in
the activity of demystification or theoretical dereification, there is in his position an optimism lacking
even in Berger and Pullberg's position, and certainly
in the 'analytic' stance in sociology. Those features
of life which may be regarded as dehumanizing are seen
by Marx as neither necessary features of the human condition for all time nor as arbitrarily legitimated ways
of seeing; rather they result at any given point in
historical time from real social relationships grounded
in the relations of production. Thus he argues:

... men develop their material production and their
material relationships alter their thinking and the
products of their thinking along with real existence. Consciousness does not determine life, but

life determines consciousness ...

and that the conception of history which he and Engels
propose, concludes that:

all forms and products of consciousness cannot be
dissolved by mental criticism ... but only by the
practical overthrow of the actual social relations
which give rise to this idealistic trickery ...
(and) shows that circumstances make men just as much
as men make circumstances.

This is not, of course, denied in any absolute sense by
many exponents of the approaches to sociology under
discussion. Since, however, the reorientation implicit
in the 'new' sociology of education was a conscious
corrective to those sociologies which denied the significance of intentionality in the explanation of human
action, it is perhaps not surprising that one moment of
this dialectic has been stressed at the expense of
another. I am therefore suggesting that in our attempt
to understand and transcend those aspects of constituted
knowledge which humanistic educators wish to reject, it
may prove fruitful to return to Marx's concern with
circumstances since, as I have suggested, it is circumstances which provide the parameters within which change
may or may not take place.

I also want to suggest that a return to the work of
Marxist-oriented writers may, in particular, permit us
to formulate (via the notion of circumstances) a critique of knowledge as it is constituted which focuses
more precisely on those aspects which may be considered
'dehumanizing' without rejecting all constituted knowledge as invalid - and without celebrating the act of
'doing knowledge' at the expense of any consideration
of the created product. In the context of this paper,
I can only tentatively suggest two lines of enquiry
which it might be fruitful to pursue in terms of
Marxist or neo-Marxist perspectives - in one case, the
manner in which circumstances may be mediated even in
the very language which we employ to formulate alternatives, and, in the other case, the manner in which
objectified knowledge may come to be treated in specific historical circumstances as a 'commodity'. In
order to approach such matters, it will be necessary
to consider not only the somewhat rhetorical statements
with which Marx repudiated his Hegelian associates, but
also the more explicit formulations of the notion of
circumstances contained in his later works, and those
of some of his twentieth century successors.

It should perhaps be made clear that what follows is in no sense an argument for the sort of analysis which views history in terms of a linear causality or a crude economic determinism. Rather, it is an attempt to take seriously a position which is neither a pure materialism nor a pure idealism, a position neatly summarized by the following words of Merleau-Ponty (1964):

> ... it is precisely this idea, that nothing can be isolated in the total context of history, which lies at the heart of Marxism with, in addition, the idea that because of their greater generality economic phenomena make a greater contribution to historical discourse - not that they explain everything that happens but that no progress can be made in the cultural order, no historical step can be taken unless the economy, which is like its schema and material symbol, is organized in a certain way.

Unless we view language as somehow outside this scheme of things, as non-ideological, it should be of no surprise that in particular historical circumstances there are difficulties in even formulating alternatives to the status quo. If we view circumstances, or particular configurations of social relationships, as 'making men' as well as being made by men, it may also be appropriate to suggest that, through the dialectical relationship thus implied, features of those 'circumstances' become embedded in the language which men use to construct them as 'real'. The treatment in our culture of natural and social phenomena as discrete entities rather than as 'relations', a feature to which Ollman (1971) has pointed, may then be viewed, not as an arbitrary peculiarity of that culture, but as an example of the embeddedness of circumstances in the very way that we conceive of those circumstances. The fact that our language provides us with a vocabulary for describing what 'is' and is deficient in a vocabulary of 'becoming', or the fact that our way of formulating 'teaching' divides the process (as Adelstein (1972) suggests) into 'those who do the thing and those to whom it is done', may, in such a view, not be coincidental (and thus readily open to an infinitude of alternative definitions). It could rather be that it is symptomatic of the class division of our society, mediated not only in its educational system (as Adelstein argues), but also in features of our prevailing language, of commonsense experience as well as of scholarship.

In a consideration of such issues we enter the ground

of the debate between the 'Critical Theorists' and the
more 'orthodox' Marxists. While Marx stresses the
importance of the development of productive forces and
of a revolutionary mass as the prerequisites of change,
and thus suggests:

> If the material elements of total revolution are not
> present ... then it is absolutely immaterial, so far
> as practical development is concerned, whether the
> idea of this revolution has already been expressed
> a hundred times ...

the 'Critical Theorists', in their more pessimistic
moments, have seemed to question even the possibility
of expressing that 'idea' - as the language of
'bourgeois science' increasingly dominates our existence so that 'instrumental rationality' and 'one-
dimensionality' become features of the way we perceive
'reality', which are potentially 'immune to their own
falsehood'[19]. Both positions, however, do at least
offer theories against which other ways of seeing may
be tested and their ideological import assessed - they
provide a stance from which particular forms of 'rationality' may be criticized, including those aspects of
the 'natural attitude' which are forgetful of human
being. They avoid submission to a total relativism - a
feature of some approaches to phenomenology - which
would make the import of any critique questionable for
all practical purposes, and place 'commonsense' on a
level with all other forms of theorizing. As Shroyer
(1971 and 1972), who has been responsible for some
recent attempts at an 'optimistic' reformulation of
Critical Theory, suggests:

> Whereas Husserl found the unfounded claims of the
> 'natural attitude' to be a basic fact of the
> Lebenswelt, a critical theory of the constitution of
> society would seek to comprehend the fact that the
> everyday world is saturated with claims whose valid-
> ity has not been questioned. Thus, a more adequate
> theory of the immanent relation of truth to the
> constitution of social reality would be concerned
> with the emergence and 'sedimentation' of false-
> consciousness.

Although such a theory has hardly been developed, it
suggests a direction for enquiry which might well offer
deeper insights into the nature of the parameters of
that 'culture of positivism' which, I have suggested,
will not prove a simple matter to transcend.

Such formulations clearly retain notions of potentially authentic theory - and just as Marx was concerned[20] to maintain that there could be two real forms of property, an 'estranged' form (typical of capitalism) and a 'truly human' form, there is similarly no necessity to dispense with notions of theory and knowledge just because there may be 'distorted' theory and 'estranged' knowledge. Such a suggestion seems, however, to be implicit in some of the more extreme demands that we celebrate 'theorizing' and 'doing knowledge' irrespective of the nature of the theory and knowledge thus produced. Rather than assuming that 'authenticity' may be recovered with such ease, it may prove more fruitful to consider the production of knowledge in our society in terms of the analogy with 'commodity' production, suggested in the rhetoric of the deschoolers, though not developed there in any detail. An attempt tc fill out such a notion in terms of a more detailed analogy with the theory of commodity fetishism found in the mature work of Marx might, I suggest, permit valuable insights into the distortion of knowledge in our society without any abandonment of the notion of objectified knowledge as such. This approach might seem to minimize the possibility that there could be immediate and dramatic changes in the way we experience knowledge, but it would not ultimately deny the possibility of such liberating transformations. The expressions 'commodity knowledge' and 'banking education' do, of course, already capture to a degree the significance of the social context of knowledge production and consumption - and large sections of Illich's Deschooling Society are particularly suggestive in this respect. However, while his analysis of the role of schooling as a 'pre-alienating' institution in late capitalist society has considerable plausibility, it may be that Illich's failure to consider in any detail a theory which would explain the origins of prevailing perceptions of knowledge has led to his utopian suggestions about how it might differently be perceived. He claims that 'each of us is responsible for his own deschooling' (whatever that might mean), a proposal not unlike the suggestion that man should recover the memory that the world is his own production. Illich, in fact, recognizes that a significant barrier to the transformation of our perceptions of reality will be 'the resistance we find in ourselves', but tells us that we must overcome that resistance. It is at this point that I am suggesting that the Marxian theory of fetishism provides us with an analogy which suggests a more complex formulation of the manner in which knowledge may come

to be treated as a commodity, a formulation which
suggests that the transcendence of such a perception of
knowledge will require considerably more than the act
of a defiant will.

An analogy between conceptual production and commodity production has been hinted at by Horton (1971) and
sketched in more detail by Piccone (1971). In the context of this paper, it is not possible to attempt a
detailed explication of the theory of fetishism in
Capital, and I shall merely draw on Geras's (1971)
discussion of that theory to suggest that, if it is
applied to the process of conceptual production, it
implies that the sorts of analyses offered by Esland,
Gorbutt and Vulliamy have led us only a limited way
along the path towards that liberating conception of
knowledge which seems to be offered by a possibilitarian
sociology. In terms of the 'practice of freedom', it
may take us little further than what I have termed the
analytic stance, except that its adherents retain a
faith that there is potentially a path beyond theoretical dereification. Sociologists who express the
limitations of the 'naturalistic outlook', in which the
producer of knowledge fails to see anything but what
the conceptual constructs created by himself allow him
to see, and those who proceed to 'thematize' the
process which produced that way of seeing, may not,
in doing so, necessarily permit the transcendence of
that outlook. We may suggest that their activities expose but one of the two aspects of fetishism -
'mystification' - and not the other - the perceived
domination of the produced product which may continue
to constrain the individual and limit his possibilities
for the realization of human being. One possible way
of understanding this process would be to develop an
analogy from Geras's account of the problem in relation
to capital and apply it to another social product,
knowledge. We may then argue that fetishism gives rise
to something more than mere illusion, so that demystification cannot be regarded as equivalent to a dereification of categories as they are experienced in
everyday life. Geras suggests that 'pending the destruction of bourgeois society, capital remains an objective form, a social object, whose content and
essence are accumulated labour, which dominates the
agents of that society'. It may also be that knowledge
produced in the context of capitalist relations of
production will continue to be perceived by many in a
manner difficult to transcend: as external and oppressive rather than 'truly human' and liberating, even
when, at the analytic level, its categories have been

recognized as human products and not natural ones.

SOME IMPLICATIONS

The implications of these thoughts are that, while the parameters within which ways of conceptualizing and experiencing knowledge may be readily redefined are themselves 'social' (in the sense suggested by Williams (1973) when he urges us to consider 'base' as well as 'superstructure' in terms of activities and relationships), the undifferentiated thesis of the social construction of knowledge involves an implicit danger of underestimating the constraining nature and resistance to subversion of particular ways of seeing. While few sociologists would ultimately deny the significance of material circumstances and social relations in our consciousness and experience of reality, there has perhaps been a tendency in some manifestations of 'new directions' to overemphasize the significance of sociological theorizing and demystification in the transformation of lived reality. As a consequence, the utopianism implicit in such stances has sometimes led to a premature celebration of the politics of everyday life at the expense of more conventional forms of political confrontation, whether institutional, national or international. It is important, I am suggesting, for those concerned with radical change in education that a similar tendency does not pervade our consideration of the politics of school knowledge.

It may well be, of course, that sociologists do not wish to engage in pursuits which go beyond demystification and prefer to leave to others decisions about whether perceived reality is to be actively challenged, but there is, within some of the formulations of the 'new' sociology of education, an implicit claim to be doing more than that. Certainly this is a feature of the 'possibilitarian' position, while the 'analytic' orientation seems often to involve an acceptance that the activity of doing sociology must forever remain divorced from decisions about political commitment in the world. The stance, which I am proposing here, would be open to criticism from both perspectives since, although it draws on important insights implicit in a variety of 'new directions', it proposes something of a reorientation of studies to a more thorough consideration of those 'structural' aspects of societies upon which particular 'forms of life' are predicated. It does not, in itself, overcome the gap between theory and practice but recognizes that the difficulty of

generating alternatives to what 'is', and of overcoming
the dichotomy between theory and practice, are problems
which must be faced in a wider arena than the college
seminar or the school classroom. This must particularly be the case with those projects for change which
are, to adopt Williams' terminology, 'oppositional'
rather than merely 'alternative' in relation to the
dominant culture. This is not to deny the value of the
activities of Gorbutt, Vulliamy et al, nor is it to
suggest that we should abandon our attempts to implement
alternative classroom strategies. It is, however, to
question the extent to which such activities ultimately
permit us to avoid just those problems which were
raised by the more structural analyses of educational
ideologies which, as I suggested earlier, the 'new'
sociology of education sought to supersede. More importantly, it is to argue that teachers seeking radical
changes in prevailing definitions of education are
unlikely to attain success in isolation from other
movements concerned to redefine their own 'realities'.

In some senses, of course, the answers to such problems may already be immanent in the perspectives which
have contributed to the 'new' sociology of education.
I trust, therefore, that this attempt to set down my
own rather different views of the immediate possibilities of redefining the reality of education will, in
no sense, be taken to signal my unwillingness to engage
in further dialogue with those whose work I have discussed in the course of this paper, and that they
themselves will feel that it is fruitful to continue
that dialogue. For me, perhaps the most significant
point to be drawn from a phenomenological perspective
on knowledge is that writing accounts and formulating
theories - the activities in which I have here been
engaged - should not be considered as privileged activities outside the mainstream of social life, but
rather as involving, along with all aspects of our
lives, the elements of commitment, contingency and risk
and the recognition that things may not be as they seem.

NOTES

1. I use the term 'reification' here because the critics imply that the status of academic subjects as human
products is forgotten in the work of many writers. In
some cases, they would also want to argue that the
denial of such a status has attained a theoretical formulation and such work is thus an example of 'mystification'. There is, however, some confusion in the literature between the notions of 'objectified' and 'reified'
knowledge. In this paper, I attempt to follow the usage of Berger and Pullberg who argue that 'objectification' is anthropologically necessary, and use the term
'reification' to cover those cases of objectification
which are in an 'alienated mode' - i.e., where the
implication is that the products of consciousness
attain a thing-like character to that consciousness.
See BERGER, P. and PULLBERG, S. 'Reification and the
sociological critique of consciousness'.

2. Gorbutt's terminology for the distinction between
a 'conventional' and a phenomenologically-informed
sociology follows that of WILSON, T. P. (1971) 'Normative and interpretive paradigms in sociology' in
J. D. Douglas (Ed): Understanding Everyday Life.

3. See GOULDNER, A. W. (1971) The Coming Crisis of
Western Sociology and FRIEDRICHS, R. W. (1970) A
Sociology of Sociology.

4. See, for example, YOUNG, M. F. D. (Ed) (1971)
Knowledge and Control and COSIN, B. R. et al (Eds)
(1971) School and Society.

5. The contrast between Garfinkel's ethnomethodology
and the 'possibilitarian' sociology of Goffman and
Berger is nicely expressed by O'Neill in his essay
'Reflexive sociology or the advent of Alvin W. Gouldner'
in O'NEILL, J. (1972) Sociology as a Skin Trade.

6. Garfinkel, for instance, is concerned to stress
that his ethnomethodological studies are not in search
of humanistic arguments. GARFINKEL, H. (1967) Studies
in Ethnomethodology.

7. For some examples of 'Analysis', see McHUGH, P.
et al (1974) On the Beginning of Social Inquiry.

8. See, for example, BARTHOLOMEW, J. (1974) 'Sustaining hierarchy through teaching and research' in

M. Flude and J. Ahier (Eds) Educability, Schools and
Ideology. This offers an alternative interpretation of
ethnomethodology to the one proposed here - and suggests that it has more in common with the 'possibilitarian' position than I have allowed.

9.   GORBUTT, D. op cit. There is a similar optimism in
the proposals of BARTHOLOMEW, J. (1973) in 'The teacher
as researcher - a key to innovation and change Hard
Cheese, 1.

10. These terms follow the usage proposed by KEDDIE, N.
(1971) Classroom knowledge in M. F. D. Young (Ed)
Knowledge and Control.

11. See FREIRE, P. (1972) Cultural Action for Freedom,
FREIRE, P. (1972) Pedagogy of the Oppressed.

12. The notion of a 'third world' of objective knowledge is derived from the work of POPPER, K. (1972)
Objective Knowledge.

13. The term 'culture of positivism' is not wholly
satisfactory in this context, since the term 'positivist' has a wide variety of applications. It is used
here, as stipulated in the paper, to signify a culture
in which knowledge tends to be treated unreflexively
and the 'given' to be taken for granted as 'fact'.

14. For the Popperians, of course, the criterion for
the assessment of knowledge would be one of 'falsifi-
ability' rather than of 'verifiability'.

15. This is not to suggest that the philosophers of
science have not been interested in such issues. For
a discussion of the foundations of science and commonsense from a phenomenological perspective, see
KOCKELMANS (1969) The World in Science and Philosophy.

16. For two recent contributions to this debate, see
PRING, R. (1972) 'Knowledge out of control' in
Education for Teaching, Autumn, and YOUNG, M. F. D.
(1973b) 'Educational theorizing: a radical alternative',
in Education for Teaching, Summer.

17. This difficulty is recognized in Young's attempt to
address this problem. See YOUNG, M. F. D. (1973)
'Taking sides against the probable' Educational Review,
Vol. 25 (3).

18. The quotations from Marx-Engels are taken from
EASTON, L. D. and GUDDAT, K. H. (Eds) (1967) Writings of
the young Marx on Philosophy and Society.

19. See, for example, MARCUSE, H. (1964) One Dimensional
Man. The recent work of Habermas stresses the emancipatory potential of language in its capacity to express
the distinction between appearance and essential reality.
For a recent statement of Habermas's position in relation to Marcuse and Marx, see FRANKEL, B. (1974) 'Habermas
talking: an interview' in Theory and Society Vol. 1.

20. For a useful discussion of this point, see
MARCUSE, H. (1972) Studies in Critical Philosophy.

REFERENCES

ADELSTEIN, D. (1972) 'The philosophy of education' or
'The wisdom and wit of R. S. Peters' in T. Pateman (Ed)
Counter Course: A Handbook for Course Criticism
Harmondsworth: Penguin Books.

BANDYOPADHYAY, P. (1971) One sociology or many? Some
issues in radical sociology Sociological Review Vol. 19
(1).

BANKS, O. (1971) The Sociology of Education (2nd Edition)
London: Batsford.

BARTHOLOMEW, J. (1973) The teacher as researcher - a
key to innovation and change Hard Cheese 1.

BARTHOLOMEW, J. (1974) 'Sustaining hierarchy through
teaching and research' in M. Flude and J. Ahier (Eds)
Educability, Schools and Ideology London: Croom Helm.

BERGER, P. (1966) Invitation to Sociology: A Humanistic
Perspective Harmondsworth: Penguin Books.

BERGER, P. and PULLBERG, S. (1966) Reification and the
sociological critique of consciousness New Left Review 35.

BERNSTEIN, B. B. (1969) 'On the curriculum' now published in B. B. Bernstein (1975) Class, Codes and
Control, Volume 3 London: Routledge and Kegan Paul.

COSIN, B. R. et al (Eds) (1971) School and Society
London: Routledge and Kegan Paul.

COTGROVE, S. F. (1967) The Science of Society London:
George Allen and Unwin.

DAVIE, G. E. (1961) The democratic Intellect Edinburgh:
Edinburgh University Press.

EASTON, L. D. and GUDDAT, K. H. (Eds) (1967) Writings
of the Young Marx on Philosophy and Society New York:
Anchor Books.

ESLAND, G. M. (1971) 'Teaching and learning as the
organization of knowledge' in M. F. D. Young (Ed)
Knowledge and Control London: Collier-Macmillan.

ESLAND, G. M. (1972) 'Pedagogy and the teacher's
presentation of self' in G. M. Esland et al The Social
Organization of Teaching and Learning Bletchley: Open
University Press.

FLUDE, M. and AHIER, J. (Eds) (1974) Educability,
Schools and Ideology London: Croom Helm.

FRANKEL, B. (1974) Habermas talking: an interview
Theory and Society Vol. 1 1974.

FREIRE, P. (1972) Cultural Action for Freedom
Harmondsworth: Penguin Books.

FREIRE, P. (1972) Pedagogy of the Oppressed
Harmondsworth: Penguin Books.

FRIEDRICHS, R. W. (1970) A Sociology of Sociology New
York: The Free Press.

GARFINKEL, H. (1967) Studies in Ethnomethodology
Englewood Cliffs, New Jersey: Prentice-Hall.

GERAS, N. (1971) Essence and appearance: aspects of
fetishism in Marx's 'Capital' New Left Review, 65.

GORBUTT, D. (1972) The 'new' sociology of education
Education for Teaching Autumn 1972.

GORZ, A. (1966) Sartre and Marx New Left Review, 37.

GOULDNER, A. W. (1971) The Coming Crisis of Western
Sociology London: Heinemann.

GREENE, M. (1971) Curriculum and consciousness Teacher's College Record Vol. 73, (2).

GREENE, M. (1972) Defying determinism Teacher's College Record Vol. 74 (2).

HIRST, P. (1965) 'Liberal education and the nature of knowledge' in R. D. Archambault Philosophical Analyses and Education London: Routledge and Kegan Paul.

HIRST, P. and PETERS, R. S. (1970) The Logic of Education London: Routledge and Kegan Paul.

HIRST, P. (1971) What is teaching?   Journal of Curriculum Studies Vol. 3 (1).

HORTON, J. (1971) 'The fetishism of Sociology' in J. D. Colfax and J. L. Roach (Eds) Radical Sociology New York: Basic Books.

ILLICH, I. (1971) The alternative to schooling New York Saturday Review 19th June, 1971.

ILLICH, I. (1971) Deschooling Society London: Calder and Boyars.

KEDDIE, N. (1971) 'Classroom Knowledge' in M. F. D. Young (Ed) Knowledge and Control London: Collier Macmillan.

KOCKELMANS, A. (1969) The World in Science and Philosophy Milwaukee: The Bruce Publishing Company.

MARCUSE, H. (1964) One Dimensional Man London: Routledge and Kegan Paul.

MARCUSE, H. (1972) Studies in Critical Philosophy London: New Left Books.

McHUGH, P. et al (1974) On the Beginning of Social Inquiry London: Routledge and Kegan Paul.

McLELLAN, D. (1969) The Young Hegelians and Karl Marx London: Macmillan

MERLEAU-PONTY, M. (1964) Sense and Non-Sense Evanston: Northwestern University Press.

MUSGROVE, F. (1968) 'The contribution of sociology to the study of the curriculum' in J. F. Kerr (Ed)

Changing the Curriculum London: University of London
Press.

OLLMAN, B. (1971) Alienation: Marx's Conception of Man
in Capitalist Society London: Cambridge University
Press.

O'NEILL, J. (1972) Sociology as a Skin Trade London:
Heinemann.

PATEMAN, T. (Ed) (1972) Counter Course: A Handbook for
Course Criticism, Harmondsworth: Penguin Books.

PHENIX, P. H. (1962) The use of the disciplines as
curriculum content Educational Forum 26.

PICCONE, P. (1971) Phenomenological Marxism Telos No. 9.

POPPER, K. (1972) Objective Knowledge London: Oxford
University Press.

POPKEWITZ, T. S. (1972)   The craft of study, structure
and schooling Teachers' College Record Vol. 74 (2).

POSTMAN, N. and WEINGARTNER, C. (1971) Teaching as a
Subversive Activity Harmondsworth: Penguin Books.

PRING, R. (1972) Knowledge out of control Education for
Teaching, Autumn 1972.

ROSZAK, T. (Ed) (1969) The Dissenting Academy
Harmondsworth: Penguin Books.

SARTRE, J-P. (1974) Between Existentialism and Marxism
London: New Left Books.

SHROYER, T. (1971) 'A reconceptualisation of critical
theory' in J. D. Colfax and J. L. Roach (Eds) Radical
Sociology New York: Basic Books.

SHROYER, T. (1972) The dialectical foundations of critical theory Telos No. 12.

VANDENBERG, D. (1971) Being and Education: An Essay in
Existential Phenomenology Englewood Cliffs, New Jersey:
Prentice-Hall.

VULLIAMY, G. (1973) Teaching sociology: a new approach
New Society Vol. 23, No. 544, 8th March 1973.

WHITTY, G. J. (1973) Competing Definitions of Social
Studies: Some Observations on the Possibilities and
Problems of Change in the School Curriculum Unpublished
M.A. Dissertation, University of London.

WILLIAMS, R. (1973) Base and superstructure in Marxist
cultural theory New Left Review 82.

WILSON, T. P. (1971) 'Normative and interpretive paradigms in sociology' in J. D. Douglas (Ed) Understanding
Everyday Life London: Routledge and Kegan Paul.

YOUNG, M. F. D. (Ed) (1971) Knowledge and Control: New
Directions for the Sociology of Education London:
Collier-Macmillan.

YOUNG, M. F. D. (1973a) Taking sides against the probable:
problems of relativism in teaching and the sociology of
knowledge, Educational Review Vol. 25 (3).

YOUNG, M. F. D. (1973b) Educational theorizing: a
radical alternative Education for Teaching Summer.

1.2
Philosophers, Sociologists and Knowledge in Education

John Ahier

THE DICHOTOMIES

Since the publication of Young's *Knowledge and Control* sociologists have now joined the philosophers of education in the study of the curriculum. One cannot help welcoming such a move in the study of education, bringing to the forefront, as it does, the problem of ideology and the functioning of the state in this respect, along with the possibility of breaking with the earlier exclusive concern for equality of opportunity.

One's optimism is tempered, however, by two things. Most of the sociologists seem content to stay within the identity offered them by the very curriculum examined; that is, they believe there is a distinct sociological approach to the pre-given object, the curriculum, in which sociology is but one subject. Secondly, in spite of superficial differences, they remain indebted to both philosophical and educational thinking. Thus, what we tend to find in the 'new' sociology of the curriculum is an expression of the dilemmas of those working within the ideological apparatus of the state. There is not an analysis of the location of the salaried, state-employed petty bourgeoisie, but a continuation of ideological debate vital to petty bourgeois concerns, given its intermediate structural position and primary existence in the ideological sphere. My suggestion in this paper is that this 'educational thinking' moves within a pre-set area, never generating an alternative to philosophical problems.

What is the nature of this ideological area, the area of thought bounded by 'extremes' which are reducible to sides of philosophical dualities? Briefly, we can expose two types of thinking about education and knowledge in general, and certain connections can be suggested between these two types and the development

of the ideological apparatus of the state in capitalist
formations. To begin with, there can be located within
this area two general notions concerning the nature of
knowledge. On the one hand is the view that there is
some pure knowledge possessed and protected by educated
men, who reveal its secrets to those seeking entry to
the educated community. This may be contrasted with
the practical approach to knowledge represented by
various forms of pragmatic thinking. Here it is exploratory and utilitarian rather than revelatory and pure.
Next there may be seen to be two views regarding the
scope of knowledge in educational institutions and the
extent to which initiation into it is claimed to provide an understanding of the whole society. In one
case, holistic visions are encouraged and the process
of learning is one of coming to see and to feel the
whole culture or society. The emerging identity of the
person who knows is bound up with his moral identity
with regard to his society. In the opposite view,
conceptions of man and society are piecemeal and at low
levels of generalization. Moral insights are seen to
be generated by games, for example, and getting on together in practical activities. Knowledge itself is
more concerned with means.

Considering the two notions of education, I believe
it is unhelpful to call one elitist and the other egalitarian. Certainly the first kind of thinking has been
associated historically with situations where education
has functioned to give a selected group the credentials
for the administration of the state, and to make clear
the distinction between those with authority and those
without. The second, however, can serve, in a different fashion, to perpetuate a social order which, when
regarded from beyond the bounds of the professional
educator, may be equally lacking in egalitarian character. The first type of thinking sees men in academic
centres, the universities, doing work vital for the
state's moral condition. In times of universal education, the maintenance of the distinction between the
esoteric and the exoteric, possibly combined with the
necessity of preserving the allegiance of the masses,
is considered to be problematic by those who think in
this way. According to this type of sentiment, the
solution is to give glimpses of the 'heavenly yang
substance'[1], or the geist; to foster a simple faith
without the theology. Teachers, in this case, are
perceived as representatives of the spirit of the high
culture. They are likely to be ordered hierarchically
in accordance with their proximity to the academics
themselves. In the opposing view, this division

between the esoteric and exoteric is less pronounced or
lacking. Here 'community' or 'occupation' is stressed
at the expense of 'society' or 'culture'. Knowledge is
seen to be organized around practical affairs and
secular occupations. Intelligence is considered more
important than insight, and intrinsic arguments concerning the value of knowledge are not entertained.

These polarizations have dominated discussion and
thinking among those concerned with education during
this century. On the issue of academic freedom, for
example, there have been those who argue for universities set apart and uninfluenced by business or the
market. They, in turn, faced the criticism that such
an isolation tended towards elitism and/or ineffectual-
ity. Similarly, there have been arguments about the
'community school', which some considered to be a step
towards true democracy, whilst others thought it an
excellent means of restricting aspirations and social
mobility (Everett, 1938). In the same mode is the
present debate concerning whether it is justified to
give an academic education to some pupils and not to
others[2]. But perhaps the most significant aspect of
this dichotomous thinking in Anglo-Saxon educational
theorizing has been the fact that where 'pure knowledge'
became less secret it has tended to lose its scope -
its ability to handle universals. The opening up of an
audience, with universal education, has been paralleled
by closure in terms of application.

My argument is that much of the debate and thinking
which is encapsulated within these antipathies is
'education-bound'. The tensions which make up the arguments reflect the histories of the class which depends
upon its education.

Now for Marxist theory, the problems which are most
closely related to these issues concern the functioning
of the state as a balance for fractions of capital, the
particular role of the petty bourgeoisie vis-a-vis this
balance, and the significance of internal divisions in
the petty bourgeoisie between the state-employed and
the self-employed. Until fairly recently[3], there has
been little work of this nature which may help to
reconceptualize our understanding of education and so,
initially, there must be a reliance upon Weberian
research into what has been called the social positions
of 'men of knowledge' (Znaniecki, 1940). This work has
produced some studies of the changing beliefs of these
groups in relation to their perceived functions. One
such study, by Ringer (1969), uses Weber's previous
example of the Chinese mandarin to look at the ideas

and social position of Weber's fellow academics in
Germany. Ringer's thesis is that at a certain point
between an agrarian economy and full industrialization,
when the landholder is losing his claim to legitimacy,
yet the owner of industrial capital has not established
his, a monarch may rule bureaucratically through a
mandarin group. Under pressure, self-justification
demanded that this group distinguished itself from both
the 'merely civilized', in this case the aristocracy,
and from the practical thinking, materialist bourgeoisie. They did this, especially during their decline,
by emphasizing their culture and their elevating, holistic and synthetic thinking. This was contrasted to
the 'culture of the trader' as Sombart (1915) described
the British way of thinking.

These men's views of education and educational
institutions are of interest. During the period which
Ringer investigates, they can be seen as struggling
to keep the universities as pure centres of cultivation,
untainted by business or industry. Sensing their decline they emphasized, even further, the idea of
impracticality, seeing it as the best guarantee of
freedom from outside interference - a factor which had
not bothered them during their ascendancy in the
Wilhelmian bureaucracy. As for education in general,
they saw it as concerned with 'social orientation',
establishing the idea of service to the totality. It
might be said that through moral education they could
keep some way of influencing the course of events.

To suggest a specific alternative, Ringer's case
may be compared with that of the American 'men of
knowledge'. Chomsky (1969) has, in fact, used the term
'mandarin' to describe these academics, but it was
C. Wright Mills (1966) who documented their quite
different development. During the period when the
German mandarins were showing concern for what many saw
as the destructive forces of science, industrialization
and democracy, American universities were forsaking
idealism. Mills showed the great increase in the number of university courses in science with a utilitarian
or professional basis at the end of the nineteenth
century, and the great increase in student demand for
secular training to which the universities openly
responded. Where, to the German theorist, universal
education was to be concerned with 'social orientation',
or establishing the idea of service to the community,
American discussion of the moral aspects of education
dealt with few such holistic notions. Educational
theorists like Dewey maintained the image of a good

society as one organized like a small, rural community,
and Mead (1908-9a) discussed moral education in terms
of bringing children to play games with a spirit of
sportsmanship. The study of history to him was a way
of showing how people have worked together, and not an
introduction to the national culture and legal state
(1908-9b).

Of interest for this paper are the similarities
concerning the ways in which these issues have been
understood by intellectuals and educational theorists
from each tradition, by their critics, as well as by
the writers who have referred to such groups. They
may be seen as debating within similar bounds, as
suggested at the beginning of the paper. In the case
of the United States, for example, men like Hutchins
(1936) have posed a broad, classical, humanist education based on the 'great books of Western civilization',
against that which they thought to be the practicalism
and neglect of the mind characteristic of a pragmatic and
vocational curriculum. The answer Chomsky produced
to what he perceived as a problem about the social role
of the intellectual was the creation of an unattached
intelligentsia. This was not unlike the conception of
Mannheim, which was itself a typical product of the
latter's own German background.

SOCIOLOGY OF THE CURRICULUM IN
BRITISH EDUCATIONAL THOUGHT

By a comparison, now, between some conventional
English philosophy of education and an attempt at a
sociology of the curriculum, I want to attempt to show
the actual results of these restrictions. The point is
not that British philosophy of education has followed
the American or German cases, or that changes in the
ideological sphere are paralleled exactly in these
countries. Even within a Weberian framework, it is
difficult to locate in Britain a separate grouping of
men distinguished by their knowledge alone. British
intellectuals' quiet sense of confidence has come from
the company they kept rather than any specific mandarin
function they performed in the transition to capitalism.
On the other hand, American pragmatism, and the related
professionalization of the universities, has had little
intellectual effect here, except in the lower strata of
educational institutions.

Any philosophical analysis of a concept such as that
of 'the educated man' is likely to make clear that such

a creature remains, in English language and culture,
the man initiated into the academic disciplines. Most
certainly he has not been educated in a vocational
fashion, nor is he one who knows all about 'worthy home
membership'. In Liberal Education and the Nature of
Knowledge Hirst, an important representative of present
philosophy of education in Britain, analyses and justifies liberal education in terms of the pursuit of
knowledge alone. His criticisms of other writers on
education are based on the conviction that one cannot
understand mental abilities, or qualities of mind and
their development, without having a clear idea of the
forms of knowledge in which thinking may proceed. He
argues that 'there can be effective thinking only when
the outcome of mental activity can be recognized and
judged by those who have the appropriate skills and
knowledge, for otherwise the phrase has no significant
application'. Accepting that knowledge may also be
organized into 'fields' held together by subject matter
or practical concerns such as education itself, Hirst
still considers that it is the forms which are the
fundamental divisions. Only they are said to have
different central concepts which are internally related,
one to another, by particular logical structures. It
is also claimed that the different forms have their own
criteria or tests of validity, as well as their special
techniques of explanation. Included among such forms
are history, the arts and the natural sciences.

Some aspects of Hirst's analysis resemble, covertly
at least, the type of resolution the German academics
made of the antipathies previously mentioned. There is
the notion of the individual being progressively initiated into these forms of knowledge which are maintained by men who already understand the criteria.
There is a distinct difference maintained between such
knowledge, along with the understanding it brings, and
the mastery of mere details in a specialist or technical course. But whilst, in Hirst's writings, there
are implicit notions of a hierarchy of authority and
legitimacy, with the universities as centres of pure
learning at the peak, there are few holistic or inte-
grating terms in this symbolic system. Few questions
of membership are raised overtly. The immediate identities of British academics appear as those of historian, scientist, philosopher and so on.

With regard to the 'new' sociology of the curriculum,
it is likely that Hirst would be highly critical, especially concerning their relativization of that which
he would consider to be fundamental to any thought or

knowledge claims. One may presume that he would detect
a lack of distinction between knowledge and belief,
cause and reason, and a lack of concern for the rules
of simple logic. Conversely, in the work of two sociologists of education I wish to consider here, there are
some superficial disagreements with the views Hirst
represents. Michael Young, in an indirect reference
to Hirst, finds that criticisms of curriculum reform
like those of John White, which are 'based on an absolu-
tist conception of a set of distinct forms of knowledge'
merely serve to justify such constructs. Young goes on
to say that 'unless such necessary distinctions or
intrinsic logics are treated as problematic, philosophical criticisms cannot examine the assumptions of
academic curriculum'. Of course, if these distinctions
are necessary, then in a real sense, they cannot be
questioned by philosopher or sociologist, for one's
very questioning would depend upon them. Certainly
Young nowhere examines the fundamental distinctions on
which Hirst's case appears to rest. More significantly,
so long as he keeps the debate within education and
represents a sociology against a philosophy of education, then he cannot truly be said to be able to move
to a position from which it is possible to carry out
such a task. My argument is that in spite of some
apparent conflict there are some important similarities
between the position of thinkers like Young and Hirst
at the more fundamental levels, and that these similarities are more interesting than their differences.

How, then, do sociologists such as Young and Esland
look at the issues of knowledge in education? Primarily
they are concerned with the problems of explaining the
ways within which knowledge is socially organized. To
do this they turn to two areas of sociological theory.
The older traditions in the sociology of knowledge are
used to place 'educational knowledge' in a wider perspective concerned with the social influence on ideas
in general. Mention is made, for example, of a Marxian
approach to education in capitalist societies, which, it
is claimed, sees schools as a tool of the ruling class,
along with a Weberian view that special kinds of knowledge are used by some groups to justify the ascendancy
of some administrative groups. More recent ideas,
developed from the work of Mead and Schutz, are also
considered to throw light on the ways in which teachers'
and pupils' definitions of that which constitutes knowledge in educational institutions are created, maintained and changed.

It is worth noting the way in which they can list such diverse figures as possible contributors to a sociology of the curriculum. This must indicate that here is another claim by another subject from within the academic curriculum to be able to explain a pre-given object and thus setting itself firmly within the limits of empiricism. In a similar way Hirst's (1966) analysis of the forms of knowledge gave a safe place for a particular kind of philosophy - an 'institution-alized philosophy' (Gellner, 1968) where the 'distinct philosophical enterprise' is the clarification of con-cepts in everyday use. The way in which these sociolo-gists approach education is, therefore, likely to be within the dichotomies suggested. On examination we find that not only do their ideal typical distinctions express these dualities but one side is favoured in their sociology. Esland (1971), seeking to show the relationship between knowledge, pedagogy and the ways in which members of the teaching profession see the child, sets up two idealized models of thinking. The psycho-metric, which is empiricist, individualistic, and emphasizes the innate is contrasted with the epistemological model, which is said to have an active image of the child. Where the former encourages approaching the child as a 'deficit system' which is initiated into pre-existing, external thought forms, the latter is said to consider him as arranging know-ledge and developing interpretational schema. It is claimed that knowledge is reified along with the child in the psycho-metric model, but in the epistemological, it is perceived as dialectical. It is implied that the present philosophers of education, with their emphasis on worthwhileness (Peters), and their clarification of the public forms into which children are to be led (Hirst), fit within the psycho-metric model.

If these distinctions are meant to represent sides in the present educational debate, there is little doubt where Esland's sympathies rest with his use of the terms 'reification' and 'objectivistic' and his faith in the changes which will result from adoption of the epistemological paradigm. We find him committed to a particular sociology represented by theorists like Mead and Schutz. Such a commitment, however, does not permit him, in his research proposals, to examine the history of these very dichotomies in educational think-ing. Instead, there is both a sympathy with one side and an acceptance of both as data at the ideological level. Allying himself with a theorist so imbued with American Pragmatism and Progressivism, G. H. Mead, the

holistic aspects of the issues are defined out by
virtue of such a resolution of the dichotomies. The
pre-existence and exteriority of forms of thinking are
questioned in a mistaken way for the sake of a misdirected polemic against the philosophers. It is
misdirected because whilst we may agree that these men
produce analyses of knowledge and education which can
reflect the ideology of some class or group, this in no
way undermines the utility of such analysis. Getting
clear, by reference to public criteria, what has been
meant by being educated is no necessary evil.

The result of Esland's wanting to examine the social
construction of knowledge, but within what has been
termed in sociological theory the 'action framework',
is that he is pushed by the logic of the argument into
considering the area where personal negotiation and
bargaining is associated with different knowledge outcomes; the area of education and its institutions.
The possibilities of action may be preserved, but only
within certain educational or professional confines.
If structures are considered he feels he is reifying
and dehumanizing. If they are not, his thesis and
research are restricted. Mead's faith in the school
community and education informed the latter's concept-
ualization of the settings for socialization and vice
versa. Subsequent use of his ideas, such as that by
Esland and others, encourages similar conceptions.
When combined inevitably with a belief that talk of
structure de-activates man, the scope of thinking and
action is reduced.

Young (1971) does not show the same shyness of structure as does Esland. Both in his Introduction and in
the first chapter of his work there are criticisms of
Meadian-based research. His reservation is that such
work can only look at the level of interaction, and
that one has to investigate 'structural contingencies'
which influence the definitions which are made available in these interactions. Links are forged between
the school organization, the curriculum and the social
structure, but because of their rigidity and form, and
the formula that men make history but against a back-
drop of 'structural contingencies', these links appear
to restrict the thesis within the same philosophical
and educational bounds as Esland's. The picture is of
a hierarchical ordering of knowledge tied to a hierarchically controlled society. What analysis can this
suggest of the social formation? Inevitably it is a
simple one in terms of the distribution of quantities
of power which are used in the conflicts for respect

and status. Ideology, here, must amount to ideas put
about by a group to present an image of itself as
worthy of respect and its interests as universal interests.

Young, like others who arrive at this position, then
proceeds to take two very doubtful steps in his argument. The first raises the whole question of relativism. The second illustrates a suspect tying together
of structural change with a particular form of cultural,
educational change. First, in a part of his thesis
which he may claim was fathered by Marx, he argues that
'those in position of power' try to define 'what is to
be taken for knowledge', and dictate how it is to be
organized and distributed. This seems to be a particularly mechanical interpretation, very similar to that
which may be found in some radical criticisms of Western
societies with their capitalist controlled mass media.
Such a view implies a false idea that it is the bourgeois class or a power elite that produces ideas, as
opposed to the whole of bourgeois society. This prevents one from seeing, as Mepham (1972) has argued that:

> The effective dissemination of ideas is only poss-
> ible because, or to the extent that, the ideas thus
> disseminated are ideas which, for quite different
> reasons, do have a sufficient degree of effective-
> ness both in rendering social reality intelligible
> and in guiding practice within it for them to be
> apparently acceptable. It is the relation between
> ideology and reality that is the key to its domin-
> ance.

Attempting to forge links between the organization of
school knowledge and the social structure on the common
dimension of stratification, Young says that where
knowledge is highly stratified 'there will be a clear
distinction between what is taken to count as knowledge
and what is not ...' This is a mistaken way of looking
at the matter, for those theorists and educators who
maintain the hierarchical curriculum are not deciding
'what is to count as knowledge'. Defending poetry in
preference to bingo, the philosopher of education does
not claim that there is no knowledge of the latter.
He argues only that the former is more worthwhile and
that one ought to spend one's life pursuing such
knowledge[4]. Nor is he making some absurd claim which
can only be upheld by some force or other. Even within
Young's type of analysis, one must be able to distinguish clearly between the possibility that some kinds
of knowledge find their way into the curriculum because

of the support of powerful groups and the confusing
notion that some men have the power to define what is
true.

Secondly, examining the hierarchical organization of
knowledge, Young establishes a connection between high
social status and certain kinds of knowledge - literate,
abstract, individually studied and unrelated to daily
life. Following his criticisms of the structural
functionalist notion that some knowledge has high status
because it is more needed by society, he is forced by
the logic of conventional criticisms of this theory
into believing that if this organization of knowledge
were upset, then there would be a 'massive redistribution of the labels "education", "success" and "failure",
and thus also a parallel redistribution of rewards in
terms of wealth, prestige and power'. Like so many
conventional sociological criticisms of structural
functionalism, he maintains the forms in which the
systems and sub-systems are related in that theory,
insofar as they are seen as expressions of the central
value system, and only seeks to challenge the legitimacy or true morality of these values themselves.

Not only does this suggest a too direct and idealist
connection between what goes on in the ideological
apparatus of the state and the economic and political,
it also represents a restricted view of what would
constitute any significant ideological change. Because
the distinctions between the types of knowledge on
which he concentrates reflect the built-in antipathies
in educational thinking, moves within these will only
change strictly educational conceptions; that is,
achievements hitherto not seen as educationally significant may gain in such significance. There is, however,
no necessity for the social distinction of the new kind
of rewards to be different. In other words, destrat-
ification or restratification of educational knowledge
within the distinctions he makes would not constitute
a 'revolutionary alternative' except for those who rely
on a particular kind of knowledge to distinguish themselves from the proletariat, i.e. the petty bourgeoisie.

I have suggested that some of the organizing principles in the work of both Esland and Young may be
located within the confines which necessarily enclose
educational debate. I now wish to show how, in spite of
their critical stance towards current philosophy of education, they share, in an equivocal fashion, at least
some of Hirst's basic distinctions and attendant problems. One of the divisions analysed by Hirst (1965) which
is of interest here is that between the natural and

social sciences. The unquestioning acceptance of this
division suggests that some a priori status must be
accorded to it. Behind this particular case there must
be the assumption that those factors which distinguish
social from physical science are more significant than
their similarities. Such arguments for the distinctiveness of social science have placed emphasis on the
fact that it is concerned with persons' intentions and
ideas, and in the context the use of the notion of
'cause' is illegitimate.

Such problems are far from being solved in the philosophy of the social sciences, and one may doubt
whether the form in which they are often discussed,
fostering as it does a commitment to one side or the
other, is a satisfactory one. In the polemic of Young
and Esland, the form and vigour of the debate are continued. They rely, in their attacks on the Positivism
of previous sociologists, on the a priori distinctions
which must be, in one form or another, at the basis of
Hirst's separation of forms. There are the same superficial difficulties with such a position. For example,
any claim that all social phenomena are equally and
necessarily concerned with ideas and intentions tends to
overlook the humanly constructed yet physical aspects
of a social environment. More serious for Young is
that, combined with the attack on Positivism, there is
also an attempt to open up to enquiry 'the dogmas of
rationality and science'. Now, while some advocates
of a rational and scientific education may be dogmatic
in their beliefs, it is more than confusing to pose
notions of dogmatic reason and science. The problem
with Young's position is such that it casts a general
suspicion on the possibility of a scientifically constituted object with related forms of experimentation.
Given the critique of Positivism, we are impelled by
the argument to consider society as basically people
and their relationships, and, because of the primacy
given to meanings and reasoning, these relationships
must remain in essence those of differing respect and
legitimacy in accordance with different values.

CONCLUSION

It could be said that I have merely forced these two
sociologists into the same framework by imputations of
similarity with Hirst. My concluding point is that
there are differences between Young and Esland on the
one hand, and Hirst on the other, but, given their
starting points, these differences operate within that
framework to the point of rendering any ensuing debate

between them of limited value, at least for the development of a theorized understanding of education in society. Given (a) the relative lack of boundary between occupants of the primary ideological institutions and the bourgeoisie because of the specific development of the state in Britain; and (b) the primacy among occupants of the subject identities which Hirst found so significant as to turn into a *priori* distinctions; and (c) the hierarchy in these subjects, which Young found so important as to lead him to believe that its rearrangement would have revolutionary implications, then the distinguishing feature, their relativism, is understandable. It may be seen to do three things at the same time. In the first place, because of the assumed relation between universities and the ruling class, it may be seen as a possible way of relativizing the structure on which they depend. In the second place, it can serve as an instrument with which to call into question the legitimacy of other 'subject-based' men of knowledge who are perceived as being above the sociologist in the hierarchy. But finally, and inevitably, it brings the self-inflicted wounds of relativism, when the sociologist's own knowledge can be of no more relevance than that of anyone else.

NOTES

1. See WEBER, M. (1948) The Chinese Literati in H. Gerth and C. W. Mills (Eds) *From Max Weber* London: Routledge and Kegan Paul.

2. See WHITE, J. (1969) The curriculum mongers: Education in reverse, *New Society* 6th March 1969; and Education in reverse, *New Society* 2nd May 1968. See THOMPSON, K. (1970) Not so simple, *New Society* 30th April 1970 for criticisms.

3. Recent work by N. Poulantzas has gone some way to filling this gap, e.g. *Fascism and Dictatorship* London: New Left Books, 1974.

4. Nor is the 'ought' here made explicit, but only suggested by an extension of the trancendental argument concerning truthfulness to show that there is some kind of moral obligation to pursue the truth in some curriculum activity. viz. BECK, A. W., Does ethics and education rest on a mistake?, in *Education Philosophy and Theory*, III, p.I-II.

REFERENCES

CHOMSKY, N. (1969) American Power and the New Mandarins
Harmondsworth: Penguin Books.

ESLAND, G. (1971) Teaching and learning in M.F.D. Young
(Ed) Knowledge and Control London: Collier-Macmillan.

EVERETT, S. (1938) The Community School New York:
Appleton Century.

GELLNER, E. (1968) Words and Things Harmondsworth:
Penguin Books.

HIRST, P. (1965) Liberal education and the nature of
knowledge in R. D. Archambault (Ed) Philosophical
Analysis and Education London: Routledge and Kegan
Paul.

HIRST, P. (1966) Educational theory in J. W. Tibble
(Ed) The Study of Education London: Routledge and
Kegan Paul.

HUTCHINS, R. M. (1936) The Higher Learning in America
New York: Yale University Press.

MEAD, G. H. (1908-9a) Moral training in schools in
Elementary School Teacher IX p.327.

MEAD, G. H. (1908-9b) The problems of history in the
elementary school in Elementary School Teacher IX p.433.

MEPHAM, J. (1972) The theory of ideology in Capital,
Radical Philosophy No. 2.

MILLS, C. W. (1966) Sociology and Pragmatism New York:
Oxford University Press.

RINGER, F. (1969) The Decline of the German Mandarins
Cambridge: Harvard University Press.

SOMBART, W. (1915) Handler und Helden: Patriotische
Bessinnungen Munich.

YOUNG, M. F. D. (Ed) (1971) Knowledge and Control
London: Collier-Macmillan.

ZNANIECKI, F. (1940) The Social Role of the Man of
Knowledge New York: Columbia University Press.

1.3
Education as Reproduction:

A critical examination of some aspects of the work of Louis Althusser

Michael Erben and Denis Gleeson

A Marxist Structuralist perspective in the sociology of education provides alternative questions and frameworks for analysis to those advanced by Structural-Functionalist sociology. Its particular strength lies in its capacity to examine questions of power and cultural reproduction. This paper attempts to examine the work of Louis Althusser (1971), as an example of such a perspective[1]. Althusser critically analyses the organization of schooling as a feature of both the reproduction of production, and of ideological processes. While a Structural-Functionalist approach sees existing relations between education, economy and society as 'given' and functioning to maintain the necessary conditions for technological survival, Althusser's work radically questions the nature of such relations in terms of their role in the maintenance of ideology and control. However, we would claim that while such an approach succeeds in analysing the ideological character of schools as agents of cultural reproduction, it fails to adequately address the processes through which those who work in schools may act to influence both the conditions of their work, and the wider social context of which schooling is a part.

It is, we feel, crucially important, and in keeping with Althusser's own formulations, that his work be examined critically. As Gane (1974) has stated:

> Althusser's works are 'investigations'. Their demand to the reader is clear, they are not to be regarded as elements of a completed system, but as

* A modified version of this paper first appeared in Educational Studies, Vol.1, No.2, June 1975, titled: Reproduction and social structure, comments on Louis Althusser's sociology of education.

systematic interventions into specific conjunctures
of theory and ideology.

We want to argue that within Althusser's influential
essay *Ideology and Ideological State Apparatuses* there
are conclusions and prescriptions at variance with what
we would see as the character of Marxist theory. In
relation to education, it particularly neglects the
importance of the actions of teachers and students. In
Britain, where teachers and students at all levels are
questioning the various ways in which capitalist relations are expressed, it is necessary that these teachers and students be regarded as important.

Althusser in his attempt to explain the nature of
the processes and mechanisms of the relations of production unwittingly highlights certain ambiguities in
his position, and it is the intention of this paper to
illustrate these by focusing attention on the most
overlooked aspect of his writings, namely his analysis
of education in capitalist society. We focus on the
neglected aspects in Althusser's examination of the
relations of education and production by examining the
notion of reproduction as it relates to knowledge,
ideology, and education. Reservation is expressed concerning Althusser's over-emphasis upon the 'crushing'
influences of apparatuses[2] which condition man in his
pursuit of the maintenance and reproduction of production. Four related issues are raised:

1. Althusser fails to examine how men acquire a sense
    of social structure within production relations,
    and, therefore, inadequately considers how know-
    ledge is produced;

2. he over-emphasizes the consumption of knowledge at
    the expense of the production of knowledge;

3. Althusser's notion of reproduction tends to advance
    a passive model of socialization and assumes a
    reified model of a system tightly policed by a
    'conspiracy' of apparatuses in dominance; and

4. Althusser fails to explain how radicals emerge
    from, escape from, and engage with the 'crushing'
    influences of State Apparatuses.

While the essay puts liberal revisionism in its
place, it equally inhibits teachers and students from
considering the possibility that they may be concerned
with struggle and change. Its message not only leaves
teachers completely flattened and speechless, but it

is likely to reinforce the idea that radical change is
beyond their frames of reference. Questions about what
goes on in schools which are neglected by Althusser, in
particular the ways in which knowledge becomes transmitted, constructed and legitimized, are crucial in
order to begin to understand the contexts and conditions
of schooling. Moreover, there would appear to be a
distinct disparity between current reformist policy and
actual school practice. The 'liberalization' of educational policy would seem to have led to a situation
in which increasing importance is attached to academic-
ally high status pupils. At the same time, any serious
critical consideration of the existing relations between
education and production, which alienate the vast
majority of working-class pupils, is neglected. It
could be argued therefore, that such a contradiction
not only reflects the persistence of the political and
social hierarchy, but also raises important questions
for both the pupil and the radical teacher concerning
how they define such problems as deviance, under-
achievement, deprivation and truancy. Clearly, they
are both being asked to work within pre-given and
largely unquestioned definitions of their own situations
rather than being given the opportunity to redefine and
reshape that situation in the light of their own critical experiences. If this then is the case, surely the
'real' problem facing teachers and pupils is that they
are engaged in a confrontation which is not entirely
of their own making. They are both located in antagon-
istic relations of struggle which (if not articulated
and demonstrated in a united fashion) reflect their
respective positions within the relations of production. It is here that potential for radical change
lies.

In claiming that the initial descriptive theory
of the State advanced by Marx must be explored further
in order to develop the analysis, Althusser claims his
own theory as a scientific advance. He takes Marx's
descriptive theory of social formations in relation to
the view of education which claims that schools are
neutral institutions purged of ideology and devoted to
propagating rational and objective forms of knowledge.
Further, he suggests that just as priests failed to
question religious processes in the past so, in like
manner, teachers today fail to question the ideology
involved in educational processes. His writings raise
important criticisms of the ways in which the teaching
and learning, as well as the transmission and evaluation of educational knowledge, become part of the
fetishism of commodity consumption. Such a thesis

therefore opposes the liberal reformist claim that education may not only compensate for society but also
revolutionize it as naive and reactionary[3].
Althusser's writings, like the work of Meszaros (1970),
call into question all forms of reformism and gradualism.

In his essay, Althusser (1971) analyses the relations between production and the construction of knowledge, which provide the ideological basis for the
reproduction of the pre-conditions of production.
Althusser suggests that the ultimate condition of production is therefore the reproduction of those conditions. That is, in order to produce, there must
initially be the pre-conditions to ensure production:
that as a pre-condition for survival, capitalist society must institutionalize mechanisms for the planning
and management of reproduction and innovation. Reproduction is concerned with two key areas, (a) materials,
capital resources and skills; and (b) a competent,
reliable and well behaved (passively socialized) labour
force. The reproduction of the conditions of production and production itself are therefore interrelated.
Althusser states that:

> Like every metaphor, this metaphor suggests some-
> thing, makes something visible. What? Precisely
> this: that the upper floors could not 'stay up'
> (in the air) alone, if they did not rest precisely
> on their base[4].

In other words, basis and superstructure act in a
reciprocal relation. However, Althusser attempts to
refine discussion of the superstructure by adding
another dimension to the traditionally accepted
Repressive Apparatuses. He argues that two inextricably related forms make up the superstructure:
Repressive State Apparatuses, with such agencies as
the armed forces and police, and Ideological State
Apparatuses, which are characterized by such agencies
as the law, the family, the Church, the unions, the
media and education. While recognizing that this distinction is a 'play on words' and not absolutely clear-
cut, Althusser states that:

> What distinguishes the Ideological State Apparat-
> uses from the (Repressive) State Apparatus is the
> following basic difference: the Repressive State
> Apparatus functions 'by violence', whereas the
> Ideological State Apparatuses function 'by
> ideology'.[5]

For Althusser the school system is a crucial Ideological State Apparatus facilitating and ensuring the reproduction of the essential conditions for capitalist institutions to adapt, survive and innovate. He states:

> Here unlike social formations characterized by slavery or serfdom, this reproduction of the skills of labour power tends (this is a tendential law) decreasingly to be provided for 'on the spot' (apprenticeship within production itself), but is achieved more and more outside production: by the capitalist educational system and by other instances and institutions.[6]

Althusser perceives the functions of the School as two-fold: (a) to transmit the necessary 'know how' required to work and transform the means of production; and (b) to transmit the necessary discipline and respect for existing relations of production. The mechanism of the school, then, not only reproduces skills required in production, but also passively socializes pupils into requirements of their future work situation. Althusser maintains that most teachers are unwitting servants of such an ideology and have little choice in avoiding the service of its interests. The major problem with such an analysis is that it tends towards a typically functionalist view of the school, which is seen as passively responding to the 'needs' of society.

Central to such a thesis is a preoccupation with the problem of order in society in which the basis is perceived as over-determined by the superstructure. Apparatuses here take on self-regulating natures to ensure order within the Body Politic through violence (Repressive State Apparatus) and trickery (Ideological State Apparatus). However, we have to ask to what extent this analysis adds anything to Marx's analysis of production in Capital, and also, to what extent it refines revolutionary theoretical practice. Williams (1974) has stated that:

> The Althusserian concept of Marx's scientific object is not Structuralist as is so often alleged. Marx's vebindungen, specific combinations of invariant elements which define the modes of production, are not turned into structuralist combinations where results and the occupants of the places are irrelevant[7]. The problem (our emphasis) is that Althusser's concept of the scientificity of Marx's object is uncomfortably Structuralist ... What Althusser offers is more a rejection of vulgar

Marxism than a worked out theory of the ideological
instance in the social formation.

It might be further added that Althusser's reference
to his own 'play on words' recoils upon itself. His
analysis of Apparatuses exaggerates those over-determin-
ing structures of dominance, and ignores processes which
characterize men as active producers of knowledge and
social change. The danger is that the 'up in the air'
metaphor may have been allowed to run away with itself,
which is a problem shared by other systems theorists
(who allow their model to take on a reality of its own).
Indeed, Althusser has spared few pains in condemning
this mistake in others elsewhere:

In the creation of knowledge as a 'model', we find
the real and the concrete intervening to enable us
to think the relation, i.e., the distance, between
the 'concrete' and theory as both within theory
itself and within the real itself, not as in a real
outside this real object, knowledge which is produced precisely by theory, but as within this real
object itself, as a relation of the part to the
whole, of a 'partial' part to a superabundant whole.
The inevitable result of this operation is to make
theory seem one empirical instrument among others,
in other words, to reduce any theory of knowledge
as a model directly to what it is: a form of theoretical pragmatism (Althusser and Balibar, 1970).

Althusser's reading of the nature of reproduction proceeds along a different path from that of Marx in
that he assumes the consent implicit in social contract
theories. In one form or another, theorists, such as
Hobbes, Rousseau, Weber and Parsons, have placed great
emphasis on examining those constraints concerned with
the problem of order which have limited men's actions
and choices when coming to terms with doubt and violence. Here men give up their 'natural' freedoms for
those of the corporate Leviathan organized for the
protection of the General Will; the overriding concerns become the establishing and maintaining of the
social order, and not the questioning of that order.
Like other such analyses, Althusser's cannot account
for how and why men 'deviate' from the protection of
the Leviathan. He makes any examination of intention,
motive or change apparently trivial in his reified
account of processes of social reproduction.

Althusser's emphasis on the problem of order leads
him into a position in which he fails to understand the

nature of disorder and radical doubt. Having failed to
examine how men 'deviate', he has similarly failed in
the task he has set himself of understanding the mechanisms of social formations, and therefore, the nature
of the Leninist weak link. His analysis approaches
a positivistic interpretation of knowledge as being
'out there' and external to the passive learner, who is
perceived as manipulated by dominant mechanisms and
social formations outside his control. Referring to
both Althusser and Habermas, O'Neill (1972) writes:

> ... both are adding babies to the Marxian bathwater
> which then becomes even more, and not less, essen-
> tial to their displacement. ... Althusser returns
> theory to the savage practice of the Hobbesian state
> which provides the very occasion for political
> theorizing.

Such dilemmas in Althusser's writings are revealed when
he examines the mechanisms for the reproduction of
knowledge; how such knowledge is produced by men inter-
subjectively experiencing the relations of production
is excluded. Althusser claims to seek explanations of
how knowledge is produced, but his analysis tends
towards a description of its consumption rather than
its production.

Not only are the questions which Althusser sets
himself functionalist in nature, but also his use of
language assumes a functionalist 'rhetoric'. For example, he asks:

> What exactly is the extent of the role of the
> Ideological State Apparatuses? What is their im-
> portance based on? In other words: to what does
> the 'function' of these Ideological State Apparat-
> uses, which do not function by repression but by
> ideology, correspond?[8]

His analysis rests on an oversimplified equilibrium
model in which the main features (Ideological State
Apparatuses and Repressive State Apparatuses) complement one another inter-dependently; the former ensuring the maintenance of, and innovation in the system
through ideological mechanisms (schools as ideological
software); and the latter ensuring maintenance through
policing the system with threats of violence (armies
as repressive hardware). There are parallels here, for
example, with Parsons' attempts to use pattern variables
to explain the maintenance of social order.

For Althusser, the school system reproduces the conditions of production, and this may be on a simple or
on an extended scale. His descriptions, however, are
worked out only in the most perfunctory way, providing
a wholly inadequate account both of the reproduction of
labour power in the school, and the nature of political
activity surrounding this process. Even at the analytic level, the distinction between Ideological and
Repressive State Apparatuses seems almost too arbitrary
to have any explanatory value. Althusser himself says
that although the two areas overlap and interconnect,
they are still predominated either by ideology (Ideological State Apparatus) or violence (Repressive State
Apparatus). This is to misunderstand the character of
institutional social reality in two ways[9]. First, at
the level of procedure, we know that some institutions
'behave' as though they were other institutions. For
example, we know that certain schools have organization-
ally or ideologically more in common with certain
prisons or other 'total institutions' than with other
schools. Similarly we know by observation, that organizations vary in their characteristics on a total/open
continuum, and also that the majority of schools have
many of the characteristics of Goffman's (1961) 'total
institution'. Second, the patterns of interaction in
schools and other institutions could usefully be analysed
in terms of models generated from studies of prisons[10].
It is a characteristic of Althusser's functionalist
tendency that the vocabularies of meanings associated
with individuals in particular situations are neglected;
and the potential of such situations for political
activity is missed. The basis for politically available situations is by-passed and any possibility of a
'weak link' denied. There is a contradiction therefore, between his functionalist description of the
school, and his argument that the reproduction of the
social relations of production can only be a class
undertaking, realized through a class struggle.

It is precisely not enough, for example, for
Althusser to state that the Repressive State Apparatus
provides a 'shield' behind which the school is allowed
to reproduce the relations of production. Further
analysis of the position is necessary in order to formulate any kind of political strategy. It is just at
this point that there has been witnessed action -
students and teachers, both separately and together,
feeling the strength of their power, and harnessing it
against specific aspects of capitalist oppression.
This is, in many ways, just the kind of activity that
Althusser (1969) has argued for elsewhere; but here

again, as Ranciere (1974) has shown, Althusser does not
fulfil the promise of his own rigour when the situation
moves to action. It is not enough for Althusser (1971)
to patronise:

> ... those teachers who, in dreadful conditions,
> attempt to turn the few weapons they can find ...
> against the ideology ... in which they are trapped.[11]

It is more important to engage with them in struggle,
rather than, as Althusser can be seen as doing, scupper-
ing the ship while it is still in port. It is within
the activity of Marxism that answers to questions about
Marxism lie. Clearly, what counts as a valid or legitimate explanation must inevitably require the examination of competing scientific theories which then raises
all kinds of relativistic issues. The outcomes of
such considerations are not necessarily resolved by
appeals to reason or the presumed self-evidence of
truth or science, but rather through the critical examination of the intentional actions and processes of
control exercised by those in the dominant positions
of power. The engagement in struggle we are concerned
with means active engagement, and not that practised
by bourgeois empiricist sociology; for, as Althusser
has shown, empiricism is guilty of a fundamental confusion in that it cannot finally differentiate between
the object of study and the studying subject. An
empiricist conception of knowledge implies that the
subject first perceives knowledge as 'out there', and
then proceeds to distill from this its essence, and to
eliminate in the process those inessential things that
might serve to obscure the essence. The final possession by the subject of this essence (the object) is
then characterized as knowledge. Here is the point of
departure for Althusser's critique of empiricism. This
conception of knowledge with its two real parts (object
and abstracted essence) is actually proposing that knowledge is to be found in the essence of the real object.
The knowledge of reality is thereby conceived as part
of that reality which is tautologous. As a result of
this process, Althusser et al (1970) argue that we have
fallen '... into empiricist idealism (by confusing)
thought with the real by reducing thought about the
real to the real itself.' For him, therefore, empiricism is untenable because the knowledge of the object
is part of the object itself. What is missing is the
relation between men and knowledge, and the analysis
of prevailing consciousness linking it, as Mills (1959)
has put it in his discussion of empiricism, to 'social

and historical structures'. Without the engagement
that he has demonstrated in his critique of empiricism
as necessary, Althusser's statement that the school may
be the site of class struggle becomes largely meaning-
less. His analysis of education in Ideology and
Ideological State Apparatuses can lead, we argue, to
a state of inaction, justifying the avoidance of areas
exactly where there may be weak links in the chain of
capitalist coercion.

Althusser's lapse demonstrates a purely reflectionist approach in that he does not allow situations to be
constructions of reality. However, he seems to be the
victim of his own castigations at a deep level in the
functionalist and reflectionist assumptions expressed
in his essay, where he implicitly denies the effective
possibility of the power of specific situations. This
is not to say that situations are merely the composite
of random accidents with the economy being determinant
in the last instance. Althusser (1969) in his critique
of Engels has said about the latter 'host of accidents'
that[12]:

> It is astonishing to find Engels in this text pres-
> enting the forms of the superstructure as the source
> of a microscopic infinity of events whose inner
> connection is unintelligible[13].

Althusser further states in the same essay:[14]

> What makes such and such an event historical is not
> the fact that it is an event, but precisely its
> insertion into forms which are themselves historical

In Ideology and Ideological State Apparatuses however,
Althusser cannot recognize the power of specific situations on account of the limitations of his functionalist tendency. Meszaros (1970) has stated that:

> A comprehensive and dynamic socio-historical theory
> is inconceivable without a force, positively inter-
> ested in social transformation as its practical
> ground.

The school (teachers and pupils) can represent, in
real situations, the arena for such a positive interest
in social transformation.

We are not arguing that there is no overall Marxist
theory of the relationship between schools and social

structure, but rather that Althusser's attempted deline-
ation of the position of the school is a gross oversimplification of any actual situation. The character
of dialectical experience does not reside in the realization of a free subjective aim, but in a conditioned
subjective aim. Neither does it reside in a purely
'out there' exterior world, but in the awareness,
through action at the intersection of the conditioned
subjective aim and the exterior world, of an ongoing
process of realization. As Laing et al (1971) state:

> Marx put his thought in very precise terms. If, for
> example, one wishes to act on or influence (agir)
> an educator, then one must act on or modify the
> factors which condition him.

The 'one' can be the educator himself, other educators,
or students or pupils acting within their own situation
in a process of transformation.

In Reading Capital Althusser states that:

> The structure of the relations of production deter-
> mines the places and functions occupied and adopted
> by the agents of production, who are never anything
> more than the occupants of these places, insofar as
> they are the 'supports' (Trager) of these functions.

This at first appears adequate as a description of the
reciprocating and restrictive influences of capitalist
relations of production, the agents of production, and
the functions of production, as these factors influence
occupants in the system. However, what does this
interpretation tell us of the meanings which men give
to this predicament? Not unlike Parsons, Althusser
portrays a model of man as a puppet or cultural fool
constrained completely by agents or mechanisms of the
system. In over-emphasizing those passive features of
socialization to the exclusion of active features,
Althusser fails to consider adequately the ambiguities
in production which influence men's abilities to make
decisions in the face of intimidation, fear and violence. The exposure of such a failure does not necessarily mean a retreat into a Marxist humanism.

If we are left with the conclusion that Althusser
has a functionalist tendency in his analysis of social
order and adaptation, what are then the implications
that arise for his theory of the relationship between
education and reproduction? For Althusser, the mechanism of the school not only reproduces specific skills

but also reproduces types of pupils with thought processes (consciousness) and attitudes that are largely
related to a respect for the workings of existing production relations (discipline). The learning of such
processes is a long apprenticeship of instruction in
obedience. This takes two forms. First, pupils learn
to respect the conditions of production (time, loyalty,
honesty, the law, property); second, they learn specific skills and tasks to implement the means of production. Teachers who are critical of such a process,
Althusser argues, can do little to change events and
are destined to serve the interests of a ruling ideology, subjugated to a system 'which is bigger than they
are and (which) crushes them'[15]. Althusser, here and
elsewhere in his essay, is doing little more than re-
echoing what Durkheim has had to say about the nature
of the school. In fact, a seemingly important part of
Althusser's thesis is but a repetition of Durkheim, or
the notion of what has been called the 'hidden curriculum'. The analogy between Althusser's analysis of the
school and that of Parsons is not dissimilar, although
perhaps for different ideological reasons. Parsons
(1959) writes of 'our' interests in the functions of
the school in the following way:

> Our main interest, then, is in a dual problem:
> first of how the school class functions to internal-
> ize in its pupils both the commitments and capac-
> ities for successful performance of their future
> adult roles, and secondly of how it functions to
> allocate these human resources within the role
> structure of the adult society.

Not only are there similarities between the concepts of
system and socialization used by Althusser and Parsons,
but also both writers base their 'theory' on similar
assumptions. This leads Althusser into the uncomfortable position of a contradiction concerning the nature
of theory and beliefs. On the one hand, he wishes to
advance a view which supports the rationality of scientific explanations (theory) over the irrationalities
of myth and illusion (ideology), and yet on the other
hand, he fails to make explicit the criteria upon which
his own theory is based.

Furthermore, Althusser (1964) advances a paradoxical
definition of pedagogy based on the ascendant position
of teachers 'initiating' the novice into forms of
'worthwhile' knowledge. He states that:

> The objective of the pedagogic function is to

transmit an established body of knowledge to students
who do not possess that body of knowledge. The pedagogic situation rests therefore on an absolute condition of inequality between the individual who
knows and one who does not.

The impact of such a view reveals a central ambiguity
in Althusser's position because, on the one hand, he
wants to argue the distinction between ideology and
science, and yet, on the other, he defines the transmission and reception of knowledge in terms of an uncritical acceptance of the superior knowledge of the
teacher standing ascendant over the naive learner. As
Ranciere (1974) points out:

> The two theses complement each other, but absolutely
> contradict each other as well ... But didn't the
> science/ideology distinction precisely imply the
> deepest and most justifiable suspicion towards the
> knowledge of teachers?

It is as though Althusser is oblivious of the import for
his work of theoretical traditions other than his own
(as noted previously in his reductionist conception of
institutions). When, after a descriptive sociological
passage in Ideology and Ideological State Apparatuses,
Althusser says,

> I only wish to point out that you and I are always
> already subjects, which guarantee for us that we are
> indeed concrete, individuals, distinguishable and
> (naturally) irreplaceable subjects[16].

he is stating very little that is new. Much symbolic
interactionist and 'phenomenological' sociology has
been making such statements for a considerable length
of time.

Althusser however, does not, it must be stated, fall
into the relativism of much of the phenomenological
school of sociology. For example, he has demonstrated
that although the Hegelian contradiction appears to be
full of the complex cross-currents of determination and
therefore appears to be over-determined, such a contradiction is, in fact, relativist. That is, although it
describes a complexity of occurrences in each moment of
its progress as it experiences its own essence, this
essence is the product of all those past essences it
has been which now haunt the present. Finally, these
essences are just allusions to the original essence,
and the Hegelian contradictions are nothing other than

the complexity of a cumulative 'internalization'. A
position based on Hegelian phenomenology does not, then,
provide for the conditions available to effectively
'act' in a 'new' realizable way on the present - to
confront the current moment, as Lenin would have put
it, or be part of the articulation of a conjuncture,
in Althusser's (1969) terminology.

History has shown Althusser to be crucially inadequate in his description of Ideological State Apparatuses. The events of 1968 left Althusser's formulations
languishing because they analysed that situation as
'incorrect' for revolutionary struggle. Insofar as
total revolution was concerned, Althusser was right,
but in an important Marxist sense he was wrong. This
was not because there has been some 'reform' as a
result of 1968, but because the direct confrontation
produced both change in the institutions, and a conscious awareness that struggle and political consciousness are inextricably linked[17]. The subsequent organization of courses in terms of content, relevance and
participation, were altered beyond recognition in many
French universities. This movement for change was so
strong that it has now percolated down to lycees,
perhaps the most educationally conservative and traditional state school sector in Western Europe. And most
importantly, while we recognize that much conventional
school practice in France has now become enmeshed in a
move of gradual reaction, we would argue that the
initial stimulus for change did not initially come from
the politics of gradualism.

It would be a mistake to imagine that extra-
parliamentary areas of action are merely 'one off' experiences in moves to radicalization. They are features,
rather, of late capitalism that have emerged in numerous
areas (e.g., Black Power in the United States, Women's
Liberation, Civil Rights in Ulster), and have established themselves as sites of class struggle. Raymond
Williams (1971) has stated:

> It seems to be true that in late capitalist societies
> some of the most powerful campaigns begin from spec-
> ific unabsorbed ... experiences and situations.
> Black Power in the United States, Civil Rights in
> Ulster, the Language Movement in Wales, are experi-
> ences comparable in this respect to the student
> movement and women's liberation. In their early
> stages, these campaigns tend to stress as absolutes
> those local experiences which are of course authen-
> tic and yet most important as indices of the crisis

of the wider society.

One might add specifically to this the movement in
schools represented by radical students and teachers.

The strong Soviet influence on China in educational
matters is a case that demonstrates most effectively
that the arena of activity can change the character of
that arena, and may even precipitate a mass advance.
As reported by Frazer (1965), students in China demon-
strably complained about the arena of their activity,
for example, the number of courses:

> Take the school education specialization in our
> department as an example. The first year consists
> of eight subjects, involving twenty-six hours of
> lectures a week. Besides the five hours of psychol-
> ogy which is a specialization subject the rest are
> almost entirely political theory and culture courses.
> Even the teachers do not know the reasons for such
> courses. For instance, the Modern Literature
> Selection professor once remarked in the classroom
> 'I do not know why first year education requires
> this course, but anyway it is good for you'.

and further, the method of classroom teaching:

> The teaching attitude, and comprehension of the
> material of some teachers are not satisfactory to
> students. For example, in Logic, for the past year.
> It has consisted of the teacher reading his lecture
> notes and the students taking them down like record-
> ing machines. Some students, after attending a
> two-period class, have to spend more than that much
> time to verify and supplement their notes. The
> teacher relies on his notes to lecture, and if he
> should lose a few papers, he will not be able to
> continue with his lecture ... Though incessantly
> talking about cultivating the students' independent
> work ability and coordinating theory with practice,
> the teachers, in practical teaching, only emphasize
> note-taking.

It was within this situation that Mao strove for criticism of the particular situation, and in May 1956
presented his famous slogan: 'Let a hundred flowers
bloom, a hundred schools of thought contend'. It was,
partly, as a response to certain politically active
students and teachers that Mao encouraged the Cultural
Revolution. It was a member (Nieh Yuan-Tzu) of the
Philosophy Department of Peking University who first

brought the Cultural Revolution out into the open when she attacked the President of the University for suppressing a play critical of a policy of Mao's. Mao instructed that her criticisms be broadcast to the nation. The poster Nieh had put up attacking the University President, and therefore implicitly Mao himself, was called by Mao 'China's first Marxist-Leninist dazibao' (Hinton, 1972). Marx said that education is most adequately realized when control is situated as close as possible to the individual - education then, perforce, becoming the concern of each member of society. Marx condemned state control of education in the normal sense as vehemently as he did ecclesiastical control[18].

In Althusser's 'discovery' of certain areas of sociology, it seems that he is aware of a number of criticisms that have been lodged against him, and is demonstrating that his formulations are more 'human' than may have appeared. Along with this 'discovery', in Ideology and Ideological State Apparatuses he reaffirms his criticism of Hegelian Marxism (Lukacs, the Frankfurt School, etc) namely, that in this tradition, history, no matter by how circuitous the route, is reduced to the consciousness of individuals. This criticism he has previously explained in Reading Capital:

> History then becomes the transformation of a human nature, which remains the real subject of the history which transforms it. As a result, history has been introduced into human nature, making men the contemporaries of the historical effects whose subjects they are, but - and this is absolutely decisive - the relations of production, political and ideological social relations, have been reduced to historicized 'human relations', i.e. to inter-human, inter-subjective relations. This is the favourite terrain of historicist humanism.

Althusser has in Ideology and Ideological State Apparatuses, then, as it were, a crucial deposit in the bank - a humanity that is not a humanism. Yet, in the practice of his own essay, because of his inadequate description of particular processes, he actually draws the map of a site of a possible genuine class struggle in a functionalist, reflectionist and self-defeating manner.

As has been remarked elsewhere[19], the essay under discussion shows Althusser at his best and at his

worst. Part of his discussion of ideology is revealing,
but alongside it is a muddled, mistaken and inactive
formulation of Ideological State Apparatuses. Although
Althusser is successful in his analysis of the contradictions within capitalist educational systems, his
very recognition of the problem fails to take into
account possibilities for dynamic change within situations themselves. In order to comprehend such possibilities for radical change in education, there is a
need to go further than just the examining of the
'problems' as evidence of wider political contradictions. It is within the activity of men experiencing
such contradictions that they may act to transform
realities. Althusser's description of education as
reproduction tells us very little that is new; we need
to understand more fully the experiential conditions
under which such a process takes place. Althusser is
merely telling us 'what we know', rather than considering how 'what we know' may be made problematic in order
to enhance those conditions through which change may be
possible. 'Alternatives' cannot be constructed as a
priori solutions, or 'stuck on to' an exploited radical
situation, but are reached through theoretical advances
formulated in the experience of contradiction and practical action. Therefore, we argue that in order to
demystify ideological oppression in education there is
a need initially to question what counts as a 'problem',
in terms of the experience of such oppression, by those
who work and study in education. It is one thing to
describe education as reproduction, but it is another
to explain this phenomenon as transcendable. It is
this problem, neglected in Althusser's thesis, with
which this paper has been concerned.

NOTES

1. See ALTHUSSER, L. (1971) 'Ideology and ideological
state apparatuses' in L. Althusser Lenin and Philosophy
and Other Essays (Trans. B. Brewster) London: New Left
Books, pages 121-173.

2. The term apparatus refers to Althusser's concept of
Ideological State Apparatuses, by which he refers to
the non-repressive institutions of social control -
religion, the family, education, etc.

3. A stance that embraces most sociologists of education as well.

4.   ALTHUSSER, L. (1971) p. 129.

5.   ALTHUSSER, L. (1971) p. 138.

6.   ALTHUSSER, L. (1971) p. 127.

7.   See ALTHUSSER, L. and BALIBAR, E. (1970) Reading
Capital (Trans. B. Brewster) London: New Left Books.
pages 165-181.

8.   ALTHUSSER, L. (1971) p. 141.

9.   This is illustrated in the long tradition and
debates in Organization Theory from Weber on to
Silverman.

10. See Erving Goffman, Asylums: essays on the social
situation of mental patients and other inmates;
R. D. Laing and D. G. Cooper Reason and Violence: a
decade of Sartre's philosophy 1950-1960, 2nd Edition.

11. ALTHUSSER, L. (1971) p. 148.

12. ENGELS, FREDERICK 'Engels to J. Bloch in Konigberg'
(1890) Karl Marx and Frederick Engels: Selected Works
in Three Volumes Moscow: Progress Publishers, 1969-
1970), III, p. 487.

13.   ALTHUSSER, L. (1969) p. 119.

14.   ALTHUSSER, L. (1969) p. 126.

15.   ALTHUSSER, L. (1971) p. 148.

16.   ALTHUSSER, L. (1971) pp. 161-162.

17.   See for example, on this point, Jean-Paul Sartre,
Between Existentialism and Marxism, 118-137.

18.   Karl Marx, Karl Marx and Frederick Engels:
Selected Works in Two Volumes Moscow: Foreign Languages
Publishing House, 1962, 1, 38, 519, 520, Karl Marx,
Critique of the Gotha Programme, Karl Marx and
Frederick Engels: Selected Works in Three Volumes,
op cit, III, 28-29.

19.   Anon., 'Marxism without Marx' Review article:
Louis Althusser (1971) Lenin and Philosophy and Other
Essays; The Times Literary Supplement, 5th December

REFERENCES

ALTHUSSER, L. (1964) Problemes etudiants La Nouvelle
Critique 152 (January, 1964).

ALTHUSSER, L. (1969) For Marx (Trans. B. Brewster)
London: Allen Lane, The Penguin Press.

ALTHUSSER, L. (1971) 'Ideology and ideological State
apparatuses' in L. Althusser (Trans. B. Brewster)
Lenin and Philosophy and Other Essays London: New
Left Books.

ALTHUSSER, L. and BALIBAR, E. (1970) Reading Capital
(Trans. B. Brewster) London: New Left Books.

FRAZER, S. (Ed) (1965) Chinese Communist Education:
Records of the First Decade Nashville: Vanderbilt
University Press.

GANE, M. (1974) Althusser in English Theoretical
Practice, 1, 1974.

GOFFMAN, E. (1961) Asylums: Essays on the Social Situation of Mental Patients and Other Inmates New York:
Doubleday.

HINTON, W. (1972) Turning Point in China: An Essay on
the Cultural Revolution New York: Monthly Review
Press.

LAING, R. D. and COOPER, D. G. (1971) Reason and
Violence: A Decade of Sartre's Philosophy 1950-1960
(2nd Edition) London: Tavistock.

MESZAROS, I. (1970) Marx's Theory of Alienation (2nd
Edition) London: Merlin.

MILLS, C. W. (1959) The Sociological Imagination New
York: Oxford University Press.

O'NEILL, J. (1972) Sociology as a Skin Trade: Essays
Towards a Reflexive Sociology. London: Heinemann.

PARSONS, T. (1959) The school class as a social system:
some of its functions in American society Harvard
Educational Review XXIX (Fall 1959).

RANCIERE, J. (1974) On the theory of ideology: the
politics of Althusser (Trans. M. Jordin) Radical

Philosophy, 7 (Spring, 1974).

SARTRE, J-P. (1974) Between Existentialism and Marxism
(Trans. J. Matthews) London: New Left Books.

WILLIAMS, K. (1974) Unproblematic archaeology a review
article of M. Foucault (1972) The Archaeology of
Knowledge London: Tavistock in Economy and Society,
III, 50, 1st February 1974.

WILLIAMS, R. (1971)   Who speaks for Wales? The Guardian
3rd June, 1971.

1.4
Ivan Illich and Deschooling Society:

The politics of slogan systems

Michael W Apple

INTRODUCTION

One of contradictions that seems so odd at first
glance is the fact that people who are being so thoroughly challenged by others often read them, teach
them, and thus, sometimes are even converted by them.
Perhaps the best current example of this phenomenon is
the work of Ivan Illich. His interest is in abolishing
schools, yet his books consistently find their way on
to book lists in classes within schools of education.
Courses containing present and future teachers for the
very schools he wants to eliminate, discuss (and even
get tested on) his ideas. It is hard not to see the
paradox here. It could be explained by Marcuse's
provocative notions of repressive tolerance and co-
optation where an institution opens its doors to radical ideas only to discuss them to death within the
framework these radical ideas want to criticize. Or,
it could be that educators themselves are riddled with
self-doubt and are seriously questioning the role they
play in society. Any explanation would probably need
pieces of both interpretations of Illich's 'popularity'
among school people. However, explaining the paradox
is less important for our own analysis here than seeing
what Illich himself is actually about, exploring his
strengths and weaknesses, and pointing to some possibilities for action.

In this paper, I have tried to provide a basic outline of his educational criticisms that would represent

the more extensive treatment found in his many (though
often repetitious) writings on deschooling. Thus, the
reader should not assume that this analysis deals with
all of Illich's points. In fact such a treatment would
be impossible in an essay of this size. Rather, what
I shall do is point out the major aspects of his arguments, and at the same time raise a number of criticisms
of him; ones that may seriously detract from his potency. While Illich is provocative, he is also sometimes
wrong. For example, in parts of this analysis it will
be necessary to compare Illich's position to the
Marxist tradition since he is seemingly indebted to it,
yet he oddly misappropriates parts of it. He thereby
weakens his arguments and runs the risk of making complex dilemmas seem easy to solve.

In a number of places throughout this essay, I have
specifically chosen to let Illich speak for himself.
This is done for two reasons. In the first place, it
is helpful to get the style of an argument. In Illich's
case this is actually quite important since style and
content blend together, each complementing the other.
Secondly, by letting Illich speak, the systematic ambiguity of his writings will be evident. As we shall see,
this ambiguity is of no small moment in enabling various
groups of people, people who might otherwise disagree,
tune into certain aspects of his critique of the process
of schooling and his suggestions for deschooling society. The ambiguity also has the opposing tendency,
however, of being less than efficacious in leading to
effective action by these groups.

At the outset, let me note that Illich is not talking
about schools in advanced industrial societies, but
about schools universally as they are found in capitalist, socialist, and Third World countries as well. The
roots of evil lie in the phenomenon of formal schooling,
not in any particular economic form. Furthermore, he is
not talking about increasing public expenditure to
create alternatives to our dependence on schools. The
answer is not new and more costly devices that will
make people learn. Instead, what Illich (1971a) en-
visions is a new type of relationship, but still an
educational one, between men and women and their environment. But this requires some fairly radical rethink-
ing not just about schools, but also about such
deep-seated things as our dominant attitudes towards
growing up, our perception of the types of tools available for learning, and the quality and structure of our
day to day lives.

For Illich (1973) the fundamental choice we must

ultimately make is that between 'more efficient education fit for an increasingly efficient society and a
new society in which education ceases to be the task of
some special agency'. Now this is somewhat different
from what educators and the general public are used to
hearing, to say the least. Because of this, it is easy
to dismiss the notion of deschooling as patently absurd
in the face of the way life really is. Yet, as I shall
argue, Illich's fundamental weakness does not lie in
his being totally unrealistic - he very consciously
wants not to accept reality - but rather in his inability to deal with the complexity of changing what he
perceives are the problems themselves. We shall have
to look more closely at this in the next section.

DESCHOOLING AS VISION AND SLOGAN SYSTEM

It is wrong, I think, to argue against Illich because he is unrealistic. That is not what he is about.
That is, Illich wishes to create a vision of different
educational relationships, to posit a new reality based
on trust and overt interpersonal need. In so doing, he
must ignore current institutional practices as a basis
for future educational ones. By creating a distinctly
different picture, one that is at times nearly madden-
ingly vague, he hopes to enable people to disclose
possibilities for educating themselves and others that
go beyond what currently exists[1]. In essence, that
almost seems to be Illich's plan, to show that there
are alternatives to those basic practices now dominating
the educational process so that individuals and groups
of people can engage in self-conscious reflection and
action on these 'unreal' possibilities. One test of
Illich's notions, hence, becomes their fruitfulness in
stimulating our imagination, in forcing us to reflect
on the taken-for-granted nature of a good deal that
educators do. Here it is important to remember his
priestly background and the critical place vision
plays in religious thought, for in this tradition utopian prospects precede (and unfortunately too often take
the place of) political action and argumentation.

In order to give power to any imaginative vision of
alternative social relationships, it is quite important
to illuminate the problems of current institutional
practices. In more philosophical terms, one bears
witness to the negativity of current relationships.
This is close to a dialectical method of enquiry. One
must call forth the contradictions, the antithesis, the
negativity within any existing position so that these

contradictions can stand against the commonsense of that position. Only through the interaction of the negative and the taken-for-granted elements of an accepted position can a radically different alternative arise. Only when the negative characteristics of schooling - and here he means the very basic and fundamental structures of the institution - are used as lenses to focus on the supposedly positive elements of schooling, only through the contradictions of what schools are supposed to accomplish and what they actually do accomplish, can progress towards 'true' education arise.

The notion of 'true' education is obviously the key here. For Illich (1971b), education involves the conscious choice by an individual or group to learn something, to 'school' oneself. As such it is a self-determining process not a compulsory activity that is forced upon an unwilling or unknowing student.

> I believe that only actual participation constitutes socially valuable learning, a participation by the learner in every stage of the learning process, including not only a free choice of what is to be learned and how it is to be learned, but also a free determination by each learner of his own reason for living and learning - the part that his knowledge is to play in his life.

Based on this position, in Illich's view, a good system of education must fulfil at least three purposes. Those individuals or groups who desire to learn must have access to adequate resources at any time during their lives, not just during the years usually set aside for formal schooling. Thus, technology must play a crucial place in the process of deschooled education. Quality education must also challenge the ideas of institutional certification by providing access for those people who want to share their wisdom with others who might want to learn it from them. Obligatory curricula become unnecessary. Finally, a system of education that proposes to be excellent must furnish an opportunity and the means for individuals to make public any issues or challenges they wish to make before the body politic (Illich 1971a).

But how is one to deal with the complex problem of organizing people and recreating institutions (or creating new institutions) to fulfil these three purposes? Illich (1971c) would argue that, starting from the stance that the proper question to ask about education is not 'What shall someone learn?', but

rather 'What kinds of things and people might learners
want to be in contact with in order to learn which may
enable them to define and achieve their own goals?',
he proposes four networks. Each of these grows out of
his conception of 'left-convivial institutions', networks of individuals or groups that 'facilitate client
initiated communication or cooperation'. These networks of educational resources are ideal types that are
more visionary than made to fit existing social arrangements. They include the following:

1. Reference Services to Educational Objects - which
facilitate access to things or processes used for formal learning. Some of these things can be reserved
for this purpose, stored in libraries, rental agencies,
laboratories, and showrooms like museums and theatres;
others can be in daily use in factories, airports, or
on farms, but made available to students as apprentices
or on off hours.

2. Skill Exchanges - which permit persons to list
their skills, the conditions under which they are willing to serve as models for others who want to learn
these skills, and the addresses at which they can be
reached.

3. Peer-Matching - a communications network which
permits persons to describe the learning activity in
which they wish to engage, in the hope of finding a
partner for the enquiry.

4. Reference Services to Educators-at-Large - who can
be listed in a directory giving the addresses and self-
descriptions of professionals, para-professionals, and
freelancers, along with conditions of access to their
services. Such educators could be chosen by polling
or consulting their former clients.

Illich has little desire to make these proposals
into recipes that would give a step-by-step syllabus
for deschooling and establishing such networks. Once
the vision is established, given his underlying faith
in the nature of individuals as striving for 'self-
realization' (Gotz, 1974), there will be a growing
motivation to fulfil the possibilities inherent in the
alternatives he proposes. This overly confident view,
as we shall later see, may provide some decided difficulties in Illich and his even more optimistic
followers. However, the broadness itself that this
view embodies may be helpful in a variety of ways.

Most proposals that have sought to change the nature
of schooling, be they curricular proposals or those

aimed at even more substantive alterations, are slogan systems. By calling these proposals slogan systems, I do not mean to denigrate them; rather, it is important to note that these systems of ideas are not usually 'scientific' or 'provable' in the way we usually talk about science or proof. Instead, slogan systems are founded on strong social and valuative commitments and have certain characteristics that may make them successful in changing everyday practices in schools[2]. They do not aim essentially at producing new information or explaining social interaction as much as they aim at altering (often substantially) the usual patterns of things that had up to that time been accepted as given in schools. Logically the difference might look like this: scientific - if X, then Y; proposal from a slogan system - if you want Y, then do X. The imperative, the commitment (Y), must be acceptable if the proposal is to be effective. But the effectiveness of a slogan system is even more complex than simply a viable social commitment.

To be effective in moving people to action a slogan system must have certain specific aspects[3]. It must be broad enough to encompass a wide variety of people who might otherwise hold disparate views. In this way, it acts as an umbrella to cover a diversity of social, political, and educational interests and enables people who have these interests to work together. But broadness is not sufficient. The slogan system must also be specific enough to give concrete suggestions for action to these committed groups and individuals so that the broad proposal 'makes sense' in terms of their modes of operating in day-to-day life. This is a tenuous balance, obviously. If it is too broad, it has little power to give tactical guidance to the people who fit under it. If it is too specific, it risks alienating a large portion of its original adherents who disagree with some of the concrete suggestions.

Yet another characteristic of a successful slogan system is its ability to stimulate the imagination, to provide a means for going further than what is given. In essence, it needs what might be called 'the power to charm', the imaginative capacity to attract both disciples and opponents (see Komisar and McClellan, 1961). Given the immense amount of space devoted to discussion, both pro and con, of Illich's thought on deschooling in books, journals, and elsewhere, it is difficult to find fault with him here.

A good example of a relatively successful slogan system in the recent past was Bruner's (1960)

articulation of the structure of disciplines movement.
It was open enough to draw upon both advocates of
'child-centred' education and those who felt that some
aspects of the progressive movement debased the importance of sophisticated and disciplined enquiry into
the disciplines of knowledge. By combining a discovery
emphasis with subject matter specialization, it was
able to give concrete suggestions for changing educational practice without eroding a significant extent
of its support within a broad based movement. As an
aside, however, it is interesting to note that even
with its success as a slogan system, it is possible to
argue that the discipline-centred movement was much
less effective than most educators suppose in actually
bringing about significant change in the patterns
which dominate classroom life[4]. Thus, even if a proposal meets all of these characteristics there is no
guarantee of its success in altering social or educational practice. This is at least partly due to the
inability of the field of education, and perhaps especially the curriculum field, in dealing with the political and economic complexity of institutional innovation[5].

The 'failure' of the discipline-centred movement to
substantially transform the process of schooling, however, can at least partially explain why the notion of
deschooling has found a number of adherents even among
educators. If these ameliorative curricular and educational reforms continually do not live up to their
promise, then the questions might be asked, 'Is it the
very nature of the institution that must be changed?'
or 'What alternative frameworks can be designed that
are more effective in enabling significant educational
dialogue to emerge?' These are the questions that
Illich wants to take seriously.

This process of questioning is complemented today
by the existence of significant groups of people whose
appraisal of most if not all of the dominant institutions of advanced industrial society is quite critical.
Not only do these institutions, and schools among them,
perform in a manner that does not alter the relative
distribution of knowledge, power, and economic resources that exists now, but they are linked together in
such a way that cultural, economic, and political
challenges to prevailing institutional structures
logically must include the school. It is difficult to
censure, say, economic structures in a society, structures that seem to keep millions of people in poverty
or in a state of anomie and alienation, without at the

same time transferring these feelings to a rather
immediate institution, the school. Thus, a coalescence
of forces combining serious and often warranted questioning of nearly all of the major institutions of a
society and the perceived inability to make schools
significantly more 'humanized' makes for more fertile
ground than usual for a proposal such as deschooling
and the slogan system in which it is encased. These
conditions could cause a number of people to reject the
current 'reality' of schools and search for ways to
find a new one based on someone like Illich.

While one should not carp about the 'reality' of
Illich's vision, it is quite possible to point to decided weaknesses in his programme, that is, if Illich
has put forward his alternative as a serious proposal
for action rather than only as a model or mirror against
which we are to see the decided problems of current
educational practices. If the idea of deschooling
society is 'merely' a notion that enables us to reflect
upon the differences between what we think education
should ideally be like and our inability to come close
to that ideal, then the test of its usefulness would
be its ability to stimulate our thought. However, if
the idea is intended to be more than this, to provide
ways in which self-conscious agents can begin acting
differently, then its fruitfulness must also be determined by its success as a political programme.

It is here that one of Illich's major weaknesses can
be found. He provides a slogan system that can enable
a number of disparate groups to come together and perhaps begin to talk and clarify their goals. This is
primarily due to his description of the contradictions
of industrial society - the possibilities to feed,
clothe, educate, and make life fulfilling because of a
society's wealth and technological power on the one
hand, while there are such things as the deterioration
of life in cities and our environment, massive poverty
and inequality, and alienating nd unfulfilling work
on the other. However, while this illumination of the
contradictions of a modern industrial order is relatively accurate, he does not provide specifics, an
effective programme that can be employed by these individuals and groups once these goals have actually
been clarified. In fact, it may well be the case, as
Gintis (1973) has argued, that Illich's rather broad
and ethereal programme is a 'diversion' from the rigorous conceptual, organizational, political and ultimately
personal analyses and commitment that may be necessary
to effectively modify the conditions to which Illich

points.   I shall have more to say about this later in
our discussion.

CONSUMPTION, REALITY, AND THE HIDDEN CURRICULUM

But what are the conditions of a modern industrial
order that Illich points to and how does formal schooling in bureaucratic institutions fit in? Central to
this argument is his analysis of the hidden curriculum
of schools, the tacit teaching of certain social norms,
values, and dispositions that are 'guaranteed to produce a universal bourgeoisie', a class of consumers who
treat all aspects of knowledge as commodities. It is
not the subject matter, per se, the overt curriculum,
that teaches these things; instead, it is the very
structure of the school as an agency that certifies
competence which communicates these hidden perspectives.
This is perhaps best stated in a quote from Illich
(1973) himself:

> The hidden curriculum teaches all children that econ-
> omically valuable knowledge is the result of prof-
> essional teaching and that social entitlements
> depend on the rank achieved in a bureaucratic pro-
> cess. The hidden curriculum transforms the explicit
> curriculum into a commodity and makes its acquisition
> the securest form of wealth. Knowledge certificates
> - unlike property rights, corporate stock, or family
> inheritance - are free from challenge. They with-
> stand sudden changes of fortune. That high accumu-
> lation of knowledge should convert to high personal
> consumption might be challenged in North Vietnam or
> Cuba, but school is universally accepted as the
> avenue to greater power, to increased legitimacy as
> a producer, and to further learning resources ...
> The hidden curriculum makes social role dependent
> on the process of acquiring knowledge, thus legitim-
> izing stratification. It also ties the learning
> process to full-time attendance, thus illegitimizing
> the educational entrepreneur.

Illich (1971c) goes on:

> Everywhere the hidden curriculum of schooling init-
> iates the citizen to the myth that bureaucracies
> guided by scientific knowledge are efficient and
> benevolent. Everywhere this same curriculum instills
> in the pupil the myth that increased production will
> provide a better life. And everywhere it develops

the habit of self-defeating consumerism of services
and alienating production, the tolerance of institutional dependence, and the recognition of institutional rankings. The hidden curriculum of school
does all this in spite of contrary efforts under-
taken by teachers and no matter what ideology pre-
vails.

Thus a consumer consciousness is effectively taught to
students in schools. But that is not all, for, according to Illich, the very real human need for further
learning is translated by this hidden curriculum into
a demand for further schooling instead. Knowledge, a
term that should signify intimacy with others and shared
life experiences, is remade by the school into professionally packaged products and marketable credentials.
Here, then, personal knowledge is (and must be) discredited, since students must be taught to consume ever
more packages of official 'public' wisdom. In this
way, students learn not to trust their own judgment and
to turn themselves completely over to the hands of
therapeutic institutions, institutions which may actually cause many of the social problems modern society
faces. That is, the hidden curriculum, and the attitude
towards knowledge that coheres with it, produces
disciplined consumers of bureaucratic instructions
ready to consume other kinds of services and treatments
from institutions other than the school that students
are told are good for them. It is important, as Illich
(1971b) points out, that modern techniques of persuasion
be used to make the individual consume 'packaged'
learning in a self-motivated fashion. Thus, many of
the reforms of schooling are really devices that condition students to be happy in institutions that prevent
them from clarifying their actual educational, economic,
and social situations.

The internalization of the hidden curriculum by
students has important social and political consequences other than those noted so far. First, by
learning to be a 'consumer of pre-cooked knowledge',
the individual also learns not to react to 'actual'
reality but to the reality that teams of certified experts have seen fit to distribute as a commodity. The
student becomes politically powerless because the avenues of access to reality are controlled by the therapeutic institution, and the world behind the packaged
recipes becomes what Illich calls neutral and hygienic,
devoid of significant conflict and drama. The role of
the school is to make certain that the process itself

is accepted as natural, as the world tout court by students[6].

The second major consequence concerns the nature of schooling as a mechanism of social and economic control. Schools actually contribute to the maintenance of an already unequal society; they 'conspire against the poor and disenfranchised'(Postman, 1973). Schools provide through their sorting and channelling functions a labour force that is differentiated according to existing economic needs and social stratification (Gintis, 1973). And this very economic model and the system of social stratification which arises out of it completes the circle by confirming individuals and groups in the slots they have been 'trained' for. Thus, schools provide the fundamental mechanism for maintaining an unequal and oppressive economic and social order. They control people and they are ultimately central to the control of an economy.

Now Illich is certainly not alone in seeing schools as primarily institutions of social control. While Illich is a bit too reductive himself in perceiving schools as only agents of social control, the position that the educational structures of, say, the United States as they grew and developed represented conscious attempts to socialize (and ultimately control) large groups of people, and especially the masses of immigrants, has been articulated by several revisionist historians of education (see for example Karier et al 1973).

There is a paradox here though. While Illich obviously is against schooling as a formal mechanism of education, and this is his 'radical' aspect, he can be interpreted as really part of a long line of liberal reformers who believe that education is the fundamental avenue for changing society. That is, while schooling itself is condemned by Illich as a means of education, the faith that education offers the basic strategy for institutional and cultural change is even stronger than in most of the past progressive educational reformers. This enables a number of people, who would not otherwise look twice at his proposals, to feel more comfortable with them since the problems of our society are still perceived as profoundly educational. However, this is still a relatively small percentage compared to the others who reject him outright.

Perhaps one of the major reasons many individuals feel uncomfortable with Illich's approach as well as his conclusions is something I mentioned earlier in this discussion, the fact that behind most of the questions educators ask is a model of how thinking should be carried on (Mannheim, 1970). This involves two things. First, the model inclines us to ask ameliorative questions and to accept only those answers that fit existing conditions and assumptions. This is something of a normative framework that looks askance at basic research, at investigations that do not seem to have some visible relationship to current classroom problems. Thus, for example, difficult conceptual issues such as whether the concept of, say, 'learning' itself is really as useful as we believe are shunted aside or not even considered (Apple, 1973a).

Second, and, for our interpretation of Illich, quite important, is our tendency to neglect the contradictions and negativity built into each of the accepted ways we usually go about schooling children or valuing that schooling. That is, for Illich (and here he has borrowed a bit from Marx, though he could have made it more powerful) each intellectual and social institution has its contradictions, its negative elements, already built into it and as the process of the institution unfolds these contradictions get larger and larger. Therefore, as formal schooling reaches more people (supposedly a positive element), more people are turned into passive consumers who can be manipulated and the more schools reinforce existing social and economic distinctions that are generated out of the economic structure of a society (the contradiction and negativity)[7]. Unfortunately, while Illich's approach is an interesting beginning and is perceptive in describing some of the very real problematics of current institutional practices, it fails where it needs to be strongest. This failure is twofold. First, it does not offer significant hope for more than individual action. Second, it tends to be naive in what is really required to change widespread conditions in advanced industrial societies like our own.

ON THE DIALECTIC OF INDIVIDUAL AND GROUP

The vision of men and women that Illich seems to hold is obviously an optimistic one. Not only are people ('Man') self-creating and capable of self-direction, but any institution that fetters man, that prevents this potential from evolving, must be explained and either reconstructed or eliminated. Thus, schools act as barriers to this self-directing and creative process. They prevent individuals from realizing their

human potential and actually work against a person even
perceiving the need to fulfil these constitutive properties of man. This optimistic view of man is shared by
many radical critics and, in fact, is the initial grounding of some of Marx's own early work. This confident
stance, though, presents a weakness in Illich's analysis,
one that poses much less of a problem in the Marxist
tradition due to its complementary focus on the complex
relationship between the individual and the group.
Illich looks to each individual on his or her own to
engage in the sort of questioning and institutional rec-
reation he advocates. Each separate person is responsible for his or her own enlightenment (Gintis, 1973).
What is missing here is any real sense of the importance
of collective commitment, of the possibility that historical change may be the result of mass movements which
embody the creative potential of each individual
(Ollman, 1971).

   This absence is evident in his proposal for left-
convivial learning webs as well; for his suggestion
actually substitutes an entrepreneurial relationship for
the existing schooling process. It is the ethic of the
small businessman able to sell his wares on an open and
competing market. This in itself is rather dispersive
and fragmenting of community. It also does little to
account for the fact that the structure of the open and
competing market may have had a strong impact on why
schools are as Illich sees them[8]. This is one of the
many paradoxes in the notion of deschooling. Its analysis of what may be taught through the hidden curriculum
in schools in insightful, yet its suggestions for change
may in fact lead one back to the very elements that
could have caused the problems in the first place.

   It is interesting to note here that the United States
has had an extensive history of what could be called
'entrepreneurial radicalism'. From the Jacksonian to the
Populist era, for example, a number of militant groups,
among them the wheat farmers of the plains, metal miners
in the West, and poor whites and blacks in the South,
fought against the domination of society by business.
However, they struggled to find mechanisms to provide
the economic foundation for a society of small producers (Harrington, 1972). Illich, a person who begins
his arguments by censuring a society which produces a
universal class of petty bourgeoisie, finds himself in
odd ideological company, then, if he is serious about
the changes he advocates.

   All this is not to say that individuals have no part
in any realistic scheme for changing institutional

arrangements. Quite the contrary is the case. In fact
it is ultimately a question of individual responsibility
to begin the questioning. However, what gives this
critical process potency is the linking of individuals
with others who are also engaged in similar activity.
Now the broadness of Illich's slogan system does this to
some extent. But this is not merely a strategy of finding people in the here and now who share like commitments. It also includes a search for traditions in the
past that have struggled with the questions now before
these people. In Illich's case, this tradition lies in
something akin to the Marxist Humanism movement
(Kolakowski, 1968). Unfortunately, the ties to this
tradition are missing in his analysis. I say unfortunately for the reason that critical potency is enhanced
when a group can find its roots and hence can identify
with a movement that is, and has been, larger than
itself. A struggle against, say, repression is made
legitimate and at the same time the pressure for immediate 'victory' is tempered by a historical perspective
that illuminates the arena in which painfully slow progress can be made. A reader of Illich has no sense of
this tradition and, thus, they have difficulty using
him as an entry point into present or past groups that
have been and are now confronting the basic institutional
structures of, say, advanced industrial economic orders
like our own. Here again Illich does not provide a
mechanism by which individual and collective commitment
can evolve. In saying this, I do not mean that one
should appropriate a tradition whole, without criticism,
without questioning. The act of criticism is especially
important in dealing with any of the number of extant
'Marxist' and 'Neo-Marxist' positions. Rather, one
grounds oneself in it and goes beyond the parts that are
not utile; but it is impossible to go beyond what one
does not know and Illich does not help one know.

SHOULD SCHOOLING BE THE CENTRAL FOCUS?

Another problem arises with the idea that schooling
provides the fundamental place for changing a given
social order. The central role given to schooling by
Illich (1971a) is shown in his argument that any political programme to change society that does not explicitly see the necessity for deschooling as well is simply
not revolutionary. In his eyes, a political programme
must be evaluated primarily according to the following
criteria: 'How clearly does it state the need for
deschooling, and how clearly does it provide guidelines

for the educational quality of the society for which it aims?' This is the case because shcools are not merely dependent variables, but instead are the 'major reproductive organs of a consumer society'; they are the essential mechanisms for producing institutional dependence and the habits and expectations of a 'managed consumer society'.

To the criticism that schools are reflections of other social structures and that conditions in schools are symptomatic of other social ills, not strong constitutive elements themselves, Illich answers that schooling is actually the largest single 'employer' in this society. If one counts students within the varied institutions of education and people employed or affiliated with education, teaching , or other cultural structures, then one comes up with the rather startling figure that sixty-two million people are 'employed' in schools (again including students in the category of school-related workers), while only a slightly higher figure, eighty million, work elsewhere. Hence, the theory of deschooling merely recognizes the fact that a large proportion of work in this society is engaged in producing demands for goods and services that are necessary to keep an economy growing. Since the schools perform the most important role in producing these demands and are such significant institutions economically in terms of employment, then, according to the theory's proponents, disestablishing them is a truly revolutionary act in changing these other social structures as well (Gotz, 1974).

While there is a danger in reducing the argument over the role of the school in an industrial order to a chicken and egg debate, the question of the roots of the problem is critical. It is possible to argue that the conditions to which Illich points - the increase in bureaucratic consciousness and the growth of social welfare institutions and therapeutic conceptual models, the alienation and compulsive consumption, the 'universal bourgeoisie' - are not dependent on the schools. While Illich never quite states that schools are the originating cause of social ills (and in fact occasionally points to economic roots) he comes quite close to this position by implication given his focus on the school as a central agency in advanced society. This places formal education and the bureaucratizing consciousness which dominates it in too much of a vacuum. It neglects the economic nexus that at least partially explains why such symptoms emerge. It also places unwarranted limits on appropriate avenues for action.

While educational, social, and political ideologies
and institutions cannot totally be explained by economic
analysis (and this is one of the misinterpretations of
Marx by all too many individuals)[9], to ignore it as a
major factor in analysing the dynamics of these ideologies and institutions of a society is questionable.
Without it, there is a tendency to see the educational
mechanisms of a society as underlying causes, as opposed
to actually being symptomatic of much larger economic
and cultural configurations. Parts of this economic
explanation of the growth of alienation, 'oppressive
institutions', welfare, etc., are set out by Schroyer
(1973):

> All advanced industrial societies are committed to
> the stimulation of economic growth (indicated by
> GNP, per capita income, and levels of investment)
> which creates social dislocations that increase the
> need for social amelioration. Societal planning and
> organization to increase economic growth has con-
> flicting consequences because the revolutionizing of
> production deepens the collectivizing trends that
> uproot communities, individuals, and the environment.
> In this general sense, the dynamic of all advanced
> industrial societies recurrently results in a contra-
> diction between the priority of economic growth and
> its social costs and consequences. It is this con-
> tradicting tendency that promotes the extension of
> bureaucratic organizations to deliver goods and
> services to those groups that suffer from rapid
> economic development, e.g., occupational and regional
> obsolescence. This generally results in the in-
> creasing integration of the individual into the web
> of bureaucratized organizations, concerned with work,
> education, government services, and so forth, and the
> resultant growth of 'dependent participation' and
> manipulated consumerism ... (This interpretation
> stresses) the sociocultural consequences of stim-
> ulated economic growth that makes the work experience
> and everyday life less intelligible, transforms the
> human milieu into a technologically determined sys-
> tem, and systematically blocks symbolic communication
> by the superimposition of more and more technical
> rule and constraints derived from rationalizing
> processes.

Even if Illich is correct about the importance of
schools in the process of instilling ideological rules
of action in students, and here he is probably more
correct than in some of his other points, he does not

go far enough in seeing the relationship among economic
institutions, ideological production, and social agencies such as the schools. A more appropriate appraisal
of the nexus between 'repressive' educational institutions and a larger society, between knowledge production
and economic production, could be found in the work of
the critical social theorist Jurgen Habermas[10]. Starting out with a utopian concept of non-repressive
interpersonal communication - the ideal speech situation
- Habermas constructs a framework for analysing modern
society and the ways in which scientific, therapeutic,
and rational/bureaucratic ideologies are related to
existing institutions, ways that prevent significant
social change from arising. What makes it more interesting than Illich (though more difficult to read as
well) is his combination of Wittgenstein's later work
in linguistic philosophy with the reconstructed Marxism
of Adorno and Horkheimer (1972)[11]. This is done in
such a way as to illuminate the close connections between the styles of personal action, interpersonal
communication, and economic relationships of a society
on the one hand and the interest structures of the knowledge producing sciences and institutions on the other.
In essence, by showing the control orientation of modern
institutions (something Illich certainly recognizes)
and dialectically relating it to the rationality of
control in the modern physical and behavioural sciences
which provide the technical expertise for policy making
based upon and within these institutions, Habermas is
able to get much closer than Illich can to the problem
of institutional reification (Schroyer, 1973). In so
doing, he also gives a clearer picture of the possible
steps specific groups can take towards emancipation
from these widespread rubrics of control. Furthermore,
he does not shy away from pointing to the complexity of
any serious analysis of advanced industrial society and
the factors that must be considered in changing it.
Illich's own analysis seems rather weak in comparison.
Ignoring complexity is beneficial in stating positions
in a broad enough fashion to gain support; it is less
so if one wants to engage in knowledgeable action.

Etzioni's (1971) argument is instructive in regard
to this complexity. He argues that many of the institutional forces of our society may tend to make
children passive, dependent, and alienated. However,
he raises serious questions about the reliance on
deschooling for social change. In essence, in contra-
distinction to Illich's tacit espousal of a position
that holds that by 'changing children' one sets in
motion major forces that will also change society,

Etzioni asks if it is realistic to assume that the institutional forces that act to support the existing
economically and politically stratified structure of our
society will sit back and allow educational resources to
be used against them. Furthermore, he raises the interesting and potent issue that deschooling, the eradica-
tion of formal educational institutions, serves to turn
children over to a number of other problematic institutions including the authoritarian family and an exploitative labour market. It thus ignores the magnitude of
the problem of changing a given social order.

These points are rather telling. However, there may
be political and practical reasons for focusing on
schools, not the reasons Illich gives, but reasons of
another sort. Granted the problems are much deeper than
even Illich himself realizes, but schools can be a proper
focus for change for at least three reasons of another
sort. First, they provide a testing ground, though not
always a conscious one, for tactics and strategies that
enable people to see the possibility of reasserting
their role in the crucial argumentation over the means
and ends of the institutions that distribute goods and
services to them. Second, by often dealing with issues
piecemeal, one structure at a time, concrete progress
towards creating more economically, educationally, and
socially responsive institutions can be effected. After
all, there are children 'living' in these schools now,
and they must not be forgotten in Illich's or anyone
else's attempt to create conditions for long-range
institutional change. Third, focusing on the schools
may lead to the clarification of where the real problems
may lie. That is, our attempts and failures at making
significant and lasting changes in schools may lead
people to ask even more basic questions about the generally unresponsive nature of other organized structures
in advanced industrial societies, and, hence, these
attempts can be educative acts in the best sense of the
term.

I do not mean in this section, however, to be totally
negative concerning Illich. After all, if his goal is
to stimulate imagination and argumentation through his
vision then he has found some measure of success. He
also provides what is at times a telling appraisal of
certain conditions which are found in schools and this,
combined with suggestions growing out of an analysis
of his weaknesses, as we shall see can lead to some
possibilities for action on the part of educators and
others.

CRITICAL SCHOLARSHIP AND CRITICAL ACTION

A major point, and one that Illich does expressly
recognize, is the potential for social control in the
knowledge that is taught in schools. This occurs in
two types of knowledge. First, as we saw in Illich's
treatment of the hidden curriculum, the social norms
and values expressed in and by the basic structural
properties of schools communicate to students 'the way
life really is' in a society, though this may in fact
be a distorted picture of reality. Children internalize
these knowledge forms simply by being in the school for
a number of years. The knowledge, as Jackson (1968)
noted, is learned 'merely' by participating in the
activity of school life. Second, and here Illich is
weaker than he should be, the selection of 'cognitive'
knowledge in the school curriculum also effectively
communicates a somewhat distorted view of reality (see
Bourdieu, 1971), a view that often supports political
and intellectual quiescence rather than conflict and
serious questioning by students. For example, investigations into the forms of knowledge found in science
and social studies curricula indicate that there is a
massive presentation of an ideology that ignores the
importance of conflict and basic argumentation in these
fields and social life in general. Assumptions of consensus, both intellectual and normative, seem to dominate the knowledge itself (Apple, 1971). Not only is
this an unrealistic presentation, but it embodies the
interests and world views of only a limited representa-
tion of society and may cause students to have negative
perceptions on the uses of conflict in making needed
changes in society.

Investigations like these and many of the arguments
offered by Illich can be better understood by again
referring to the similarities they have to Marxist perspectives. According to this position, basic forms of
knowledge and the criteria of selection and organization of this knowledge are not necessarily neutral, but
are valuative in nature. They may, in fact contribute
to and be a mechanism of political domination. Apparently 'objective' knowledge is often only partial
knowledge, meaning structures that come from and legitimate the most powerful elements of a society[12]. The
Marxist notion of 'false consciousness' is helpful
here. The dominant consciousness of social groups is
thought to be a reflection of their place in the economic and political structure of a society. The
oppressed and minorities (in traditional Marxist theory
the proletariat and even the bourgeoisie) have views of

the world - of what is important to know and to do, to
produce and consume - that are 'untrue'. These views
are distortions of reality that support the economically and politically powerful classes and groups of
society. They are taught to the less powerful groups
through these people's participation in the major institutions of society from economic structures to the
family to the schools[13]. For Illich obviously and to
a lesser extent for the investigators of the relationship between ideology and curricular knowledge, it is
the school that is the central institution in effectively communicating this ideologically ridden false
consciousness.

One thing that does arise from a serious treatment
of these ideas is the necessity of seeing many educational problems in a larger context. Not all (or perhaps even most) of our questions can be solved or even
adequately posed in a 'learning' framework. By the
very fact that learning language is apolitical, it
covers the relationships of power, expertise, and money
that control a good deal of the process of schooling in
the United States. Once this larger political and economic context is revealed, then part of the task of
committed educators is to engage in the rigorous historical, analytic, and empirical scholarship necessary
to show how many of the tools, categories, perspectives,
and ideologies of education provide unquestioned support
for this socio-political framework[14]. Models of what
might be called critical scholarhsip need to be developed that take as one of their fundamental tasks the
illumination of the concrete mechanisms by which this
support for existing and often problematic institutional
structures is marshalled in education.

This points to a problem with Illich. One of the
dangers of someone like Illich writing about education
is his lack of insight into the fact that many committed individuals are and have been delving rather
deeply into the issues he raises. For example, he argues
that an educational revolution requires as one of its
facets a totally new orientation to educational research, one that does not merely seek to optimize the
quest for efficiency within the existing institutional
framework (Illich 1971c). Now many people will agree
with this, and in fact that is exactly the point.
There are and have been numbers of committed educators
who are seeking to establish a critical framework for
educational scholarship, who are proposing new models
of educational research and activity based on in-depth
analysis of the strengths and very evident limitations

to those models now in use[15]. This also points to the
need for historical insight in the field so that the
roots of this critical tradition (in people such as
Counts, Rugg, and others) are not lost.

This is not to say that Illich is always wrong in
making these arguments. Rather it is to say that if
Illich's assertions are to go beyond mere stipulations,
a good deal of further investigation is required in a
number of areas. Perhaps one of the most important
places to begin would be in what might be called the
sociology of school knowledge. This type of study has
important implications for curriculum thought, for
example. We need to critically examine not just 'how
a student acquires more knowledge' (the dominant question in our efficiency-minded field), but 'why and how
particular aspects of the collective culture are presented in school as being objective, factual knowledge'.
How, concretely, may official knowledge represent
ideological configurations of the dominant interests in
a society? How do schools legitimate these limited and
partial standards of knowing as unquestioned truths?
(Wexler, in press). These questions must be asked of
at least three areas of school life: (a) how the basic
day-to-day regularities of schools contribute to these
ideologies; (b) how the specific forms of curricular
knowledge reflect these configurations; and (c) how
these ideologies are reflected in the fundamental perspectives educators themselves employ to order, guide,
and give meaning to their own activity[16].

But besides these important areas of scholarly investigation there are concrete and practical arenas for
action on the part of committed educators to which
Illich (usually unconsciously) points. For instance,
an issue that Illich raises but does not go deeply
into is the necessity of a change in our attitudes
towards growing up. He very much wants to argue that
the possibilities of choice and responsibility that
students have today are conditioned by the economic
needs of our society. The capacity for significant
choice and the process of taking responsibility for
one's own growth have atrophied in 'schooled societies'.
One of the tasks of concerned individuals, then, is to
expand both the range of choices available and, if I
may go further than Illich, the right of students to
make these choices.

Historically, it is the case that childhood has
become more and more a protected status and has
expanded upwards in age to include individuals who in
previous times would have been accorded all the rights

of adults. Aries' (1962) excellent treatment of the history of childhood documents the interaction of economic and social necessity with the increasing contraction of the range of options 'children' are entitled to have and the situations they may honestly confront without total simplification by 'adults'. That is, it is not naturally preordained that students should be protected from choice and should have few rights. This is very much a historical condition. It is also interesting to note that at the end of the nineteenth century many of the people in the United States who attempted to create institutions such as more 'humane' schools and juvenile homes ultimately provided mechanisms that abridged already existing rights of children. They, thereby, contributed to the trend to which Illich accurately points (Platt, 1969).

These facts, though, open up an area of action where considerable progress can be effected - that of student rights. The Supreme Court in the United States has ruled that schools are not places where constitutional guarantees are lost. The student does not leave his or her rights at the door when entering the schoolhouse. Exactly the opposite is the case. If education is to be more than mere training or indoctrination, then controversy, argumentation, and conflict must be an integral part of it[17]. Because of this, it is all the more imperative that the constitutional rights of students concerning freedom of speech, of access to information, or procedural and disciplinary activity, be upheld, re-established, and strengthened wherever possible. Action by educators can be centred around several concrete proposals here which while focusing on schools (something Illich might feel somewhat uncomfortable about) can lead to the significant expansion of the rights of students and an alteration of our commonsense attitudes towards growing up. Bills of student rights can be established in schools. Educators can help students clarify the causes of their discontent and help them focus on strategies for dealing with these problems. They can teach students their rights in as honest a fashion as possible. Furthermore, through their professional organizations, educators can lobby for organizational backing and monetary support for student rights advocacy and the judicial proceedings that may arise from the conflict over them[18].

This can be taken even further if one treats seriously the question of the role of an educator in what is to some degree a political struggle. The work of John S. Mann is exceptionally important in this regard.

He argues that part of the task of politically oriented
educators (and we all are since it is exceptionally
difficult for education to be neutral activity) is to
affiliate with political movements and use the educational expertise they possess in programmes that will
assist these movements in the political education of
workers, youth, and others who are oppressed. In this
way, one goes beyond Illich in linking oneself with
those concrete traditions that I discussed earlier in
this essay.

It is possible to argue based on the analysis of
Illich presented here that what is needed is a two-fold
or at least a dialectical outlook on the process of
social and educational change. The primary focus of
economistic Marxists is upon changing the material
forces of society so that the distribution and control
of goods and services is more just and equitable.
This is rather reductive in that all economic, educational, and social problems are reduced to their basis
in the modes of production of a given collectivity,
e.g., what social class controls the wealth of a country and lives off the surplus value produced by the
labour of a larger, poorer group. Now this may or may
not be an accurate explanation of social and economic
stagnation and crisis in modern capitalist societies.
However, even if it is accurate, its fundamental weakness lies in its lack of any coherent treatment of both
character structure and the specific means or mechanisms by which individuals and groups of people are socialized into accepting as given, and indeed even yearn-
ing for, the ways in which goods and services are
produced and distributed. That is, an examination of
the economic roots of how a social order operates is
incomplete without at the same time engaging in an
investigation of the institutions whose job it is to
instill and reinforce in the young the dispositions
and propensities, the hopes, fears, and anxieties, that
enable the economic roots to keep functioning (Brown,
1973). And here is where Illich in his admittedly
vague, 'unreal', and even sometimes wrong way, can at
least stimulate the questions that might profitably
be asked in a more specific and disciplined approach.
The 'economic' and the 'characterological' are com-
plexly intertwined with the former still probably more
fundamental than the latter, and educators need much
greater sophistication in their analyses than has .
heretofore been the case. If Illich does not offer
the sophistication, he at least offers an interesting
problem both in refuting where he is wrong and going
beyond where he is too simple.

One idea should be kept in mind in the future.   If
it is the case that schooling is dialectically linked
to other more fundamental institutions of a modern
industrial society, then attempts at making more permanent changes in the formal mechanisms of education
(even towards Illich's own proposals) may require substantive critique and change of the institutions which
surround the school. Therefore, educational commitment
must go hand in hand with political, social, and even
aesthetic commitment. Obviously such a realization
makes it even harder to deal with; but then honest
appraisals need to accompany knowledgeable action.
Perhaps Illich is oddly correct here. One starts by
taking responsibility for making oneself knowledgeable.
Then, it will be possible for knowledge and action to
be joined.

NOTES

1.   The concept of disclosure models is critical here.
While these models do not seek to be pictorial representations of reality, they do seek to consciously
bracket taken-for-granted perceptions and to create new
'paradigms' that will enable more fruitful descriptions
and possibilities to emerge. See, e.g., Ian Ramsey,
1964, Models and Mystery.

2.   I do not mean to infer here that science itself is
not committed (though this may be tacit in science
rather than overt) to social and valuative interests.
As I have argued elsewhere, these interests may be quite
strong in scientific rationality in advanced industrial
societies. See Michael W. Apple, 1975, 'Scientific
Interests and the Nature of Educational Institutions',
in Curriculum Theorizing: The Reconceptualists (Eds)
William Pinar and Paul Klohr, and Trent Schroyer (1970)
'Towards a Critical Theory for Advanced Industrial
Society', in Recent Sociology Number 2.

3.   Here I am drawing upon the lucid analysis of slogan
systems found in B. Paul Komisar and James McClellan
(1961) 'The Logic of Slogans', in B. Smith and R. H.
Ennis Language and Concepts in Education.

4.   See Sarason's (1971) The Culture of the School and
the Problem of Change. There are, of course, analytic
and programmatic problems with the structure of disciplines approach besides this lack of effect. See, e.g.,

the work of Fred Newmann and Herbert M. Kliebard.

5.   For a comprehensive treatment of the problem of
curricular innovation, which unfortunately limits
itself to only educational issues, see the entire issue
of Interchange 3, No. 2/3 (Winter, 1972).

6.   See ILLICH, I. (1971c) The breakdown of schools:
a problem or a symptom? Interchange No. 4 Spring 1971.
On the notion of the world tout court, see BERGER, P.L.
and LUCKMANN, T. The Social Construction of Reality
(1966).

7.   Merton's notion of 'latent dysfunction' is similar
here, except that structural functionalism tends to
see society in static terms, while, say, Marxist positions see social flux and conflict as the usual occurrences. See MERTON, R.K. (1968) Social Theory and Social Structure. For the Marxian emphasis on social flux
and change, see OLLMAN, B. (1971) Alienation: Marx's
Conception of Man in Capitalist Society and APPLE, M.W.
(1971) The hidden curriculum and the nature of conflict
Interchange 2, No. 4 (Spring, 1971).

8.   The best treatment of Illich's acceptance of an
entrepreneurial (but small scale rather than corporate)
society can be found in H. Gintis,'Toward a political
economy of education'.

9.   Marx, himself, was not an economic determinist in
the strict sense of the word. See Ollman (1971).

10.   There are exceptional problems in translating
Habermas' analyses into English. The most accessible
(in terms of readability) work is Jurgen Habermas
(1970) Toward a Rational Society.

11.   cf., ADORNO, T. and HORKHEIMER, M. (1972)
Dialectics of Enlightenment and JAY, M. (1973) The
Dialectical Imagination.

12.   See WEXLER, P. (in press) The Sociology of
Education: Beyond Equality Indianapolis, Bobbs-Merrill.

13.   For a detailed treatment of 'false consciousness'
see MARCUSE, H. (1964) One Dimensional Man (Boston:
Beacon,) and the exceptionally well written portrayal
of the ideas of 'estrangement', 'alienation', and
'class interests' in Ollman, (1971).

14.   See APPLE, M. W. Common-sense categories and
curriculum thought, in Schools in Search of Meaning,
ed. James B. Macdonald, et. al. (Washington: Association for Supervision and Curriculum Development, in
press).

15.   See, for example, the work of Huebner, Mann,
Kliebard and others. Much of this perspective can be
found in Pinar and Klohr (Eds.) (1975) Curriculum
Theorizing: The Reconceptualists.

16.   cf., Michael W. Apple (1973b), The adequacy of
systems management procedures in education, in
Perspectives on Management Systems Approaches in Education, ed. Albert H. Yee; Michael W. Apple (1974), The
process and ideology of valuing in educational settings,
in Educational Evaluation: Analysis and Responsibility
eds. Michael W. Apple, Michael J. Subkoviak, and Henry
S. Lufler, Jr., and APPLE, M. (in press), 'Common-sense
categories and curriculum thought'.

17.   cf., the decision written by Supreme Court Justice
Fortas in Tinker vs. Des Moines Independent Community
School District, 393 U.S. 503, 511 (1969).

18.   Michael W. Apple and Thomas Brady (1975b), Towards
increasing the potency of student rights claims, in
Schooling and the Rights of Children eds. Vernon,
F. Haubrich and Michael W. Apple. See also John S. Mann
The student rights strategy, Theory Into Practice 10,
No. 5 (December, 1971), 353-362.

REFERENCES

ADORNO, T. and HORKHEIMER (1972) Dialectics of Enlightenment New York: Herder and Herder.

APPLE, M. W. (1971) The hidden curriculum and the nature
of conflict Interchange 2, No. 4 (Spring 1971).

APPLE, M. W. (1973a)'Curricular design and cultural
order' in N. Shimahara Educational Reconstruction:
Promise and Challenge Columbus, Ohio: Charles Merrill.

APPLE, M. W. (1973b) 'The adequacy of systems manage-
ment procedures in education' in A. H. Yee (Ed)
Perspectives on Management Systems Approaches in
Education Englewood Cliffs, New Jersey, Educational
Technology.

APPLE, M. W. (1974) 'The process and ideology of valuing in educational settings' in M. W. Apple et al Educational Evaluation: Analyses and Responsibility Berkeley: McCutchan.

APPLE, M. W. (1975a) 'Scientific interests and the nature of educational institutions' in W. Pinar and P. Klohr (Eds) Curriculum Theorizing: The Reconceptualists Berkeley: McCutchan.

APPLE, M. W. and BRADY, T. (1975b) 'Towards increasing the potency of student rights claims', in V. F. Haubrich and M. W. Apple (Eds) Schooling and the Rights of Children Berkeley: McCutchan.

APPLE, M. W. (in press) 'Common-sense categories and curriculum thought' in J. B. Macdonald et al (Eds) Schools in Search of Meaning Washington: Association for Supervision and Curriculum Development.

ARIES, P. (1962) Centuries of Childhood New York: Random House.

BERGER, P. L. and LUCKMANN, T. (1966) The Social Construction of Reality New York: Doubleday.

BOURDIEU, P. (1971) 'Systems of education and systems of thought' in M. F. D. Young (Ed) Knowledge and Control London: Collier-Macmillan.

BROWN, B. (1973) Marx, Freud, and the Critique of Everyday Life New York: Monthly Review.

BRUNER, J. (1960) The Process of Education Cambridge: Harvard University Press.

ETZIONI, A. (1971) 'The educational mission' in D. U. Levine et al (Eds) Farewell to Schools??? Worthington, Ohio: Charles A. Jones.

GARTNER, A. et al (Eds) (1973) After Deschooling What? New York: Harper and Row.

GINTIS, H. (1973) 'Towards a political economy of education: a radical critique of Ivan Illich's Deschooling Society in A. Gartner et al (Eds) After Deschooling What? New York: Harper and Row.

GOTZ, I. L. (1974) On man and his schooling Educational Theory 24 No. 1 (Winter 1974).

HABERMAS, J. (1970) Towards a Rational Society Boston:
Beacon.

HARRINGTON, M. (1972) Socialism New York: Bantam.

ILLICH, I. (1971a) 'Education without school: How it
can be done?' in D. U. Levine and R. J. Havighurst
Farewell to Schools??? Worthington, Ohio: Charles A.
Jones.

ILLICH, I. (1971b) The breakdown of schools: a problem or a symptom Interchange No. 4 (Spring 1971).

ILLICH, I. (1971c) Deschooling Society New York:
Harper and Row.

ILLICH, I. (1973) 'After deschooling what?' in A.
Gartner et al (Eds) After Deschooling What? New York:
Harper and Row.

JACKSON, P. (1968) Life in Classrooms New York: Holt,
Rinehart and Winston.

JAY, M. (1973) The Dialectical Imagination Boston:
Little, Brown.

KARIER, C. et al (1973) Roots of Crisis: American
Education in the Twentieth Century Chicago: Rand
McNally.

KOLAKOWSKI, L. (1968) Towards a Marxist Humanism New
York: Grove.

KOMISAR, B. P. and McCLELLAN, J. (1961) 'The logic of
slogans' in B. O. Smith and R. H. Ennis (Eds) Language
and Concepts in Education Chicago: Rand McNally.

MANN, J. S. (1971) The student rights strategy Theory
Into Practice 10, No. 5 (December 1971).

MANNHEIM, K. (1970) 'The sociology of knowledge' in
J. E. Curtis and J. W. Petras The Sociology of
Knowledge New York: Praeger.

MARCUSE, H. (1964) One Dimensional Man Boston: Beacon.

MERTON, R. K. (1968) Social Theory and Social Structure
New York: The Free Press.

OLLMAN, B. (1971) Alienation: Marx's Conception of Man

in Capitalist Society New York: Cambridge University
Press.

PLATT, A. M. (1969) The Child Savers Chicago: University
of Chicago Press.

PINAR, W. and KLOHR, P. (Eds) (1975) Curriculum
Theorizing: The Reconceptualists Berkeley: McCutchan.

POSTMAN, N. (1973) 'My Ivan Illich problem' in A.
Gartner et al (Eds) After Deschooling What? New York:
Harper and Row.

RAMSEY, I. (1964) Models and Mystery New York: Oxford
University Press.

SARASON, S. (1971) The Culture of the School and the
Problem of Change Boston: Allyn and Bacon.

SCHROYER, T. (1970) 'Towards a critical theory for
advanced industrial society' in H. P. Dreitzel (Ed)
Recent Sociology Number 2 New York: Macmillan.

SCHROYER, T. (1973) The Critique of Domination New York:
George Braziller.

SHIMAHARA, N. and SCRUPSKI, A. (Eds) (1975) Social
Forces and Schooling - An Anthropological and Sociological Perspective New York: David McKay.

WEXLER, P. (in press) The Sociology of Education:
Beyond Equality Indianapolis: Bobbs-Merrill.

2.0
Towards a Critical Theory

Introduction

Part of the reason why the analysis of the social relations of education tends to be treated simplistically by those writers whose work was discussed in section one lies in the very complexity of those relations. In this situation it is not difficult to comprehend the priestly, and to some extent sociological, tradition of positing utopian futures as a substitute for analysis of and action in contemporary contexts. The papers which we have chosen to include in this second section cannot claim to have entirely overcome that problem, but they do serve (individually and collectively) to point up the extent of the complexity of the relationship between school and society. In their various, and sometimes contradictory, ways they illustrate the impossibility of comprehending it in any simplistic manner and thus of achieving its transformation via any single strategy of change. All the contributors seem to us to offer important examples of the ways in which the critical historian or the critical social scientist might begin to analyse the social relations of education - though not all of them would necessarily wish to be described in such terms. For us, as for Fay (1975), a critical social science 'sees theories as analyses of a social situation in terms of those features of it which can be altered in order to eliminate certain frustrations which members in it are experiencing, and its method of testing the truth of scientific theory consists partially of ascertaining the theory's practical relevance in leading to the satisfaction of human needs and purposes'.

Something of the complexity of the issues which the critical social scientist has to confront will already have been glimpsed in the earlier contributions to this volume, and particularly in Apple's discussion of the variety of ways in which schooling is dialectically related to other institutions of modern industrial

society. A common theme in the various perspectives
proposed or discussed in this book is that schools act
as agencies of social control and serve to reproduce the
prevailing system of social relations. They differ,
however, about the nature of what is being reproduced,
about the mechanisms via which such reproduction is
achieved, and about the extent to which schools can be
regarded as merely agencies of reproduction. The different stances which they take on these issues also point
to differing conclusions about the contribution which
practical work within the field of education can make to
the attainment of a more egalitarian and liberated society, and about the concrete nature of that work.
Clearly, there are often sound theoretical and practical
reasons which lead theorists to stress particular aspects of the relationships between society, state and
schooling, and an attempt to avoid facing contradictions
between different theories by a thorough-going and superficial eclecticism could ultimately create as many problems as it seemed to solve. On the other hand, any
particular analysis of schooling is not necessarily exclusive of all the others. Thus Gintis's (1972a) critique of Illich is persuasive only insofar as its
analysis of the role of schooling in the reproduction of
the relations of production is also able to account for
the consumption orientation of schooling to which Illich
points. Equally, any analysis which concentrates upon
the economic aspects of reproduction at the expense of
the ideological ones, is liable to be inadequate.

The tendency of Illich (and Gintis with him on this
particular score) to concentrate attention upon the
hidden curriculum, while many 'new direction' sociologists stress aspects of the selection and organization
of curriculum knowledge, is a further example of the way
in which particular styles of theorizing can obscure the
complex nature of the process of schooling. Thus it
seems likely, for instance, that any further exploration
of the role of schooling in the perpetuation of that
'culture of positivism', to which Whitty referred in
section one, would indicate that the successful presentation of partial views of the world (in both senses) as
unquestioned and unquestionable truths is achieved, not
by aspects of the hidden or the overt curriculum alone,
but via the subtle relationship between them. The papers
by Gorz, Hextall and Sarup and Holly in this section are
examples of modes of theorizing which make it clear that
the nature of the overt curriculum is not something
detached from the social contexts of its production and
reproduction. These papers serve to illuminate rather
than obscure the linkages between the hidden and overt

curricula of schooling, and illustrate the embeddedness
of the social relations of capitalist society within the
social relations of schooling. These relations are
further illuminated in concrete terms in various contributions to Explorations in the Politics of School
Knowledge (Whitty and Young, 1976).

The paper by Gorz serves to reinforce the point that
those forms of analysis which remain 'education-bound'
in their exploration of the possibilities for change
are ultimately self-defeating because they fail to
recognize that classroom practices, and indeed the emergence of compulsory schooling itself, are not independent of the social division of labour as it has developed
in Western capitalist societies. At the same time, the
paper offers support for the view that 'it is impossible
to contest the division of labour (and its manifestations in the problem of classifications and qualifications often referred to as "wage differentials"),
without raising the question of education' (Lettieri,
1976). Gorz shows how the development of technology and
technical education, together with the hierarchical social relations often assumed to be technology's necessary
concomitant, reflects not the technical needs of production but the social needs of the capitalist division of
labour. This is the background to his admittedly schem-
atic account of the processes by which separations and
hierarchies, such as those between education and production, work and culture, science and technology, intellectual and manual labour, are sustained by educational
practices. He goes on to point out how the current
'crisis' in the educational system contains some real
radical potential, but only if it generates unity between technical and manual workers and an attack on the
prevailing relations of production. Finally, he makes
clear the necessity for this to be an attack which embraces work and school in a thorough-going 'cultural
revolution'.

Hextall and Sarup approach the relationship between
the institutions of school and work in capitalist society
via a rather different, but complementary, mode of analysis. In their paper they attempt to explore the circumstances and conditions which enable 'certain communities or interests to persuade and sustain certain
definitions which others find coercive and alienating'.
They adopt the process of evaluation as their focus of
attention and argue that it is internally related to
the division of labour in society. They therefore
suggest that the form of life which makes prevailing
modes of evaluation possible and comprehensible is an

alienated mode of existence, while evaluation itself
serves to sustain a sense of the social order by per-
forming and legitimating the various forms of separation
which typify that mode of existence. Thus, for example,
they argue that evaluation procedures relate to the
separation of man from man and the reduction of the
pupil's labour and its product (knowledge) to the status
of commodities. The various discrete features of contemporary schooling to which other theorists, such as
those discussed earlier, have pointed are shown by the
relational mode of analysis to be embedded within each
other. Part of the third paper, by Holly, is also
devoted to the way in which, under capitalism, knowledge
appears as alienated from the subjective learning of men
and women. While Hextall and Sarup do not perhaps entirely avoid that 'metaphysical idealism' which they
attack in McHugh (1974), Holly's attempt to offer a
materialist analysis of the specific form of education
which characterizes our present system of social relations conveys something of the dynamic of human history
which, as they admit, is missing from their own paper.

The importance of this historical dimension is particularly significant for any consideration of the possibilities for changing the social relations of and in
education, to use Holly's terminology. Holly's consideration of the dialectic between the general social
relations of society and those of the education system
exposes the weakness of the argument that there is a
simple and constant 'fit' between the institutions of
schooling and the needs of capital. Whilst there are
clearly examples where, as we have suggested, different
aspects of schooling combine to reproduce efficiently
the relations of production, there will co-exist within
schooling contradictory elements. These will generally,
but again not in any straightforward manner, reflect
contradictions within other institutions of capitalism.
In particular, to take up the point raised but not
developed by Althusser, they will reflect aspects of
class struggle and not purely aspects of class domination. This point comes out clearly in the sort of
historical analysis of American education offered in the
paper by Bowles and Gintis. This is not, however, to
suggest that all attempts to provide concrete accounts
of the relationship between society, state and schooling
renew that sense of purpose for socialist teachers
which Erben and Gleeson felt the Althusserian analysis
denied. Many historical analyses suggest such a close-
ness of fit between the economic institutions of corporate capitalism and the institutions of schooling that
there is little in the way of contradiction to exploit.

As Bowles and Gintis tell us in their contribution to
this section, much of the Marxist analysis of education
has been devoted to mapping 'the ways that schools work
to legitimate class divisions and to produce a labour
force shaped by the requirements of profitable employment in the capitalist system'. Indeed, the mapping of
this correspondence - 'an essential characteristic of
American education' - has been a major aspect of their
own work (Bowles, Gintis and Meyer, 1975), even though
they recognize that 'both the evolution of the educational system and the prospect for a liberated future
must be analysed in terms of both reproduction and
contradiction'.

The emphasis upon concrete analysis of the contradictions within the educational system and between it and
the other institutions of capitalism is then a necessary
part of any attempt to formulate realistic strategies
for socialist educators. In an earlier paper Gintis
(1972b), reflecting upon the development of a dialectic-
ally-generated counter-culture during the nineteen
sixties, regarded the struggles of 'imperfectly or con-
tradictorily socialized groups' such as students, youths,
blacks and women - operating at the point of generation
of the alienated labour force - as a vital element of
revolutionary struggle, whose activities should be
united and related to working-class politics and dominant social contradictions. In that paper, Gintis also
presented an account of the contradiction which has
emerged from the increasing tendency of the two formerly
distinct school systems of America to overlap, a point
which is echoed in the analysis of comprehensive education in Britain developed by Holly in the final part of
his paper. 'Out of this clash', Gintis argued, 'has
come student activism and scepticism, in a dialectical
movement that might have made Marx himself proud ...
The outcome, if properly capitalized upon, is revolutionary consciousness'. For Holly, the conflict offers
the possibility for teachers and pupils to develop 'what
Freire calls "dialogical relations" in learning, in
which organized learning is returned to a non-alienated
state, a subjective-social project'.

A more detailed analysis of the historical development of schooling does, however, suggest that some
qualifications of Holly's optimism may be in order, and
his analysis (Holly, 1973) of the emancipatory potential
of recent curriculum developments might also be fruitfully examined in the light of the fate of earlier
supposedly 'progressive' innovations. The work of
Bowles and Gintis suggests that, if the revolutionary

potential of education is to be realized, the 'conscious determination of history by men and women' must necessarily involve the forging of links with what Apple called the 'concrete traditions' of mass movements which embody the creative potential of each individual. Their account of American educational history certainly shows that it involved 'a conflict-ridden course of struggle and accommodation rather than a smooth adjustment of educational structure to the evolution of economic life'. They argue, however, that whereas 'working people have managed over the years to get more education ... they have managed to get the kind of education they demanded when their needs coincided with those of the economic elite'. They further suggest that the idealistic progressives working for a humanistic and egalitarian education worked largely in vain because they, rather like the deschoolers or the 'new' sociologists of today, lacked any strong grassroots support and eschewed any systematic critique of the evolving economic order. They, therefore, conclude that 'only a mass-based organization of working people powerfully articulating a clear alternative to corporate capitalism as the basis for a progressive educational system' could have had any chance of preventing the sort of selective implementation of reform which merely preserved the role of schooling in the perpetuation of the economic order.

Clearly, the dynamics of the history of education in Britain have been different from those of the United States, but there are also some broad parallels. Considerable work needs to be done to understand the 'complex relations between educational structure and economic forces' in both contexts, and particularly to develop a more adequate analysis of the role of the state in the educational system. The concrete historical studies of the demise of educational movements which attempted to challenge prevailing conceptions of education remain few (Kingston, 1976; Layton, 1973), as do studies of the explicit modes of intervention by the state into working-class lives and institutions (Frith, 1976; Johnson, 1976). However, historical studies such as these, and of the kind exemplified by the paper by Bowles and Gintis in this section, have important implications for Left theory and practice in education today. To take a specific example, much is made in this book, and elsewhere, of the failure of the Labour movement to develop a critique of the content and structure of the education that is imposed on working-class children. However, if we go back to 1926, the following resolution passed by the Labour Party Annual Conference and quoted by Jones (1976) called for:

> a workers' enquiry into education ... to determine
> how far the present books ... used in schools and the
> predominant methods of teaching and discipline foster
> a bourgeois psychology, and how far, under a workers'
> administration, this might be counteracted and a
> proletarian attitude cultivated.

As Jones goes on to say, 'this resolution draws the
clearest of lines between the interests of classes in
education. It establishes the criteria which the working-class movement and Left teachers should bring to
bear on education'. The outcome, of course, was that
this initiative, and no doubt others, became a casualty
of the largely defensive tactics of the Labour movement
in the 1930s, and appears to have been buried altogether
by the time the Labour Government came to power in 1945.
The kind of ideology-critique that was being suggested
by the 1926 conference resolution is beginning to be
made by sociologists and others, but in a manner almost
wholly disconnected from the wider Labour movement. We
have therefore important lessons to learn from historical studies of the origins and basis of support for
such a critique of education in the Labour movement of
the 1920s, as well as of the political context of its
disappearance.

On a broader level, historical analyses suggest
that the optimism with which the New Left greeted the
emergence of the so-called counter-culture is no substitute for the forging of links between radical
students and radical educators and the mass movements
of the working classes. On the other hand, the opportunities for exploiting the contradictions of schooling,
to which Gorz, Holly and Gintis point, suggest that
the contempt of some of the Old Left for the work of
radicals within the field of education is also misplaced - as, we would add, is their concern purely with
issues of access rather than of ideology. However,
such analyses also indicate that, as a result of being
virtually independent of the concrete material circumstances of working-class life, many of the progressive
educational advances developed by radical teachers
actually become seen and experienced as anti-working-
class (Jones, 1976). This, as the William Tyndale affair
has shown, can quickly be turned to the advantage of the
political Right. We feel that the papers in this section go some way towards fulfilling that part of the
task of the critical social scientist which Fay (1975)
describes as seeking to disclose how the historical
process has been such that the social order under
scrutiny is incapable of satisfying some of the wants
and needs that process has engendered. They also begin

to suggest ways in which such analyses might not simply offer 'a picture of the way a social order works', but also act as 'catalytic agents' of change within the complex of social life which they analyse - the issue which is taken up in our final section.

REFERENCES

BOWLES, S., GINTIS, H. and MEYER, P. (1975) The long shadow of work: education, the family and the reproduction of the social division of labour Insurgent Sociologist, Vol. 5.

FAY, B. (1975) Social Theory and Political Practice London: Allen and Unwin.

FRITH, S. (1976) 'Socialization and rational schooling: elementary education in Leeds, 1800-1870' in McCann, W.P. (forthcoming): Popular Education and Socialization 1800-1900, London: Eyre-Methuen.

GINTIS, H. (1972a) Towards a political economy of education: a radical critique of Ivan Illich's Deschooling Society, Harvard Educational Review, 42(1).

GINTIS, H. (1972b) Activism and counter culture - the dialectics of consciousness in the corporate state, Telos No. 12.

HOLLY, D. (1973) Beyond Curriculum London: Hart-Davis McGibbon.

JOHNSON, R. (1976) Notes on the Schooling of the English Working Class, 1780-1850 Mimeo, Centre for Contemporary Cultural Studies, University of Birmingham.

JONES, K. (1976) Progressive education and the working class Radical Education, No. 6.

KINGSTON, J. (1976) 'It's been said before and where did that get us?' in Boyle, G. and Harper, P. Radical Technology London: Wildwood House.

LAYTON, D. (1973) Science for the People London: Allen and Unwin.

LETTIERI, A. (1976) 'Factory and School' in Gorz. A. (Ed) The Division of Labour Brighton: Harvester Press.

McHUGH, P. et al (1974) On the Beginning of Social
Inquiry London: Routledge and Kegan Paul.

WHITTY, G. and YOUNG, M. (1976) Exploration in the
Politics of School Knowledge Driffield: Nafferton
Books.

2.1
Technical Intelligence and the Capitalist Division of Labour

Andre Gorz

Up to recent years, it was traditionally assumed by most Marxists that the development of productive forces was something intrinsic and intrinsically positive. Most Marxists held the view that capitalism, as it matured, was producing a material base which could be taken over by a socialist society and upon which socialism could be built. It was widely held that the higher the development of productive forces, the easier the building of socialism would be. Such productive forces as technology, science, human skills and knowledge, and abundant dead labour were considered assets that would greatly facilitate the transition to socialism.

These views were based somewhat mechanically upon the Marxian thesis regarding the deepening contradiction between productive forces on the one hand, and social relations of production on the other hand. Most orthodox communist parties clung to the view that capitalist relations of production were stifling the development of productive forces and that socialism, by tearing down the so-called superstructure of the capitalist state and of capitalist social relations, could set free at one blow a tremendous potential for socio-economic development and growth.

This view still pervades the political attitude of the Western European communist parties. They usually consider all available productive capacity, all available manual, technical, professional and intellectual skills as forces that will be valuable and useful during the transition period: socialism, so the story goes, will be capable of putting them to good social uses and of rewarding their labour, whereas capitalism either misuses them or puts them to no use at all.

* First published in 'Telos', No. 12, Summer 1972.

I shall try to illustrate that these simplistic views
no longer hold true. We can no longer assume that it
is the productive forces which shape the relations of
production. Nor can we any longer assume that the
autonomy of productive forces is sufficient for them to
enter spontaneously into contradiction with the capitalist relations of production. On the contrary, developments during the last two decades rather lead to the
conclusion that the productive forces are shaped by the
capitalist relations of production and that the imprint
of the latter upon the first is so deep that any attempt
to change the relations of production will be doomed
unless a radical change is made in the very nature of
the productive forces, and not only in the way in which
and in the purpose for which they are used.

This aspect is by no means irrelevant to the topic
of 'technical intelligence' dealt with here. It is, on
the contrary, a central aspect. In my view, we shall
not succeed in locating technical and scientific labour
within the class structure of advanced capitalist society unless we start by analysing what functions
technical and scientific labour perform in the process
of capital accumulation and in the process of reproducing capitalist social relations. The question as to
whether technicians, engineers, research workers and
the like belong to the middle class or to the working
class must be made to depend upon the following questions: 1(a) Is their function required by the process
of material production as such, or (b) by capital's
concern for ruling and for controlling the productive
process and the work process from above? 2(a) Is
their function required by the concern for the greatest
possible efficiency in production technology? or (b)
does the concern for efficient production technology
come second only to the concern for 'social technology',
i.e., for keeping the labour force disciplined, hierarchically regimented and divided? 3(a) Is the present
definition of technical skill and knowledge primarily
required by the technical division of labour and thereby
based upon scientific and ideologically neutral data?
or (b) is the definition of technical skill and knowledge primarily social and ideological, as an outgrowth
of the social division of labour?

Let us try to examine these questions. And to begin
with, let us focus attention on the supposedly most
creative and most sought after area of employment by
asking ourselves: what is the economic purpose of the
quickening pace of technological innovation which, in
turn, calls for an increasing proportion of technical
and scientific labour in the fields of research and

development?

We may consider that up to the early 1930s, the main purpose of technological innovation was to reduce production costs. Innovation aimed at saving labour, at substituting dead labour for living labour, at producing the same volume of goods with a decreasing quantity of social labour. This priority of labour-saving innovation was an intrinsic and classical consequence of competitive capitalism. As a result, most innovation was concentrated in the capital goods sector.

But this type of innovation, while keeping a decisive importance, has been overshadowed from the early 1950s onwards by innovation in the consumer goods sector. The reason for this shift is quite clear: sooner or later, increasing productivity will meet an external limit, which is the limit of the market. If the market demand becomes saturated for a given mix of consumer goods, the wider reproduction of capital tends to grind to a halt and the rate of profit to fall. If innovation were to remain concentrated mainly on capital goods, the outlets for consumer goods production could be made to grow only by lowering prices. But falling prices would slow down the cycle of capital reproduction and rob monopolies of new and profitable opportunities for capital investment.

The main problem for monopolies in a virtually saturated market is therefore no longer to expand their production capacities and to increase productivity; their main problem is to prevent the saturation of the market and to engineer an on-going or, if possible, an expanding demand for the very type of commodities which they can manufacture at maximum profit. There is only one way to reach this result: constant innovation in the field of consumer goods, whereby commodities for which the market is near the saturation point are constantly made obsolete and replaced by new, different, more sophisticated products serving the same use. The main function of research is therefore to accelerate the obsolescence and replacement of commodities, i.e., of consumer as well as capital goods, so as to accelerate the cycle of reproduction of capital and to create profitable investment opportunities for a growing mass of profits. In one word: the main purpose of research and innovation is to create new opportunities for profitable capital investment.

As a consequence, monopolist growth and the growth of the GNP no longer aim at or result in improved living conditions for the masses. In North America and tendentially in Western Europe, growth no longer rests on

increasing physical quantities of available goods, but,
to an ever larger extent, on substitution of simpler
goods by more elaborate and costly goods whose use value
is no greater - it may well be smaller.

This type of growth is obviously incapable of eliminating poverty and of securing the satisfaction of social
and cultural needs; it rather produces new types of
poverty due to environmental and urban degradation and
to increasingly acute shortages in the fields of health,
hygiene, and sanitation, to overcrowding, etc.

The point I am driving at is that the type of productive forms which we have at hand, and more specifically the type of technical and scientific knowledge,
competence, and personnel, is to a large extent functional only to the particular orientation and priorities
of monopolist growth. To a large extent, this type of
technical and scientific personnel would be of little
use in a society bent on meeting the more basic social
and cultural needs of the masses. They would be of
little use because their type of knowledge is hardly
relevant to what would be needed to improve the quality
of life and to help the masses to take their destiny in
their own hands. For example, technical and scientific
workers, though they may know a lot about the technicalities of their specialized fields, know very little
nowadays about the ways to make the work process more
pleasant and self-fulfilling for the workers; they know
very little about what is called 'ergonomy' - the science of saving effort and avoiding fatigue - and they
are not prepared to help workers into self-organizing
the work process and into adjusting production technology to their physical and psychic needs. (Moreover,
they are not generally capable of conveying their
specialized knowledge to workers holding less or different training and of sharing it with them.) In other
words, technical and scientific knowledge is not only
to a large extent disconnected from the needs and the
life of the masses; it is also culturally and semantically disconnected from general comprehensive culture
and common language. Each field of technology and
science is a typical sub-culture, narrowly specialized
in its relevance, generally esoteric in its language
and thereby divorced from any comprehensive cultural
concept. It is quite striking that though a large
majority of intellectual workers are engaged in technical and scientific work, we do not have one scientific
and technical culture, but a great number of fragmentary
sub-cultures, each of which is bent on devising technical
solutions to technical problems, and none of which is

qualified to put its specialized concern into a broader
perspective and to consider its general human, social,
and civilizational consequences. Hence this paradox
that the main intellectual activity of advanced industrial societies should remain sterile as regards the
development of comprehensive popular culture. The
professionals of science and technology, and more specifically of research and development, must be seen as
a kind of new mandarins whose professional pride and
involvement in the particular fields of their activity
is of little relevance to the welfare and the needs of
the community and of humanity generally: most of their
work is being done on problems that are neither the
most vital nor the most interesting as regards the well-
being and happiness of the people. Whether in archit-
ecture, medicine, biology, or physics, chemistry,
technology, etc., you can't make a successful career
unless you put the interest of capital (of the company
or corporation or the State) before the interest of the
people and are not too concerned about the purposes
which the 'advancement of Science and Technology' is
to serve. The so-called concern about Science and
Technology per se - the belief that they are value free
and politically neutral, and that their 'advancement'
is a good and desirable thing because knowledge can
always be put to good uses, even if it is not, presumably - is nothing but an ideology of self-justification
which tries to hide the subservience of science and
technology - in their priorities, their language, and
their utilization - to the demands of capitalist institutions and domination. This fact, of course,
should not surprise us: technical and scientific culture remains fragmented and divorced from the life and
the overall culture of the people because the object
to which it relates, that is, the means and processes
of production, is itself alienated from the people. In
a society where the means and processes of production
are estranged from the people and erected to the status
of die Sache selbst, in such a society it is not aston-
ishing that the knowledge about the means and processes
of production should be an estranged knowledge, a knowledge as reified (versachlicdet) as its object itself, a
knowledge that forbids, through its narrow concern for
a particular aspect of die Sache, a comprehensive understanding of what everything is about (warum es im
Gesamten geht).

Technical and scientific culture and competence thus
clearly bear the mark of a social division of labour
which denies to all workers, including the intellectual
ones, the insight into the system's functioning and

overall purposes, so as to keep decision-making divorced
from productive work, conception divorced from execution
and responsibility for producing knowledge divorced from
responsibility for the uses knowledge will be put to.

But however estranged technical and scientific
workers may be from the process of production, and however significant their role in producing surplus value
or, at least, the conditions and opportunities for
profitable investment, this stratum of workers cannot
be immediately assimilated to the working class, that
is, to the class of productive workers. Before making
such an assimilation - and before speaking a propos the
technical worker of a 'new working class' - we have to
distinguish: (a) situations where plants are run by
an overwhelming majority of technicians doing repetitive
or routine work and holding no authority or hierarchical
privilege over production workers; and (b)   situations
where technical workers supervise, organize, control and
command groups of production workers who, whatever their
skills, are credited with inferior knowledge, competence
and status within the industrial hierarchy.

A great number of misunderstandings have arisen owing
to the fact that sociologists like Serge Mallet have
focused attention on situation (a), whereas situation
(b) is, for the moment and for the near future, still
much more widespread and sociologically relevant, at
least in Europe. I shall therefore start by examining
situation (b) and comment later on the ambiguity of the
technical workers' protest movement, a movement which
can hardly be understood unless it is related to the
ongoing transition from situation (b) to situation (a).

II

To understand the function of technical workers in
manufacturing industries, we have to see that their
role is both technical and ideological. They are entrusted not only with keeping production to certain
pre-determined technical standards; they are also and
mainly entrusted with maintaining the hierarchical
structure of the labour force and with perpetuating
capitalist social relations, that is, with keeping the
producers estranged from the product and from the process of production.

There is ample documentary evidence for the fact
that this second aspect of their role takes precedence
over the first. But this fact has usually escaped the
attention of capitalist societies, and only the Chinese

cultural revolution has led Western observers to pay
attention to it. Until recently, it was most commonly
assumed that since industrial production in factories
or large mechanical plants requires the division, specialization and separation of tasks, it was quite natural
that minutely divided repetitive and unskilled tasks
needed to be coordinated, supervised, planned and timed
by people responsible either for part or for all of the
complex final product, or for part or all of the work
process: these people had to have both superior technical skills and intellectual and hierarchical authority.

But if we look into it more closely, we must ask:
why must labour be minutely divided? Why must the narrowly specialized tasks be performed separately by
different workers? The reasons usually given are:
(a) narrow specialization requires less skill and
training; (b) repetitive tasks enable the workers to
work faster and more efficiently.

In truth, neither of these reasons holds true[1].
Experiments conducted mainly in the United States have
demonstrated that productivity can be greatly enhanced
by enlarging the jobs and replacing repetitive assembly
line work by team work, i.e., by giving teams responsibility for a complex product and allowing each team
to organize production as it deems most convenient. In
this system, the repetitiveness and separation of tasks
are abolished and workers are incited to achieve and
to display a spectrum of skills, and to take over the
coordination, planning, timing, and even the testing of
their production. Of course, the coordination of the
different work teams and technicians or engineers
undergoes a fundamental change: it ceases to be hierarchical and authoritarian. It cannot remain such.
The system, in order to work, must rest on the workers'
consent, initiative and sense of responsibility;
relations of cooperation and mutual trust between work
teams and technicians or engineers become indispensable:
the latter can no longer give orders and demand obedience; they must seek the workers' consent and therefore have to explain and discuss each of their concerns.
Moreover, they must be at the workers' disposal, ready
to help them solve problems they meet and to achieve
improvements, modifications and innovations of the work
process, the tools and the products[2].

In this type of organization, as enacted in China
and envisioned in Europe (mainly in Italy) by political
and labour activists, sharp differences between workers
on the one hand and technicians and engineers on the

other hand tend to disappear. Production work and the
acquisition of new skills and knowledge proceed together; working and learning or studying cease to be
separated. From his early adolescence onward, everyone
is at the same time both a producer and a student. No
one is meant to remain blocked in unskilled, stupid and
'inferior' jobs: an 'evolutive profile' (or 'career')
is sketched out in each industry whereby each worker's
work is to be progressively enriched, the reduction of
working time being designed to allow free time for
studying. The work process and production technology
of course must be radically reshaped so as to allow for
the maximum display of the producers' capabilities and
creativity[3].

That such a reshaping of production technology should
be possible without increasing the social costs of production to the whole economy is a demonstrable fact;
experiments in the United States even demonstrate the
superior micro-economic efficiency of the type of work
organization that abolishes hierarchical authority and
control and appeals to team spirit and creativity.
The question to which we have to revert then is: why
is such a type of technology not generally available?
Why has capitalism consistently promoted a technology
that rests on the minute and stupefying fragmentation
of tasks: a technology that requires the hierarchic
structure of the work force and the hierarchic separation of manual and technical and intellectual labour?
Why does 'rationalization' and 'modernization' keep
replacing skilled work and work teams with unskilled
repetitive work that leaves most workers' capabilities
unemployed, that denies them the possibility of thinking and developing into complete human beings? Why
does the capitalist system instead transfer most of the
intellectual, creative and skilled dimensions of production work onto a pyramidally structured personnel of
supervisors, technicians and engineers who receive an
essentially abstract training and are instrumental in
making and keeping the workers stupid?

There is one main, fundamental reason: the hierarchical division of labour destroys the power of the
workers over the work process and maximizes the bosses'
(or their representatives') power of control over the
work force. The minute division of labour renders the
process of production totally extraneous to the workers;
it robs them of the possibility of determining how much
work they want to do, it prevents them from tampering
with work speeds. It makes them work to the limits of
their physical and nervous capabilities - a thing no

one would do unless personally committed to the purpose
of his work, and even then not permanently. In a word,
the capitalist division of labour is functional to a
system that rests on forced labour and that therefore
can rely only on regimentation and hierarchical control,
not on the workers' consent and cooperation. To sum it
all up, we have the following vicious circle: (a) since
the purpose of production is not the satisfaction of the
producers' needs, but the extortion of surplus labour,
capitalist production cannot rely upon the workers'
willingness to work; (b) the less capitalist management wishes to rely upon the willingness of the workers,
the more extraneous, regimented and idiotic work has to
become; and (c) the more extraneous, regimented and
idiotic work becomes, the less capitalist management
can rely upon the workers' willingness.
Hierarchical regimentation thus appears to be a necessity that flows from production technology; but in
truth it is built into production technology insofar as
the latter is itself a reflection of the social division
of labour.

Whether we like it or not, we must see technicians
in the manufacturing industries as key instruments of
the hierarchical regimentation required by the capitalist division of labour. Their role is to oversee the
domination of mechanical processes over living labour;
their role is to make sure thereby that the maximum
labour and surplus value is extracted from each worker.
The role is to de-qualify workers by monopolizing the
technical and intellectual skills required by the work
process. They embody the dichotomy between manual and
intellectual work, thought and execution. They hold
significant financial, social and cultural privileges.
They are the workers' most immediate enemy: they
represent the skill, knowledge, and virtual power of
which workers have been robbed. In a machine tool shop,
every one technician that is hired will turn five, ten,
or twenty hitherto skilled workers into unskilled under-
dogs, thereby enabling the boss to pay them unskilled
wage rates.

I shall conclude this section by reporting a recent
conversation with a young technician in a machine tool
factory. He had been to a technical school and was
very proud of his knowledge. He earned twice as much
as the workers he was supervising. When asked what he
knew which the workers did not, he replied, 'I have
studied calculus, mechanics, and am a good draughtsman.'
I asked him, 'Do you ever use calculus in your work?'
'No,' he said, 'but I am glad I have learned it. It's

a good training for the mind.'

I then asked him, 'What skills, besides calculus, do
you have which workers have not?' 'I have a more comprehensive insight,' he said, 'into what it's all
about.' 'Could workers acquire such an insight,' I
asked, 'without having been to a technical school?' He
replied, 'They might get it through experience, but it
would take them time.' 'How long?' I asked. 'Oh, at
least five to six years,' he said.

This technician had been to a technical school for
three years. You will have noticed that, in his view,
his hierarchical and social privileges and superiority
rested mainly on his knowledge of calculus. But he had
never used calculus in his work. Calculus was the
cultural status symbol that made him socially different
from the workers. Because it was the one thing he knew
which the others could not learn from experience, calculus gave him a sense of authority and of superiority
over them. We have here a crystal clear illustration of
the way in which the school system is instrumental in
building social hierarchization. Indeed, in our example
the technician's superiority did not stem from superior
useful knowledge. In his own words, the useful knowledge he held could be acquired by workers in five to
six years. His hierarchical superiority stemmed from
superior useless knowledge. He had been trained in
calculus not to become more efficient than a worker, but
to become superior to a worker. And the workers had
not learned calculus not because they were too stupid to
learn it, but because they were meant to remain culturally and therefore hierarchically inferior, whatever
their skill.

From a political viewpoint, we must therefore consider that there is an unbridgeable objective class distinction between technical supervisory staff and
production workers. This class barrier can be overcome
only by a powerful ideological thrust enhancing class
consciousness. Mainly in situations of acute crisis
and upheaval, technical supervisory personnel can be
brought to side with the working class and to feel one
with it. This possibility rests on the fact that technical and engineering personnel, though they hierarchically oppress the workers, are themselves frustrated,
estranged and oppressed from above. Vis-a-vis their
superiors, they are in the same situation as are their
inferiors vis-a-vis themselves. When, during radical
outbreaks in factories, the workers attack the capitalist division of labour and demand or even practice
self-rule and equal pay for all, the sheer ideological

appeal of their demand can win over technical and scientific personnel. I saw this happen in May 1968 in the Thomson-Houston plant near Paris, where research engineers came out in favour of equal pay for all. It must be added, of course, that some of them were highly politicized. We cannot expect, however, that such a demand should spring up in normal times. All we can do in times of uneasy and restless 'peace' is to impress upon technical personnel that they have more to win than to lose by the abolition of hierarchical regimentation and privilege. To prepare the ground for this abolition, both culturally and materially, technicians must be stimulated to question their role on the following basis:[4] (a) they must endeavour to distinguish between their particular technical or scientific skills on the one hand, and their role in the hierarchical division of labour, on the other hand; (b) they must endeavour to 'socialize' their particular skills, that is, to look for the ways and means whereby their superior knowledge could be made accessible to all, could cease to be a privilege, could cease to be professionally exercised by a few to the detriment of all, which entails the reshaping of the language of science and technology, a new definition of skills, of the learning process, and of the work process; and (c) they must refuse the social privileges and the hierarchical position of power attached to professionalism in the capitalist division of labour.

In short, the sharpest possible line must be drawn between specialization and privilege. Whereas specialization cannot be abolished in the foreseeable future, privilege can. There is no intrinsic necessity to attach privileges of status, power and money to certain skills. The basis for such privileges cannot be considered to be the scarcity of the more intellectual skills or of the capability to acquire them. It is questionable whether this scarcity has ever existed and it certainly has virtually ceased to exist: on the contrary, there is an actual or potential over-abundance of intellectual skill. Scarcities that can still be observed cannot be ascribed to scarce talent or lack of capability to learn, but are a result of the class character of educational institutions: as we have seen in the example of the young technician, so proud of his mathematical skill, education aims at imbuing a minority with a feeling of elitism and is instrumental thereby in reproducing the hierarchic stratification of labour required by capitalist social relations. This result is reached through teaching methods that make the acquisition of abstracted intellectual skills difficult

for children of less educated parents and by identifying
good school grades with a right to privilege and to
social promotion. The schooling system is a key instrument of social hierarchization: it registers a differentiation of skills and learning capabilities because it
produces it.[5]

III

It may seem at first that the class analysis which
we have outlined so far does not apply at all to the
growing stratum of technical and scientific personnel
which, working in big engineering firms and in so-called
scientific industries, is itself subjected to the capitalist division of labour. In Italy, France, and Great
Britain, we have witnessed in recent years mass rebellions and strikes by draughtsmen, engineering and technical personnel of the computer industry, research
workers in the laboratories and research institutes,
project engineers in large firms of consultants, etc.
In many instances, mass rebellion was motivated by the
technical and scientific workers' frustration and hum-
iliation at being submitted in their work to the same
job evaluation, fragmentation and hierarchical regimentation as ordinary workers. Where intellectual workers
no longer hold hierarchic authority over manual labour
but are themselves producers of non-material commodities
such as information, projects, patents, and innovations,
they experience the proletarianization of their labour
and their alienation through extraneous work processes
and stupefying specialization.

But we must be careful not to jump to hasty conclusions and not to miss the inherently ambiguous character
of most intellectual workers' rebellions. We cannot
consider these right away as proof that intellectual
workers join the struggle of the proletariat because
they in fact tend to be proletarianized. Such a conclusion would be legitimate only if intellectual workers
actually joined up with manual workers on a class basis
and fought together with them for common goals. Though
there are cases where this has happened, it is far from
being the rule. In most instances, intellectual workers
have not revolted as proletarians, but against being
treated as proletarians. They have rebelled (a) against
the hierarchical division, fragmentation and meaning-
lessness of their work; and (b) against their proletarianization and the loss of all or part of their social
privileges. The anti-hierarchical and anti-authorit-
arian dimension of their rebellion was, in most cases,

inextricably linked with demands aiming at recovering
some of the privileges that were attached, in earlier
times, to the intellectual workers' middle class status.
Hence the ambiguity of their protest movement, a movement that may be said to be anti-monopolist rather than
anti-capitalist, corporatist rather than proletarian.

To make clear this ambiguity, we have to examine the
kind of training most technical workers are receiving,
and their motivation in accepting such training.

Post-secondary education, in almost all countries,
is sharply divided into two branches: the more traditional liberal universities, on one hand, and the
technical and engineering schools, on the other hand.
The content and the methods of education differ significantly in these two branches. Whereas the teaching
process in universities may be rather informal, it is
quite strict and disciplinarian in technical and engineering schools. Whereas universities as a rule aim at
conveying a certain knowledge and at training students
to become intellectually self-reliant, technical and
engineering schools aim at conveying both knowledge and
practical skills, and at shaping the personality of the
student so as to make him or her fit into the hierarchical and authoritarian order of the factory or the
laboratory. University graduates are supposed to acquire and develop a critical intelligence that should
enable them to work independently as free professionals,
research scientists, private entrepreneurs or teachers;
their degree does not prepare them for a definite job
and, actually, may leave them jobless. Technicians and
engineers, on the contrary, are trained for a job they
have chosen and which they know will position them in
a definite place within the social hierarchy and the
division of labour. They have chosen this particular
kind of training and this particular job for two
reasons: (a) their social origin leaves them little
hope of becoming anything but salaried employees; they
do not have enough time and money to attempt an independent career and to run the risk of not finding a job
as soon as they graduate; (b) they are 'upwardly mobile'
and aim for a salaried position which will be 'better'
than that of an ordinary worker or employee, but which
will hardly carry them to the 'top'.

They may therefore be described as being essentially
lower middle class. Their hope of positioning themselves on an intermediate level between top and bottom
implies that they are prepared to serve unquestioningly
the goals and purposes of the ruling class. And this
is precisely what the technical and engineering schools

prepare them to do. Technical training, in its essence,
is indifferent to goals and purposes; it specializes
in paying attention to the ways and means to reach
preset goals and purposes. It dispenses a typically
subordinate culture: not one that deals with defining
the so-called higher values of society and the meaning
of things; but one that prides itself on being value-
free and therefore capable of devising efficient means
to enact any values others may set. The divorce between
so-called higher culture - the humanities, the liberal
arts - and technical skill and knowledge is an essential
part of the social division of labour as embodied in
technical education.

Technical schools and institutions are thus instrumental in producing a particular type of individual. Or,
to put it the other way around, those who will put up
with the regimentation, repressiveness, discipline and
deliberately unattractive programmes of technical
schools are the kind of persons capitalist industry
needs. They are a hand-picked minority. As you know,
a very large proportion of young industrial workers
dream of improving their qualifications and becoming
technicians and engineers. They dream of this to escape
the dreadful embarassment and boredom of repetitive
work. They could become well qualified if the education
and programmes were rendered attractive and pedagogically efficient. But the programmes are devised in such
a way as to discourage, repel, and eliminate between
one-half and three-fourths of the youngsters who would
have liked to learn.

In Europe and, to a lesser degree, in the United
States, the highly selective character of high schools
and technical and engineering schools is something
deliberate: as long as manual and unskilled jobs in
industry and the service sector represent a significant
proportion of all available jobs, the schools must produce a sufficient proportion of failures for whom the
'low level' jobs will remain the only choice. The production of failures and school drop-outs is as important
to the reproduction of hierarchical social relations as
the production of school graduates: a set proportion
of adolescents must be persuaded by the impersonal
process of schooling that they are incapable of becoming
anything better than unskilled labour. They must be
persuaded that their failure to learn is not the
school's failure to teach them but their own personal
and social shortcoming. (Conversely, those who do well
at school must be convinced that they are something
like an elite, that they will rise above the working

class and that their success is due to their hard work,
self-denial, and ambition. Technical schools make sure
that the successful graduate will feel condescending
towards workers and submissive towards those above him.)

Consciously or not, such a selective schooling system
aims at dividing the manual and technical workers into
two distinct strata, persuading the latter that they
really belong to the middle classes and are entitled to
some social and financial privileges. This attempt at
socially upgrading the technical worker is not only a
hangover from earlier times, when technicians were working as supervisors rather than as production workers:
it is also motivated by capitalist management's need to
have costly and highly productive machines supervised
and served by reliable, trustworthy people who will feel
loyal to the corporation and to the system and not be
inclined to take the technical power they wield into
their own hands, or even to demand political and economic power for the working class. People who actually
control the more or less automatic processes of vital
production must to some extent be co-opted into the
system's privileged strata and made blind to their class
position, lest the system's smooth and safe functioning
be jeopardized.

The effectiveness of this strategy of co-optation is
dependent, however, on the (subjective) reality of the
privilege it can confer. No great difficulties may be
encountered as long as the stratum of technical workers
is only a minority. But when the proportion of skilled
versus unskilled jobs becomes reversed, contradictions
tend to explode. This situation has presently been
reached in the United States and, potentially, in most
of Western Europe. Student and high school rebellions
must be seen in this perspective. Most advanced capitalist societies are presently in a period of uneasy
transition: schools must keep producing a proportion of
failures - about two-thirds in Western Europe versus
about one-third in the United States - so as to provide
the necessary unskilled labour to the economy. But it
is already clear to most that unskilled jobs are dis-
appearing rapidly and that post-secondary education is
becoming a prerequisite to finding any - however boring,
narrowly specialized and repetitive - job. The arbit-
rariness of the schooling system's inbuilt selectiveness
is therefore becoming obvious: the schools reject a
certain proportion of students not because it would be
impossible to educate them - the contrary has become
quite clear - but because, for the reasons indicated
above, the system does not care to educate them: it

must prevent them from acquiring skills and knowledge
that would make them 'unfit' for the low grade jobs.

On the other hand, as the majority of jobs tend to
require some post-secondary training, the link between
such training and the privileges it conferred in the
past can no longer be maintained. According to recent
American statistics[6], the expected lifetime income of
youngsters with one to three years of college is only
6.24 per cent higher (i.e., $119,000 against $112,000)
than that of youngsters who have a high school education.
Hence the following explosive contradiction: post-
secondary education remains selective, competitive and
requires the kind of social attitudes that would be
expected from upwardly mobile adolescents, but the jobs
onto which junior college and technical education lead
hold hardly any privilege - whether financial or social
or intellectual - over unskilled jobs: most trainees
of technical school or of junior colleges are clearly
destined to become the labourers of the technically
advanced industries and to perform the so-called 'post-
industrial society's' ungratifying and frustrating
work.

The choice confronting young technical workers is
therefore quite obvious: either, having put up will-
ingly with the regimentation and selectiveness of a
schooling system that promised them privileges and promotion, they rebel against their regimentation at jobs
that do not fulfil the system's promises and frustrate
their desire for respectability, initiative and creat-
iveness; or, they find out while still in training
that the schooling system's promises and values are a
big swindle anyhow, and they rebel against regimentation
at school first and against regimentation at work later.
Why indeed should they put up with the disciplinarian
and authoritarian training methods since 'learning' at
school will secure them neither a 'higher' social position nor gratifying work allowing for some display of
iniative and creativity? Since good performance at
school is irrelevant in both respects, well then, fuck
the school and fuck the system and instead let's do and
learn things that are enjoyable and hold some intrinsic
interest. In one word, the motivations that could in-
cite youngsters to put up with the school and with the
jobs it prepares them for are going bankrupt; the
present crisis of and revolt against the educational
system and work organization is the consequence of this
bankruptcy.

Only the last of these two attitudes holds real

radical potentialities. It goes beyond (dépasse) the
inherent ambiguity of the first attitude, which is a
rebellion against both the alienation of work and the
proletarianization of the technical workers. When
Serge Mallet and others wrote about the 'new working
class' ten years ago, they missed this ambiguity and
still drew a line (legitimately, at that time) between
the 'old' working class, caring mainly about wages, and
the 'new' one, caring mainly about 'qualitative goals'.
As technical or post-secondary education and the tech-
nicization of work become the rule, the distinction
between the 'old' and 'new' working class is becoming
obsolete, at least with younger workers. To them, technical work no longer holds much, if any, privilege over
traditional production work. They know or sense that
the technical worker, whatever his skill, is the under-
dog and the proletarian of 'technological society'.
They have learned in schools, in their early teens,
that the system channels towards technical disciplines,
studies, and professions, those whom it condescendingly
considers 'unfit for anything better'. They rightly
feel their teachers or professors to be the prefigura-
tion - or the valets - of the bosses and cops who will
exploit them and beat them down in the near future;
and their revolt against the stupidity of regimentation
at school goes hand in hand with the revolt against the
work organization and the hierarchical division of
labour. They know that their technical skills, which
will be obsolete within five years, anyhow, are no
better than traditional manual skills and hold no hope
of escape from working class boredom and oppression.

The ground is thereby laid for the political and
ideological unification of technical and manual workers
- of the 'new' and the 'old' working class - at least
in the younger generations, and for a common onslaught
against the capitalist division of labour and the capitalist relations of production.

But this objective possibility for unification must
still be made conscious by actions for the proper goals
and on the proper ground (terrain). The goals must of
necessity be those of a 'cultural revolution': destroy-
ing the inequalities, hierarchizations and divisions
between manual and intellectual work, between conception
and execution; liberating the creative potentials of
all workers which the schools as well as the work organization stifle. The ground (terrain) must be both
and at the same time the factory where the work force
is oppressed, intellectually mutilated and psychically
destroyed, and the school where the 'human material' is

shaped so as to fit into the hierarchical factory system.   The crisis of the reproduction of capitalist social relations and of the capitalist division of labour -
i.e., the crisis of the school - must reach down to a
direct attack against the hierarchical division of labour
in the factory;   conversely, the attack must reach up to
an attack against the educational system, which is the
matrix of this division of labour.   Education and production, learning and working were separated from the
means of production and from culture and society overall.   Therefore the re-unification of education and
production, of work and culture[7], is the only correct
approach in a communist perspective.

NOTES

1.   The point I am trying to make here, and which has
been very convincingly documented by Prof. Stephen
Marglin of Harvard University in a forthcoming essay,
is that technology has been shaped by capitalism so as
to secure maximum control over and exploitation of
labour, not to secure maximum production of goods.

   Control and exploitation are obviously inseparable,
but the distinction between maximum exploitation and
maximum production is a crucial one: it implies that
capitalism uses the most efficient production technology only so far as the latter is compatible with
maximum control and exploitation.   Capital's goal is
maximum profit, and since the latter requires total
power to dispose over the work force's labour, it may
well be attained - and actually has been attained - to
the detriment of the greatest possible technological
efficiency and productivity.

   The point Prof. Marglin has documented is that -
contrary to most historians' belief and contrary to
Marx's assumption - industry did not develop from a
new and more efficient technological base, but, on the
contrary, new technologies developed after the concentration of artisanal production in large factories.
The motive of this concentration was not the factories'
superior technology - they used the same technology as
the artisans - but the capitalist bosses' (the out-
putters') desire to (1) control and market the weavers'
total production which, if not physically controlled
in the factories, would have been partly embezzled;
(2) maximize the input of work, i.e. compel the weavers
to work longer hours at greater speed than they would

have done had they remained the owners of their tools;
(3) take control of all technological innovation so as
to use it for the sake of capital accumulation and not
for purposes of more immediate interest; (4) organize
production in such a way that the cycle of production
could not dispense with the capitalist's function.

It is undeniable, of course, that capitalist industry
did result in more efficient and more productive technology. But the point that must be stressed is that
production technology has borne from the beginning the
imprint of capitalist relations of production and was
shaped by them. And that, therefore, it is by no means
absurd to infer that a quite different production
technology may have developed - and may develop - if
not maximum control over and exploitation of the work
force, but - as seems to be the case in China - maximum
collective initiative and responsibility in the maximi-
zation of social production is the main goal.

Fragmented and repetitive assembly line work must
be re-examined from this angle. It is quite certain
that assembly line production contained some significant
technological advancements and the mechanization of
hitherto manual tasks. But it must also be seen that
increased mechanization has always served a double
purpose: the introduction of more efficient machinery
has usually gone hand in hand with increased intensity
(or input) of work by each labourer. It is not at all
certain that the increased productivity achieved
through repetitive assembly line technology could not
have been achieved without the fragmentation of work
into repetitive jobs. The latter served the obvious
purpose of eliminating the quite significant control
which the skilled worker had over his working speed and
working time, a control which enabled him to withhold
a good part of his labour force from the capitalist
employer. (On the very dubious effectiveness of
monetary incentives on piece work productivity and the
practical impossibility of extracting maximum production
effort from piece workers, see William F. Whyte Money
and Motivation Harper and Row, 1955; Harper Torchbooks
1970.)

The minimization of skill has been a consistent
policy of capitalist management, since it maximized the
workers' dependence and manageability and reflected the
social division of labour in its technical division.
It is therefore no accident that bourgeois social
relations should have re-emerged in all those so-called
'socialist' countries where the capitalist technical
division of labour was used as a standard method. (On

the originality of the Chinese revolution in this res-
pect, see: Marco Maccio, 'Parti, Techniciens et Classe
Ouvrière dans la Révolution Chinoise' Les Temps Modernes
August-September 1970; and Jean Daubier Histoire de la
Revolution culturelle Maspero, 1970.

2. These experiments are known in the United States as
'job enlargement' and Scanlon Plan Y. They do not
imply far reaching technological changes and rest mainly
on a different work organization using traditional technologies, e.g. assembly line work. But they give the
workers control and responsibility over the work process
and the product and allow them to display their invent-
iveness.

    Among the more accessible writings on the subject
see Judson Goodlin's articles in Fortune July 1970 and
September 1970; 'Getting at the Root of a Labour
Crisis' in Business Week, October 17th, 1970, pp. 56-57;
William F. Whyte, Money and Motivation (op cit) chap.
10 and 14; Charles Hampden Turner Radical Man
(Schenkman, Cambridge, Mass., 1970), chap VIII.

3. See Antonio Lettieri, 'Qualifiche, Scuola e Orari di
Lavoro', Problemi del Socialismo, no. 49, November-
December, 1970.

4. I am borrowing these propositions from Eduarda Masi,
'Sur l'auto-contestation des Intellectuels', Les Temps
Modernes No. 295, February 1971. See also the dis-
cussion on technicians and the division of labour in
Quaderni Placentini, Nos. 37, 38, 39, 40 and 41, and
'Division du Travail et technique du pouvoir' in Les
Temps Modernes, No. 285 (April 1970).

5. Cf. Pierre Bourdieu and J. C. Passeron La Réproduc-
tion (Minuit, 1970).

6. 'Population Characteristics' in Current Population
Reports series p. 20 and p. 60, No. 207, November 30th
1970, quoted in a forthcoming study by Sam Bowles,
professor of economics at Harvard University.

7. 'No full time studying, no full time working' is a
mot d'ordre of Il Manifesto. See the Tesi del Manifesto
(Per Il Communismo) and Rossana Rossanda, 'Scuola e
Società' Il Manifesto, No. 12, 1970.

2.2
School Knowledge, Evaluation and Alienation

Ian Hextall and Madan Sarup

In our working activities as sociologists of education, we have beccme used to operating with various
kinds of separation in mind. We are accustomed to
fragmenting and slicing our concerns and interests. We
treat the topic of education as distinct from the world
of industry or the world of politics. Similarly,
sociology (of education) is distinguished from philosophy, psychology, economics, history or administration
(of education). In our more detailed activities of
course-building we are familiar, both from our own
courses, and from those we hear about through colleagues,
students, teachers and texts, with courses which deal
with topics such as language, role theory, knowledge,
organizations, compensatory education, etc. as distinct
and discriminable topics for study. This is not only
a feature of sociology; philosophers treat Justice,
Liberty, Equality, Respect for Persons separately, and
psychologists see motivation, memory, perception, cog-
nition, learning styles, authority patterns as distinguishable one from the other. Naturally we, like others,
attempt to show the linkages between our topics for
enquiry. We may, for example, link units on language
with work on classroom interaction, or a philosopher
may refer to the concept of equality in dealing with
liberty, or a psychologist might emphasize the place of
motivation in memorization. But we want to argue that
such attempts at linkage remain fundamentally grounded
within a world of separation. They endeavour to link
what are still conceived of as conceptually separate
and distinguishable spheres. To point to an example

* This paper was originally presented at the Annual
Conference of the British Sociological Association at
the University of Kent, March 1975. It remains substantially unaltered.

we pick up later, the attempt to explore the articulation between education and the occupational sphere
continues to operate with a notion of the legitimacy
and appropriateness of treating these as separate features of the social world. In our view, Ollman's (1971)
interpretation of Marx's philosophy of internal relations addresses precisely this world of separation[1].
Further, as Ollman develops the argument, this separation may be seen as a central feature of alienation.
We found Ollman's analysis to be fertile in its suggestions as to how we might approach questions as to the
origins and implications not only of the academic
processes of 'differentiation and specialization', but
also broader issues of hierarchy, division of labour,
and alienation. With these general remarks in mind we
should now like to present a brief account of Ollman's
treatment of internal relations as a prelude to our
discussion of evaluation.

Ollman suggests that Marx's writings are often said
to be contradictory, but this is because his philosophy
of 'inter-relations' has not been taken seriously.
Marx's words, he argues, are meant to express a conception of things and their inter-relations. These inter-
relations are not fixed, however, but changing. For
Marx, concepts are many-faceted and their sense depends
on the relations which he believes to exist between
their different components – for example, property,
labour, commodity production, the division of labour,
value. Thus one of the difficulties, and challenges, in
understanding Marxism is that its subject-matter is not
simply 'society' but society conceived of 'relationally'.
Capital, labour, value, commodity, etc. are all grasped
as relations so that capital contains labour within it
as internally related and vice-versa. Relations are
internal to each 'factor', and when a relation alters,
the factor itself alters. For example, if wage-labour
disappeared, that is if the workers' relation to capital
radically changed, capital would no longer exist.

Marx also uses the same expression to refer to different things, and he often uses different expressions
to refer to the same thing. He argues, for example,
that production is at the same time consumption and
consumption is production[2]. Indeed, one of his major
points of criticism of Classical Economists was that
they saw production and consumption as related, but
failed to see that they contain one another internally.
Marx does, however, emphasize the importance of particular influences in particular contexts. Furthermore,
each social factor (e.g. property, labour, product) has

the potential to take the names of others (e.g. commodity, production, value) when it operates as they do within a relational whole. In other words, each social factor is, according to Marx, internally related to its own past and future forms, as well as to the past and future forms of surrounding factors. Subsumed in such a view, therefore, is the importance of context (for this factor, in this context, this is the influence most worth noting), history (each social factor is related to its own past and future forms), and dialectic (things may be viewed as moments in their development in, with and through other things).

From this brief exposition of the philosophy of internal relations, Ollman's use of such terms as 'function', 'factor' and 'inter-relation' may call to mind the vocabulary of functionalism. Such similarity in vocabulary conceals fundamental differences. Functionalists analyse social life in terms of discrete, isolatable entities such as the cultural system, the social system and its various sub-systems. In such a perspective, categories are conceived in a boundable, tangible way which, in spite of theoretical protestations to the contrary, in practice under-emphasize time, change and movement in the social world. It is not surprising that this process of abstraction and reification leads to an emphasis on system stability rather than social change[3]. Functionalism, then, continues to sustain the fundamental notion of the ontological 'separateness' of the distinct parts of the social system, although stressing within its particular rhetoric the functional inter-connectedness of these parts[4]. Thus, for example, the education sub-system is seen in terms of its distinctive and distinguishable contribution to the operation of the social system, and the task for analysis in such a view becomes the exploration of the mechanisms and dynamics of the bonding between part and whole. It is through this process of analytic fragmentation that it remains a theoretically viable possibility to enquire into the independent operation of the various sub-systems in an attempt to explicate the particular role performed by the sub-system within the functionalist 'scheme of things'. It is precisely this general orientation which makes possible the debate as to whether social justice can be most effectively fostered by action within the educational, political, economic or legal spheres, as if they were unrelated. What we are claiming is that in a radical sense the educational contains within itself the economic, political, moral and legal, and likewise for the other traditionally differentiated spheres. When viewed relationally, the analytic ground for the differentiation of sub-systems is transformed into the recognition of the relational incorporation of the political, legal, economic and moral within the very sense of education.

It is difficult for us to think relationally; but we may begin by asking what might be entailed in the attempt to do so. In the first place, it serves to remind us of what is so easily ignored, even though it forms an unexplicated bed-rock of much sociology; that the phenomena we select for our interpretive focus have their sense within the context from which we remove them. For this reason some of the questions we address are close to the concerns of the 'critical theorists'[5]. They also argue that the way in which the world is presented and appears to us may hide the fact that these appearances serve particular interests; the world of appearance is organized in a way that reflects interests. Thus our invitation to explore the internal relations between features conventionally treated as separate may be similarly viewed as an attempt to transcend the ideological base of the categories of conventional presentation[6]. Such a relocation of the particular within its context may well appear to be an 'obvious' point, but we would argue that its very obviousness has not prevented generations of us from continuing our work in apparent denial of its implications. Thus, we have continued to spend our working lives in 'forgetfulness' of this principle.

Our reasons for continuing such practices of separation may well be varied. We may, for example, have genuinely lost sight of a relational conception of reality within the complexity of the ways in which we encounter and perceive the phenomenal world. In our own work, we find that research and publications - say, on the topic of classroom interaction between teachers and pupils - come to us so that they address specific, separable and discrete problems which exemplify the very unrelational character of sociological and educational theory and practice. We may then present these to our students in such a way that the ideology of separateness, which, for example, treats language, leadership patterns, authority relations etc. as independent topics, becomes insidiously the very way in which we conceive of meeting our criteria for 'doing good work'. It is precisely in this tension between the detail and the context that dilemmas occur. Equally, we may well ignore the relational nature of social phenomena because we have no available means of working with the idea, even if we are aware of it. In

other words, if we operate with the conventional 'split'
between theory and methodology, the recognition of
relationality as a theoretic injunction may not be
matched by 'acceptable' modes of enquiry.

A further dilemma in the way of accepting a relational perspective is that, with regard to some of its
central assumptions, it is not amenable to what we might
see as the conventional tests of validity which characterize what has been called a prevailing 'culture of
positivism'. We do not wish to subscribe to these
conventional modes of validation, indeed, clearly they
themselves are incorporated within and transformed
through relational analysis. Nevertheless, it remains
an issue of commitment that one must accept some grounds
of operation in order to work relationally at all.

In summarizing our argument so far, to conceive the
social world relationally is to attempt to incorporate
into one another, and thus transcend, such conventional
category differences as fact and value, cause and
effect (Ollman, 1971) and idealism and materialism, by
which we order the world (see also Avineri, 1968). If
we decide to address the relationality of the social
world, then we engage in an exploration of the internal
relations between what, unrelationally, are conceived of
as separable and autonomous spheres of phenomena. In
the face of massive 'evidence' for, and legitimation of,
the unrelated character of the world, it will be necessary to stress the relation behind the alienated
appearance of unrelatedness[7]. Thus, to make a commitment to see relationally is to commit oneself to the
attempt to discern relations even when conventional
theory and research appear to offer few grounds for
presuming them. Our commitment treats sociological
incapacity to discern relations as problematic; it
does not interpret the unavailability of a relational
account of phenomena as residing in the character of
'reality'.

EVALUATION AND EDUCATION

We argued earlier that in our view to think relationally involves emphasizing particular influences in
particular contexts. For the purpose in hand, in this
context, the factor we have elected to consider is
evaluation. To evaluate in schools is to collect persons into groups to differentiate. Evaluation will always be necessary - to the extent that in evaluation
some people are categorized by others as acceptable or
unacceptable, it is a moral activity - but our

objection to it is the particular form it takes, the
way it is used to create and sustain hierarchies.

It has been suggested recently by sociologists interested in 'Analysis' that evaluation is to make reference
to standard and community (McHugh et al, 1974). They
distinguish between different systems of evaluation
such as those based upon power and science, and state
that in the former, there is little choice but to accept
the rules as there is usually some form of force. In
the latter, evaluation is usually purported to reflect
objective discernable properties; marks are allocated
to qualities and products by an evaluator who acts as
if he was the mouthpiece of nature, or rather, nature's
messenger, and whose speech is that of 'any man' (the
scientific community). Scientific evaluation is based
on the notion that reasons are required. Reasons begin
to acquire their authority as solutions to the scientific problem of evaluation when they are converted into
rules. That is to say, reasons become rules when they
are reformulated as adequate maxims for the production
of the evaluation. After all, to be rational is to
show reasons that would be acceptable to one's community.

But why is 'evaluation' problematic? Briefly, it is
because properties of a work are treated as criteria,
and these function rather like 'causes' of the decision.
It is impossible, however, to construct a necessary and
sufficient list of such causes from criteria because in
each and every case the evaluator engages in an enor-
mous amount of interpretive work. Another way of saying
this is that the connection between rules and decisions
is contingent. A vast amount of recent sociological
work has been concerned to show that rules do not formulate solutions but are more like ad hoc reconstructions
of the concrete practice of following the rule[8]. To
put it concisely, formal grounds for decisions are given
after the event. McHugh et al (1974) suggest that one
way of seeing evaluations is by not conceiving of them
as descriptions or proofs, but as methods of making
reference to the authority of community, to the form
of life that makes evaluation possible.

Now, whilst we would agree with them that evaluation
takes place within a form of life and relies on implicit
or explicit notions of communally held standards, we have
some reservations. Firstly, for us 'power' and 'science'
are not separable but internally related. In our view
power and science are not only internally related to
each other, contained within one another, but are also

related to labour, private property, the division of
labour and other factors. Our second reservation is
that their metaphysical idealism enables them to provide
for notions of standard and community which neglect what
we consider important issues: what circumstances and
conditions, for example, enable certain communities or
interests to persuade and sustain certain definitions
which others find coercive and alienating?

Though in a sense, then, evaluation is like members'
usage, the sharing of the same competencies as other
members, it is more than that; evaluation acquires its
authority in terms of grounds or auspices which are
deeper than the usage. We are arguing that though the
problematic character of evaluation is usually disguised
behind a version of 'correct form', and that this is
part of the 'culture of positivism' in which we are so
deeply entrenched, fundamentally evaluation is a moral
and political act. The form of life which makes evaluation possible, which enables us to understand it, is
the one in which both positivist science and capitalist
activity are features of alienated labour. It is the
form of life in which we all live, in which we all have
a price, where everyone has become a commodity - an
alienated mode of existence. A concrete example of the
relation between evaluation and alienation resides in
the process by which evaluation procedures separate man
from man.

By treating the product of an individual as an individual product, and by attributing the value ascribed to
that product to the individual who is conceived as
having produced the product, the ideology and manifestation of individuality is built into evaluation. In this
manner, the pupil or student is presented with his own
individuality as the crucial characteristic to take into
account in his orientation to work. Thus, one of the
features which recurs in discussion about the uses of
group work in schools by pupils, or the collective
productions of groups of students, or in relation to
team-teaching by student teachers, is the difficulty
encountered when it comes to evaluation. What is being
seen as a problem is the wrenching apart of the cooperative project in order to place it within an indiv-
idualized evaluation context. It becomes a problem for
us precisely because we have available to us no apparent
way of coping with the social action of members; rather,
we conceive of the fundamental unit as the individual.

It might well, of course, be argued that no sociologist worth his salt sees the individual qua individual,
since we all know about the concept of 'misplaced

entitivity' and the dangers of 'psychological reduc-
tionism'. This may be so, but we continue to operate
at critical points with that 'misplaced entitivity' as
our reference point. We grant individuals degrees, and
we would have no way of coping with a request for
collective awards; we move individuals up and down
educational, occupational and social hierarchies; we
imprison individuals for crimes; we treat individuals
for mental illness; and even if we provide group ther-
apy within the institution, we release patients individually. We have kids doing group projects in school,
and we value for its creativity, flexibility and
openness the collaborative learning we attempt to foster;
but we then deny our very message as we assess individually for CSE, GCE 'O' Level and 'A' Level, or at degree
level.

But, as well as encountering the ideology of individualism, children also learn other conceptions and
attitudes: (a) that children are not expected to produce
knowledge, but to reproduce it; (b) to locate themselves and others in various forms of ranking and to
evaluate themselves in relation to others according to
certain criteria; and (c) to fit into the world of the
'given' and the 'natural'.

It is being suggested that in learning certain
'appropriate' attitudes and modes of behaviour towards
knowledge, towards themselves, and towards others, not
only are pupils' preferences shaped but actually their
sense of possibilities[9]. Thus, for example, through
evaluation it becomes possible to sustain a sense of
the social order where some are experts and some are
not, some 'are scientists and some are not'.

Evaluation implies and refers to the giving of
'acceptable' reasons grounded upon implicit or explicit
notions of 'standard'. (What constitute 'good' reasons
and rules, their negotiation and legitimation are
important questions.) In schools young people are
initiated into measurement and grading, into a world
where everything is measured. It seems that once people
have the idea schooled into them that value can be produced and commensurated, they tend to accept all kinds
of hierarchies. This would appear to be part of the
strength of the culture of positivism. Within the
school context what is being evaluated is the pupil's
labour potential, his exchange value. The pupil exchanges the product of his labour for objects - house
points, grades, examination certificates.

It is through the workings of the evaluation process

that the work of pupils in school may be represented as
a feature of commodity production. We suggest that it
is possible to see teachers and pupils, by their labour,
producing or reproducing knowledge. This object,
knowledge, embodies the subjectivity of both of them,
but through commodity fetishization the relations of
subject and object are inverted[10]. All men inevitably
objectify themselves through labour. By submitting
the product of his labour to an evaluation which deals
with it by treating it as a unit of production to be
ranged alongside and compared with the work of others,
the pupil learns to see his work in terms of exchange-
value. His work thereby loses its individual purposive-
ness. Its relation to his needs and intentions is sub-
merged by being given a 'natural price' in relation to
the work of others through the intermediary mechanisms
of grades, marks, etc. We can point here to Marx's
more general sense of the alienation of labour, which
he sees as 'giving up the use-value of one's productive
activity; the most important of all human functions is
put under the control of another' (Ollman, 1971). The
object is taken away in the sense that knowledge is seen
as other than the pupil's product, it is dependent on
others, selected by 'experts', evaluated by examiners.

However, the alienation manifests itself prior to the
actual offering of the product by the pupil to the evaluator. Alienation resides in the pupil beginning to
work with the notion of evaluation (exchange) in mind.
It is not that the pupil is necessarily working for
himself when writing his essay, or doing his experiments, and then becomes alienated when he presents his
product to be exchanged in the market of record-cards
or mark-sheets. Rather, he is alienated in beginning
work with the perception in mind of treating his labour
as a commodity. As Ollman expresses it, pupils 'see
labour ... as an activity which is responsible for only
the part of value that is returned to them as wages'.
Labour is truncated to exchange-value. Parts of the
being of pupils (and teachers) are split off and undergo
their own transformation. This means that only certain
aspects of ourselves are emphasized and developed at
the cost of our wholeness. Thus man turns his labour
into a commodity. He treats his labour as a form of
private property to be disposed of through exchange.
He becomes an unfree person.

That knowledge also becomes a commodity means that
it is treated not as an object created through man's
social, creative activity, but as something abstract
and possessing an existence independent of man. Or, in

other words, the curriculum is seen not as practice,
the outcome of human production, but as 'fact'[11]. Again,
in Marx's words, 'the social character of man's labour
appears to them as an objective character stamped upon
the product of that labour'. It is in this context
that examinations are considered 'useful' as it is
through them that everything that is ours becomes sale-
able. Abstract, objective, universal, standardized
procedures are used to return to the human producer the
value which his product has. In this process of fetishization the original producing subject is reduced to
the level of an object to be bought and sold in the
market like any other commodity. The object, knowledge, that teachers and pupils produced, becomes the
abstract subject. Knowledge thus functions as if it
were a subject, and its producers become the object.
The creative potential inherent in individuals is neglected.

Given this view of pupils' labour and knowledge
production as commodity, the pupil comes to be regarded
as a passive recipient of 'banked' knowledge. Production produces not only the object, it creates a specific
manner of consumption, it creates the ability to consume
as a need. Into this knowledge he is initiated by
someone who 'knows' and literally possesses the
'subject'[12]. Teaching and evaluation may then become
matters of efficient technique and calculation. As
with the calculation of wages as exchange values in the
industrial and commercial spheres, the 'value' of children's work is seen to be calculable according to
technical laws and rules of procedure[13]. The social
relations of evaluation are mystified through the generation of models of child development, learning theories
and evaluation schemes. These are used to explain how
the exchange process was carried out and the basis on
which marks or grade-value are attached to the work of
pupils. Elaborate theories are used to address the
different abilities and capacities which pupils bring
to bear upon their school work. Complex forms of tests
and measurements are devised to make the evaluation of
this work finer, more discrete and fairer in relation
to the ages, aptitudes and abilities of pupils. And
all of this within a context of reified forms of knowledge which are seen as providing the epistemological
grounds on which pupils' work can be evaluated and
given its 'natural price'.

It is possible in this account to see a relationship
between the tenets of educational theory and 'the
positivist, neutral, objective, natural' laws and tenets

of classical economics which Marx criticized. In both cases the social relations, which are embodied within the production activity, are mystified by their treatment as issues of technical analysis. Classical economics concentrates its attention on the development and refinement of the mechanisms of supply and demand, the determination of prices of goods, the calculation of the appropriate levels of 'earned rewards' for the factors of production[14]. Through such analysis it accomplishes the fetishization of the social relations of production by confronting men with a body of natural laws of economics which treat man and his activities as the objects of those laws. As in our previous argument, the alienation of man is accomplished by the generation of 'objective' laws to regulate human activity. The laws themselves become the social subjects by treating man as their object. An example of such a process, involving a technicist view of evaluation, can be seen in the following quotation:

> Whether we like it or not, the campaigns for the abolition of the examination system are absurd. In a society with the immensely complicated and constantly changing division of labour that all advanced industrial societies need, bureaucratic grading, and therefore examinations, is unavoidable ... Our sorts of societies cannot function without a highly developed system[15].

This quotation illustrates the classic functionalist position of seeing the inter-relationships between constituent parts of the whole. We are asked to consider the interconnections between the conceptually disparate and separated segments of 'advanced industrial societies', 'the division of labour', and 'examinations as systems of bureaucratic grading'. Seen in this way the model is one of independent segments held together by their inter-relationships. Note also that 'the division of labour' and 'advanced industrial societies' (and their 'needs') are distinct entities articulated by the form of their inter-relationship, as are the postulated linkages between 'the examination system' and 'the division of labour'.

In this way, we would suggest, the author draws attention to the process of translation of the one into the other. Thus the implication may well be to consider how the examination system relates to the division of labour and is sequentially significant to it. It may then become appropriate to consider the inter-relationship between the division of labour and the 'advanced

industrial society's needs'. Because of this form of
schematization, such theorizing may be grounded in a
notion of chains of consequence which relate one link
of action to its next link of consequence, which in
turn becomes the link of action, and so on in a way
which succeeds in separating man from consideration of
the developing consequences of his action and activity.
To express it differently, a step by step conceptual-
ization of the nature of our actions, and their consequences, may constitute a way of seeing the world
which succeeds in mystifying for man the consequences
his acts have for other men.

This 'sequentialist' version also denies the relationality of temporal dimensions. Because it conceives
the linkages between evaluation, division of labour,
and industrialization in discrete and sequential cause/
effect terms, it mystifies the embeddedness of past, present and future within the temporal stages. The examination system, for example, does not merely have connections with, relate to, or lead to the division of
labour; it is internally related to the division of
labour, in the sense that it contains it. This is not
to argue some kind of mechanistic 'correlation' between
examination results and location within the occupational
structure, but rather that such an evaluation procedure
is predicated upon the division of labour. Alienation
appears whenever the division of labour is the operative
principle of economic organization. If we accept this
supposition and view education as a mode of production,
pupils' activity in schools can then be seen as a
relation and expression of activity in society.

The division of labour is part of a complex which
includes private property, exchange, class divisions.
In this section therefore we will be focusing on the
division of labour in education, how knowledge is
conceived of as private property, and the relation of
knowledge to class divisions.

It has been suggested by several writers that in the
educational context 'capital' can be thought of as
cultural capital, and that the prevailing view of knowledge in our society is as if it was private property.
Bernstein (1971) writes: 'Children and pupils are
early socialized into this concept of knowledge as
private property. They are encouraged to work as
isolated individuals with their arms round their work[16].'
The possession of knowledge as property, however, is
not the realization of personality but its negation.
The knowledge that is connected with economic rewards -
high status knowledge - is kept in such a way that it

entails non-possession by others. At our desks we work
privately, putting our arms round our work to hide what
we read and write. Access to many subjects is limited
to a selected few, and, even where access to a subject
is given, pupils are often evaluated in such a way that
they are presented with a selection of knowledge which
gives them only restricted access to the subject[17].
Like other workers, pupils have needs for objects to
fulfil their powers but they are not given the opportunity to acquire these objects. An abolition of the
relations of private property will mean the abolition
of the conditions which produce and reproduce the
private proprietor.

As we have argued, the prevailing conception of knowledge inverts the relations between the human subject
and the world of object, and thus transforms knowledge
from an object of the will into a master. To say this
is to say that men have become a predicate of knowledge.
In many of our schools, therefore, it is the product,
knowledge, that determines what the pupil does. The
power of any of the worker's products over the worker,
Marx wrote, always reflects the power of the people
who dominate it and use it as an instrument. Certain
forms of knowledge such as science and mathematics are
evaluated as being superior to others; generally they
are conceived of as being more 'theoretical', 'abstract',
less related to commonsense and to everyday life (see
Young, 1971). Now it has already been suggested that
in schools, apart from the evaluation of knowledge that
is made, pupils too are being assessed in terms of their
ability to learn the forms of knowledge that have been
designated superior. Some notion of correspondence is
used to relate the evaluation of the knowledge and the
pupil, it being assumed that the more 'intelligent' the
pupil, the more capable he is of mastering the more
'theoretical' and 'abstract' forms of knowledge.

The distinction we have made between so-called
theoretical and practical knowledge is basically the
same distinction as that between mental and manual
labour. In the school context subjects such as mathematics and science are taken to embody the abstract
intellect and often appear to be a-historical and universal - rather like some timeless version of truth.
It is salutary to remind ourselves that 'the control of
social production cannot lie with the workers so long
as such control necessitates intellectual work beyond
their scope'[18]. The crucial question then becomes:
can the division between mental and manual labour be
overcome? We would want to argue that though much of

school knowledge is experienced as fixed, it is not universal but historically specific, and as it is the outcome of men's productive activities it is therefore changeable. The disappearance of class differences would partly depend upon the abolition of the distinctions between what has been evaluated as high status, mental, and low-status, manual, knowledge. Marx wrote that the labour by which man makes himself is neither one-sided manual, nor one-sided mental, but must be both in one, no matter how they combine. Only in this way would labour possess the creativity by which man makes his history.

But for many, the situation in our schools is very different: the more teachers and pupils 'spend' themselves, the more powerful and coercive reified knowledge seems to become. It is not surprising that pupils come to dissociate knowledge from themselves, and that some of them see themselves and teachers as opposed to one another. This split is analogously a manifestation of class - an expression of reified social relations.

In this very brief account we may appear to have done nothing more than to provide a description of 'evaluation'. In one sense, we would admit that this is so, but also we have endeavoured to consider the manner in which we can place evaluation in relation to notions of individualism, commodity knowledge, hierarchy, and the division of labour. In brief, we have attempted to locate the evaluation activities with which we are familiar within the forms of social relations which ground their use. We didn't have to begin with evaluation as our starting point - we could have begun with ability, knowledge, streaming, mind, or the nature/ nurture debate, and would through these also have been able to consider social relations of production, division of labour, alienation, commodity fetishism. To express this relationality in a different form, we see Marx's concept of alienation being expressed in our focus on evaluation. If we take Marx's theory of alienation as dealing with man's relations to his activity, his product, his fellow men and his species, we hope that our work has made reference to these features. As we see it, our writing about individualism as an ideology, commodity production, reification of knowledge and the transformation of labour in exchange value, may also be seen as writing about alienation.

It was Marx's view that the ultimate task of philosophy was not merely to comprehend reality but to change it. This is, of course, the project which many sociologists of education are attempting to address. They

have drawn attention to the ways knowledge is used to
create and sustain hierarchies, and have suggested the
exploration of an alternative conception - the curriculum of 'practice' which would stress the subjective
intentions and purposes of pupils and teachers in dialogue. Such a view, in emphasizing not transmission
but collaborative production, challenges prevailing
hierarchies. What we hope we have been addressing is
something more general than the specific analysis of
evaluation we have adopted, important though we have
found that. Rather, we have attempted to point to the
mystification and domination which may be seen in the
procedures of fragmentation and separation which
currently characterize educational (and other) literature and thinking. It is important to us that rather
than seeing education being influenced by the economic,
occupational and political it be viewed as through and
through containing the economic, occupational and
political. If an important feature and property of
alienation resides in separation and segmentation it
would appear central to explore our experiences and
practices of fragmentation if we are to grasp the
contradictions of our own positions, and further, if
having grasped them we are to practically transform
and transcend them.

It is clear that our account has not considered a
number of questions which are of central importance.
Perhaps the most crucial issue is that of the relationship between our argument and the material base of the
mode of production. Undoubtedly some will view this as
an exercise in philosophical idealism. In using the
philosophy of internal relations as an organizing principle inevitably something is missed out. By treating
labour, value, etc. as forms of each other, as expressions of a common totality we have had little space
to deal with other, and perhaps even more important
aspects such as the primacy of the mode of production.
By focusing on alienation we concede that we have not
sufficiently stressed the importance, for example, of
economic contradictions, and the materialist conception
of history. We are not saying that the world would be
changed if only people were persuaded to see it through
a philosophy of inner relations. We do not believe
that converting people's ideas (upon which they then
proceed to act) is sufficient to bring about change.
Nevertheless such a view of totality is a necessary
part of our understanding, in our struggle for revolutionary change. This is surely the essence of Marx's
dialectic and praxis.

NOTES

1. It is important to note that in the course of this brief paper we cannot hope to do justice to the imaginative analysis of Marx's writings which Ollman (1971) attempts. Further, we also make no attempt to engage with the controversy over the status and validity of the philosophy of internal relations. Within the body of Ollman's book and more especially in the Appendix, he himself makes some approach to these issues. Perhaps even more fundamentally he has written a new preface to the second edition which takes up criticisms which have been made of the total framework of his analysis, and points to unresolved questions regarding the philosophy of internal relations.

2. See Marx Grundrisse p. 91. 'Production, then, is also immediately consumption, consumption is also immediately production. Each is immediately its opposite. But at the same time a mediating movement takes place between the two.'

3. By reification we mean that historical and political process wherein the products of human practice, the objectified expressions of man's interaction with other men and nature, become alienated from the actual producers and thus appear in consciousness as independent and autonomous things. In this process what are essentially conventional activities are accepted as if they were natural entities - there is no recognition of the historical character of the present social order, nor is there an awareness of the dependence of social change on human action. We therefore regard P. Berger and S. Pullberg's (1966) 'Reification and the Socio-logical Critique of Consciousness' as an idealist account. The classic exposition of reification is of course in LUKACS, G. (1971) History and Class Consciousness pp.83-222, and there is a useful discussion of Lukacs' theory by A. Arato in the journal Telos, No. 11, 1972. For an interesting analysis of the ways in which language is involved in the process of reification and how it restricts the development of class consciousness, see PATEMAN, T. (1975) Language, Truth and Politics (available from 1 Church Green, Newton Poppleford, Sidmouth, Devon).

4. See MURPHY, R. (1972) The Dialectics of Social Life. He begins with an opposition to the positivism of functionalism and has sympathies with 'dialectical reasoning'; what we would like to take issue with is the

Hegelian idealism he then uncritically adopts.

5. See HABERMAS, J. Theory and Practice, and Knowledge and Human Interest by the same author. An interesting attempt to utilize critical theory as a base for an attack upon liberal 'policy sciences' can be found in FAY, B. (1975) Social Theory and Political Practice.

6. This point is forcefully expressed in Clarence Karier's article 'Testing for Order and Control in the Corporate-Liberal State', where he illustrates the historical grounding of intelligence testing.

7. Marx wrote in Capital III: 'all science would be superfluous if the outward appearance and the essence of things directly coincided'. See Norman Geras (1971) 'Essence and Appearance: Aspects of Fetishism in Marx's Capital'. In it he writes: 'The essence which explains (contradictory tendencies), and deprives them of all appearance of contingency, is the central con-tradiction between forces of production, the increasing productive power of social labour, on the one hand, and relations of production, the continued private appropriation of surplus value, on the other. They partake of this central contradiction and, as partial facts, are only properly comprehended in relation to the social totality which they and it inhabit.'

8. Much ethnomethodological work focuses on this issue. A specific example is D. Zimmerman's article, 'The Practicalities of Rule Use'.

9. Although we would not agree with the argument he provides, this point is forcibly expressed by Illich in Deschooling Society. A comprehensive collection of articles can be found in LISTER, I. (Ed) (1974) Deschooling. In this reader, the article by H. Gintis: 'Towards a political economy of education' is of parti-cular interest both because of the Marxist critique of Illich he provides, but also because there are points of contact between his position and our own - also points of difference.

10. A useful account of the symmetry between commodity production and conceptual production appears in Piccone's article 'Phenomenological Marxism', in B. Grahl and P. Piccone, (1973) Towards a New Marxism.

11. A more detailed argument of the relationship bet-ween 'curriculum as fact' and 'curriculum as practice'

can be found in M. F. D. Young's article, 'Curriculum change, limits and possibilities' in Educational Studies vol. 1, No. 2, June 1975 and reprinted in this volume. Also the chapter on 'Ideology and the sociology of knowledge' in Alan Swingewood (1975) Marx and Modern Social Theory provides a clear, brief framework in which one can locate 'school knowledge' in context.

12. Although different in their modes of approach the fundamental conservatism of 'banking' models is considered by Paulo Freire (1972) Pedagogy of the Oppressed and Maxine Greene, (1971) 'Curriculum and consciousness'.

13. See Trent Schroyer (1970) 'Towards a Critical Theory for Advanced Industrial Society'. See also note (6) above.

14. An example of fetishization is when it is said in Keynesian economics that 'these are the laws of the economic system' as if they were natural laws like that of gravity. B. Fay, in Social Theory and Political Practice p.60, argues that the process of reification limits the horizon of possible political action by circumscribing the area within which one can act politically. This then reinforces certain structural features in industrial capitalism.

15. This is a quotation from Professor Macrae when he was speaking at the University Entrants and School Examinations Council, the Tenth Annual Conference of Teachers, November 1973.

16. See B. Bernstein 'On the classification and framing of educational knowledge', p. 56. Bernstein continues: 'only a few experience in their bones the notion that knowledge is permeable, that its orderings are provisional ... For the many socialization into knowledge is socialization into order, the existing order, into the experience that the world's educational knowledge is impermeable. Do we have here another version of alienation?'

17. See for example Nell Keddie, 'Classroom knowledge' where after describing an economics lesson she comments (p.149): 'Here it is clear that one consequence of a differential treatment of the economy is the way in which categories of analysis are made available to or withheld from pupils ... (The teacher) does not intentionally withhold the framework which would allow the

pupil to raise questions about the taxation policy as
a whole, but he does effectively prevent, by a process
of fragmentation, the question of how such knowledge
becomes available.

18. Alfred Sohn-Rethel 'Mental and Manual Labour in
Marxism'. A version of it appears in Radical Philosophy
Six 1973 (obtainable from 40 Langdon Park Road,
London N.6. 5QG). Sohn-Rethel's paper focuses on how,
with the beginning of commodity production, the abstract intellect.(pure mathematics, pure science)
effects its cleavage from manual labour. Marx's
critique of political economy was that it was false to
build ideal abstractions and set them up as timeless
universals. Sohn-Rethel extends Marx's proposition
to a proposition of epistemology to give a critique of
science as intellectual labour.

REFERENCES

AVINERI, S. (1968) Karl Marx: Social and Political
Thought London: Cambridge University Press.

BERGER, P. and PULLBERG, S. (1966) Reification and the
sociological critique of consciousness New Left Review
35.

BERNSTEIN, B. (1971) 'On the classification and framing of educational knowledge' in M. F. D. Young (Ed)
Knowledge and Control London: Collier-Macmillan.

FAY, B. (1975) Social Theory and Political Practice
London: George Allen and Unwin.

FREIRE, P. (1972) Pedagogy of the Oppressed
Harmondsworth: Penguin Books.

GERAS, N. (1971) Essence and appearance: aspects of
fetishism in Marx's 'Capital'. New Left Review 65, 1971.

GRAHL, B. and PICCONE, P. (1973) Towards a New Marxism
St. Louis: Telos Press.

GREENE, M. (1971) Curriculum and consciousness

Teachers' College Record Vol. 73, No. 2, 1971.

HABERMAS, J. (1974) Theory and Practice London: Heinemann.

HABERMAS, J. (1972) Knowledge and Human Interest London: Heinemann.

ILLICH, I. (1971) Deschooling Society New York: Harper and Row.

KARIER, C. (1972) Testing for order and control in the corporate-liberal state Educational Theory Vol. 22, No. 2.

KEDDIE, N. (1971) 'Classroom Knowledge' in M. F. D. Young Knowledge and Control London: Collier-Macmillan.

LISTER, I. (Ed) (1974) Deschooling London: Cambridge University Press.

LUKACS, G. (1971) History and Class Consciousness London: Merlin Press.

MARX, K. (1973) Grundrisse Harmondsworth: Penguin Books.

McHUGH, P. et al (1974) On the Beginning of Social Inquiry London: Routledge and Kegan Paul.

MURPHY, R. (1972) The Dialectics of Social Life London: George Allen and Unwin.

OLLMAN, B. (1971) Alienation Cambridge University Press.

SCHROYER, T. (1970) Towards a critical theory for advanced industrial society. H. P. Dreitzel (Ed) Recent Sociology Number 2 London: Macmillan.

SOHN-RETHEL, A. (1972) 'Mental and manual labour in Marxism, in P. Walton and S. Hall (Eds) Situating Marx London: Human Context Books.

SWINGEWOOD, A. (1975) Marx and Modern Social Theory London: Macmillan.

YOUNG, M. F. D. (Ed) (1971) Knowledge and Control London: Collier-Macmillan.

ZIMMERMAN, D. (1971) 'The practicalities of rule use' in J. Douglas (Ed) Understanding Everyday Life London: Routledge and Kegan Paul.

2.3
Education and the Social Relations of a
Capitalist Society

Douglas Holly

THE NATURE OF EDUCATION

   Properly understood, 'education' is the social organization of human learning; this learning being
itself a reflexive process involving the individual
psyche in relationship with the surrounding natural and
social world. It is necessary to say this at the
beginning of a paper on education because education is
often treated in sociology as though it were a product
rather than a process, an object, quantifiable like
wealth. On the other hand, when a process is envisaged
it is often treated as a natural, biological process,
measurable like age or height. Neither of these implicit assumptions can lead to a meaningful discussion
of the social nature of education because neither pays
attention to the material quality of the process involved. Each is an abstraction based on a false analogy. In the first case, the analogy is with the world
of artefacts: things are produced by human labour, so
education is 'produced' by a given input of resources,
material and intellectual. Individually this 'product'
can be bought and sold like any other commodity,
fetching such and such a price on the market for labour
skills or technical competence. This mechanistic view
ignores the relationship of education to learning and
reifies a process into an inert, determined quantum.
In this way, the 'education' level of whole classes
and nations is held up for inspection and comparison,
leading often to very simplistic conclusions. Years
of schooling, for instance, are related to political
maturity.

   The second type of false analogy is also determined

*   This paper was originally presented at the Annual
Conference of the British Sociological Association at
the University of Kent, March 1975.

and finite: learning is seen as a quasi-biological
process, and individuals can therefore be measured at
intervals of time to discover their stage of educational 'development'. The psychological model implicit
in this view is clearly behaviourist, no distinctively
human and social aspects being involved. Education is
then seen as the social organization of a basically
animal activity - learning. The conventional sociologist of education operates with the notion of an
intellectual division of labour: sociology is concerned
with the finished product, the 'terminal education
level' of a certain population for instance, while the
matter of how this product is produced is seen as the
province of the psychologist of learning. Such boun-
dary-maintenance works happily for the politics of
university departments of education: it doesn't do
much for an understanding of the social nature of the
education process.

From this account it will be seen that two forms of
mystifying abstraction converge in the sociological discussion of education - process-objectification and
mechanism. To appreciate the material as opposed to
the abstract character of education, we must be aware
of the basic involvement of social relations in human
learning and, therefore, of the inextricable connection
between the social-psychic process, learning, and the
social organization, education.

Human learning is differentiated from animal adaptation not in degree but in kind. It is precisely here
that the behaviourist perspective on psychology is
defective when applied to man: men and women do not
simply adapt to the physical world they inhabit - they
consciously change it. Learning, unlike adaptation,
involves a discovery that the physical universe will
respond to intervention and can, with application, be
controlled to the advantage of the learner. So much
is apparent to the adventurous ape. What inhibits
the learning of the ape and what promotes that of human
beings is the absence in the one case, and the presence
in the other, of a system of social relations aimed at
a cooperative mastery of the natural world. This
specifically human type of social relations is accompanied by the phenomenon of human language, since its
complexity demands a system of referential symbols,
spoken and graphic, not required in animal communication. Language, as Vygotsky (1934) demonstrated forty
years ago, is an essential component of human learning,
and the social relations called forth by cooperative
human intervention in the physical world are, in turn,

an essential ingredient of such language.

Human consciousness might be seen as in principle comprising will, the purpose of changing reality, and imagination, the faculty of conceiving a state of affairs not physically present. In this case, learning is the development of consciousness through experience of successful reality-changing and the social appropriation of a referential language with which to imagine further changes. Learning is basically therefore a subjective process which demands direct and successful experience of purposeful activity upon the external world - physical and social. It is, in this sense, self-determined, unlike that neural activity which characterizes animal adaptive learning, which is completely determined by external and prior conditions. On the other hand, human learning is dependent upon social relations to produce, via symbol-referent language, the capacity to imagine a range of alternative purposeful actions. Marx noticed this essential interplay of language and consciousness in the context of cooperative, social activity:

> Language itself is as old as consciousness ... for language, like consciousness, only arises from the need, the necessity, of intercourse with other men. Consciousness is therefore, from the very beginning a social product, and remains so as long as men exist at all[1].

At this point, in the opening sections of Capital, Marx is not concerned with a specific historical stage of social relations producing a definite, determined 'social consciousness', but with defining the species-activity of humanity in general, human social labour, the 'necessary intercourse' which produces human consciousness in general. It is Marx's purpose to demonstrate the importance of understanding the specific historical stage of social consciousness as experienced by various groups in defined social and economic relations to other groups; but first, he is concerned to indicate the species-nature of mankind - intervention in the natural world leading to mastery. This is a theme he had consistently followed from the Economic and Philosophical Manuscripts of 1844, and it recurs several times in Capital. For Marx, 'labour' is a term defining the humanity of man, the definitive activity of the species. Far from being the curse of Adam - and of Adam Smith - it is, in principle, the key to human happiness and fulfilment. Dismissing Smith's conventional view of labour as misfortune and idleness as pleasure Marx (1973) notes in the Grundrisse:

> Certainly labour obtains its measure from the out-
> side, through the aim to be attained and the ob-
> stacles to be overcome in attaining it. But Smith
> has no inkling whatever that this overcoming of
> obstacles is, in itself, a liberating activity and
> that, further, the external aims become stripped of
> the semblance of merely external natural agencies
> and become posited as aims which the individual
> himself posits - hence as self-realization, object-
> fication of the subject, hence real freedom, whose
> action is, precisely, labour[2].

The 'stripping of the semblance of merely external
natural agencies' from human purposes, and their positing as individual aims is in fact a theme more recently
developed by Sartre (1960), who speaks of the 'inter-
iorization' of 'exterior' phenomena as an existential
principle for human life. Certainly a view of the
growth of consciousness, which stresses a necessary
tension between external constraint and internal liberation, conforms well to the psychological description of
human learning. The external problem produces an irr-
itation which is only relieved by a subjective action,
an expenditure of psychic energy. Human learning is
essentially an active process. No true change in the
subject can occur without active involvement - which is
why so much that passes for 'learning' in the conventional education system, is purely temporary, effecting
no real change in consciousness.

What needs explanation, in fact, is precisely the
disjuncture in our society between the material nature
of learning and its social organization, education.
Elsewhere (see Holly, 1971) I have characterized this
disjuncture as 'alienated', using the term in the sense
employed by Marx in characterizing the general labour
process under capitalism. Marx was using the term in
a very precise sense linked to the description of a
defined set of social and economic relations between
men: having argued the basically relational nature of
human learning, I wish in this paper to show how the
social organization of these learning relations as
education is subject to the same conditions as the
social organization of human labour - how, in fact,
education can become alienated. In so doing, I wish
also to show how this state of affairs can change, to
some extent independently of changes in the general
social structure, but with implications that are far
from unimportant to it.

SOCIAL EPISTEMOLOGY

Early work on the sociology of education was far from penetrating the nature of the social relations involved. Floud, Halsey and Martin (1956), for instance, set out to explore the extent of 'educational opportunity' experienced by various social groups. In so doing, they concentrated on the question of the degree of success experienced by individuals in the development of the British school system. For their purpose, 'education' is implicitly defined as a product or determined state in the manner described above. No attempt is made to raise the question of the nature of the learning process: indeed one forms the impression that the nature of learning and, consequently, of education, is a matter of indifference to these authors. Education is taken to be a scarce commodity, and the point at issue is the equality or otherwise of its distribution. Such a-theoretical sociology is analagous to an economics which considers only the distribution of scarce resources and asks no questions about the source of wealth; no questions, in other words, about the social relations of production. Just as bourgeois economics reifies and abstracts from the material world, the world of actual men and women, conventional sociology reifies and abstracts from the world of material relations in learning. The result is the same in each case: failure to arrive at an explanatory theory for actual practice. The net outcome of such studies was a series of government reports, like those of the Crowther (1960) and Robbins (1963) Committees, which made vague references to 'pools' of untapped ability but bore little relation to the contemporary struggles for school reorganization, or the actual experience of students in schools and colleges at the time. The subsequent curriculum reform movement was a response by government and capitalist industry to malfunctions within the education system and owed very little to the social engineering attempts of the sociologists.

Since such a-theoretical sociology was unable to explain the historical process and the changes which are taking place, a later generation of sociologists have had to turn their attention, at last, to the social process. Young (1971) and his associates, for example, have had to look closely at what goes on in the classroom - the material process of education. From the point of view of this paper, the phenomenological approach employed by many of these writers, since it emphasizes the subject's 'definition of the

situation', does not pursue with sufficient energy the
connection between individual social relations in a
local context and concrete social relations in general.
It has, however, led to a very necessary issue being
raised: that of the definition of what counts as
'knowledge'. The raising of this issue places the
learning process at the centre of sociological attention - at least in principle.

In the perspective of this paper, 'knowledge' is not
originally an object, but a set of relationships among
human beings and between human beings and the natural
world, relationships which become objectified as knowledge in the conventional sense. To understand this we
must return to Marx's notion, alluded to in the passage
from the Grundrisse quoted above, of 'objectification of
the subject' through the cooperative subjugation of
nature involved in genuinely human labour. In a passage in Capital, Marx indicates the psychological effect
of such activity. In subjugating nature by a coordinated effort man 'changes his own nature':

> He not only effects a change of form in the material
> on which he works, but he also realizes a purpose
> of his own which gives the law to his modus operandi
> and to which he must submit his will[3].

This gives us, at one and the same time, a material
basis for human learning and for its objectification
as knowledge. Since education, the social organization
of learning, is based on one or another specific theory
of knowledge, arising out of one or another specific
mode of social relations, it is important to grasp some
such general or basic conception of human knowledge
and its material derivation - otherwise we are in
danger of either (a) assuming one particular historical
practice to be fundamental; or (b) floundering in a
morass of cultural relativism. Traditionalistic
philosophers of education like Hirst (1965) exemplify
the former tendency, erecting, a priori, 'disciplines
of knowledge' which turn out, on inspection, to be
very much connected with the dominant social relations
of a certain stage of capitalism as embodied within
the historically-derived conventional divisions of
British higher education. The more recent approaches
to sociology of knowledge, on the other hand, exhibit
a tendency to lack any absolute criterion. Young
(1973) for instance, in a paper first delivered to the
1970 meeting of the Conference at Durham urges the
study of curriculum as sociologically problematic and
related to a social organization of knowledge[4]. By

proceeding, however, to erect a typology of curricula
based on stratification, and directing his argument at
elucidating notions of competing status as between
types of curriculum (specialized versus unspecialized
knowledge), he leaves open the question of the basic
epistemological status of the material organization of
learning involved in these competing social strategies.

Keddie (1971), in an associated essay, comes nearer
in examining competing definitions held by teachers
and students. She recognizes that these definitions
may be based on differently-structured social experience, the teachers and the 'A-stream' students sharing
assumptions based on career orientations not shared
by the 'C-stream' students. Unfortunately, the specific
situation described is not analysed in terms of the
wider social relations of the teacher and student
groups involved, and we are left with a general impression, simply, that the 'C-streamers' were interpreting curriculum problems in a way more basic than
the teachers themselves: but quite how this is so is
left unexplained. The danger with such phenomenological sociology seems, precisely, to be a fascination
with abstract 'phenomena' at the expense of materiality.
In this case, the competing definitions of significance
implied in the way teachers and various socially-
structured student groups handle curriculum content, is
the centre of attention. While Keddie leaves us in no
doubt where her sympathies lie - with the educationally
disadvantaged C stream students - there is no indication
that this sympathy is anything but a subjective phenomenon to be compared with other subjective 'constructions of reality'.

A satisfactory social epistemology cannot be derived
from subjective relativism of this kind for two reasons.
First, phenomenological analysis cannot, by definition,
penetrate beyond the immediately present conditions,
the competing definitions avowed or implied by actors
in a given situation. We are, therefore, debarred
from considering wider social factors, more or less
distant in time or space. Secondly, even in the case
of the immediate situation, the subject's perception
or 'construction of reality' is clearly not the only
factor determining the differential status being
accorded to various types of knowledge. A viable
theory of knowledge needs, on the one hand, to take
into account the historical character of objectified
knowledge and, on the other, the nature of the social
relations temporarily determining a given stratification. To do this it is necessary to posit, a priori,

a general basis for all human knowledge, one which can be seen to be independent of the particular interests of this or that human group.

In this paper I am proposing a material basis as implied by Marx, that is one which takes the species-being of man as founded on a humanizing labour, the planned intervention in nature of men and women in social cooperation. In other words, I am proposing that knowledge is the objectified learning-relation-ships of human beings to the natural world and to one another in the subjugation of that world to their purposes.

If this is the species-nature of human knowledge, its historical character for our society, as temporar-ily determined by the present system of social rela-tions, is different. Under capitalist social condi-tions knowledge appears as alienated from the subjective learning of men and women altogether and as existing as an independent entity. This has come about as a con-sequence of the elevation of the division of labour under capitalism, into an all-embracing principle of social organization. As Marx (1961) points out:

> ... division of labour seizes upon not only the economical but every other sphere of society and everywhere lays the foundation of the all engrossing system of specializing and sorting men, the develop-ment in a man of one single faculty at the expense of all other faculties[5].

It is no surprise that this urge to specialize people should lead to the confusion of active learning with adaptive training, or that education has come to be organized as, above all, a preparation of the young for adult life. From being an active, continuous process it has come to be thought of as a passive, finite experience applicable usually to the immature.

It is, further, not difficult to see how, as a con-sequence, knowledge has come to be alienated from the knower into an objective property of society or, more specifically, the 'property', in every sense, of capital. The mental activity that is dissipated under previous forms of social-economic organization among the many, now becomes concentrated into an objectified social knowledge but, as a consequence of the peculiar historical social relations of capitalism, it is further alienated from the subjects and appropriated to capital. As Marx further observes in Capital:

The knowledge, the judgment and the will which,
though in ever so small a degree, are practised by
the independent peasant or handicraftsman, in the
same way as the savage makes the whole art of war
consist in the exercise of his personal cunning -
these faculties are now required all for the workshop as a whole. Intelligence in production expands
in one direction because it vanishes in many others.
What is lost by the detail labourers is concentrated
in the capital that employs them. It is a result of
the division of labour in manufacture that the
labourer is brought face to face with the intellectual potencies of the material process of production
as the property of another and as a ruling power.
The separation begins in simple cooperation ... It
is completed in modern industry, which makes science
a productive force distinct from labour and presses
it into the service of capital.[6]

Though in previous societies some forms of social
knowledge have existed, independently of direct subjective experience, as the conventional wisdom of the
race - myth and religion, for instance, being seen as
attributes of nature or the gods - it is only under
capitalism that practical knowledge, material experience
has been thought of as a generalized attribute of
society. It is capitalism which has constituted science
into 'a productive force distinct from labour.' It is
precisely in the character of alienated knowledge, and
particularly of 'science' in its modern sense of knowledge which is alleged to be neutral of social interests, that we must look for the alienative aspects of
the present social organization of learning.

Before exploring the dialectical development of
those social relations from Marx's time until today, it
is possible to summarize my argument so far in this
way:

1. Human learning is a socio-psychic process which
develops individual consciousness within specific
social relations: it involves the subjective exercise of purpose and the social development of a
language through which to imagine such exercises or
projects;

2. Knowledge is the social organization of individual learning into objectified systems and principles: its characteristics will vary with the
historical character of social relations at any
given time, and its structure will be itself a
feature of those relations. In our society it

appears in alienated form as a property of capital;

3. Education is the social organization of the
subjective learning process in a defined historical
situation in response to a specific mode of social
relations.   In our society, it is an aspect of the
division of labour and prepares individuals for the
class relations of capitalism.   Since it is a social
process, it is also constituted of defined social
relations, and these may change to some extent
independently of the general social relations.

The final section of this paper will be concerned
with the dialectic within and between the general social
relations of our society and those of the education
system.

THE PRESENT SOCIAL RELATIONS OF AND IN EDUCATION

As the social organization of a subjective learning
process, then, education can be seen to form part of
the general social relations of society and, at the
same time, to consist of specific social relations.
Human beings learn from other human beings, directly
or indirectly - either by having their learning systematized, or simply by using the social invention of
language to construct and reconstruct concepts of the
physical and social universe.   In the process of education, learning is systematized, given a social
organization which reflects epistemologically the social
relations of the general society, but it is also made
subject to specific, personalized social relations.
The social organization represents the social relations
of education.   Under capitalism these are exploitative,
appropriating the mental activity of the many to the
purposes of the few.   The specific, reflexive relations
are those generic to learning: they are the definitive
social relations in education.   These are related to
the general social relations obviously, but they are
not necessarily determined by them.   Under certain
circumstances, such as will be dealt with below, the
dominant purposes of capital are deflected, and conflicting purposes incorporated into social relations
within the education process.   Such an analysis is
presumably necessary to explain the fact of historical
development itself.   Learning - which is always social
learning - either reproduces existing social relations
or projects new ones.   Its systematic organization as
education contains always the possibility of conflicting versions of the world, the success of one or other

of which rests upon the dialectic interaction between
specific learning relations and general social ones.
Consciousness is either changed or maintained as a
result of this outcome. At all points, the purposive
activity of individuals is involved, though some such
purposes will be more influential than others.

The dialectic between learning relations and the
general social relations of education is related to the
contradictions which exist within these general social
relations themselves. Thus, the social organization
of learning in Britain can be seen to contain, as con-
tending moments, the organizing principles of authority
and rationality. The authority principle was incorporated by capitalism from previous feudal social
relations. The rationality principle has arisen from
the alienation of practical knowledge as capital
becomes more and more dependent on the 'productive
force of science'. Though also ideological and dominating, it can conflict with the authoritarian principle
which insists that learning is an attribute of highly-
placed people from whom it is handed down. In the
authoritarian perspective, knowledge is essentially a
mystery, conserved and dispensed in medieval times by
guilds, monasteries or orders of chivalry, in modern
times by universities and academies. The work of
Young (1973) mentioned earlier follows that of Bernstein
(1971) in noting this essentially authoritarian-
hierarchical characteristic of British education.
Unfortunately, Bernstein in particular seems to take
for granted the other principle, rationality, as an
unproblematic alternative. In fact, rationality is
as much an ideological construction as authority.
Under rationality, learning is freed from dependence
on infallible dogma as propounded by social authority
only to be made an attribute of material circumstances
directly. In both cases the learner is effectively
separated from knowledge as a consequence of subjective
experience, and confronted with it as 'the property of
another and as a ruling power'. Only, under capitalist
rationality, the alienation is complete because the
appropriation of learning is nearly universal. Whereas
in previous social orders, as Marx points out, wide
areas of life existed which required the 'knowledge,
judgment and skill' of the individual, however humble
the status of that practice, in our society, the general relations of production have trivialized the sort
of learning and knowledge readily available to the
ordinary person.

You have to go to school, in fact, to learn. But

you don't necessarily learn by going to school. This paradox has become a preoccupation for some educationalists here and in America, leading Illich (1971) in particular, to conclude that alienation arises out of the institutional organization of learning in schools. But, as we have seen, alienation arises out of the general social relations of production. Schools are an incident: their organization can be expected to reproduce those social relations.

With the development of capitalism in the hundred years since Marx wrote, the situation he described has broadened and intensified. From applying mainly to routine workers, the alienation of 'the intellectual potencies of the material process of production' has come to dominate intellectual life in general, not excluding that of the 'educated' classes. It has become a ruling power not only over those who directly cooperate in the material process, but over all who manage that process, or distribute the product or, simply, consume: in fact, over the vast majority of people.

This coalescence of authority and rationality into an alienated social intelligence has changed the role of the most highly educated from 'guardians of ideology' into 'technicians of practical knowledge', in Sartre's (1974) terms. Even they have no means of controlling or criticizing the social process which determines the direction of this alienated intelligence. Science, in particular, is no longer the authoritative formulation of specific academics: it is thought of as an objective entity sui generis. Marcuse (1964) has therefore characterized the whole process of intellectual alienation as 'technological rationality', intending thereby to express the suppression of all critical consciousness, and the substitution for it of a purely limited form of thought which simply responds to the determined requirements of technology. In this sense, 'technology' represents the social relations of capitalist production. The foundation, which Marx saw being laid a century ago, of 'an all engrossing system of specializing and sorting men', has by now been well and truly built upon so that knowledge and mental life in general are subservient to the purposes of capitalist social-economic organization.

Within this general system of social organization as it affects the cultural world, social relations in learning can often be seen as reflecting and reproducing the social relations of learning. Starting from the appropriative and productive aspects of capitalism

respectively, it is possible to trace the institutionalization of distinctive types of relations. This
may be shown diagrammatically, in Figure 1:

SOCIAL RELATIONS IN BRITISH EDUCATION:

DUALIST MODEL

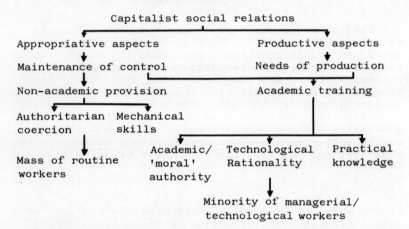

This institutionalization necessarily reflects the
classical contradition of capitalism: the productive
force set free by socializing labour is simultaneously
frustrated by the reactionary nature of its appropriation. In terms of mental life in general, as we have
noted, this results in the stultification of creative
intelligence by a pseudo-rationality which limits in
advance the development of critical thought. In terms
of socially-organized learning, it means the reproduction of repressive and manipulative relations within
the learning institutions. As Figure 1 shows, this
has affected the majority through direct oppression
and coercion. Education has represented an authoritarian provision for needs which have been oligarchic-
ally defined via legally-enforced attendance at school.
In this major sector of the institutional duality,
'learning' has consisted in the performance of routines
for training adaptive skills like reading and mechanical computation. Other activities have been performed
by analogy with these routines, and knowledge treated
as being validated through the social authority of
teachers, text-book writers and 'experts'. The 'needs',
which are the target of this provision, have clearly

related to the routine worker's ability to manage a
reality created by others. The organization reflects
social relations of exploitation and domination - the
'needs' are, in fact, those of capital.

   In the other sector, in relation to the middle
classes, learning has been socially organized to subserve
the requirement of production. Technological rationality is the form of mental activity required of those
who are to produce intellectually, in terms of managerial skills or practical knowledge (in Sartre's sense,
as opposed to critical knowledge). Social relations
here are equally dominated, but their style is the outcome of a dialectical resolution of contradictory
demands for productivity and submissiveness. What on
the cultural level takes the form of technological
rationality, on the organizational level takes the form
of rational authoritarianism or instrumentalism.
Activities are based on their alleged future utility,
and knowledge is treated as being validated through the
objective authority of its own intrinsic principles.
Education in this sector has been viewed as an attainment, in principle open to all individuals, and 'learning' consists of routines for training appropriate
responses - essay-writing, for instance, or the
application of set formulae. Performance has been
measured by examinations which test these responses,
and successful performance used as an 'objective' means
of certifying attainment. The circularity of this
process results in the controlled development of consciousness to an extent which allows a maximum of
technical competence in closely-defined 'fields' of
knowledge. The utility is that of capital. The
highest level of academic excellence is compatible with
a minimum of critical consciousness.

   The maintenance of this system of dual domination
has depended on institutional separation. Whatever the
ideological objectives of comprehensive school reform -
and Marsden (1969) has identified contradictions among
these - its true significance lies in the extent to
which institutional separation is abolished. A consequence of genuine unification of former secondary modern
schools and grammar schools is an obvious conflict
between coercive and rationalistic systems of social
relations, with a resultant questioning of both.
Similarly, mixed-ability grouping, seen as a logical
development of unification, has inevitably led to confusion about epistemological categories and pedagogic
strategies, resulting in the questioning of the conventional models. In the case of social relations

within schools, questioning has typically involved the
students. Particularly in schools where a majority
are bound for routine labour (or, increasingly with
economic instability, routine unemployment), methods of
social control are now problematic. In the traditional
situation of the 'tough' secondary modern school,
legitimated by generations of expectation based on
familial experience, coercion is seen by all as inevitable. Teachers, like policemen, are an unpleasant fact
of life; pupils are potential law-breakers, in school
and out. In the new situation of the urban comprehensive, with a growing complement of graduate teachers
originally destined for the academic sector, and an
element of would-be academic students, coercion comes
to be resented by students. At the same time, it
becomes a bone of contention among teachers, with the
younger more academically-trained rejecting physical
coercion, and the older calling for a return to more
clearly defined authority relations. In this situation,
'discipline' tends to be a preoccupation, with relatively little basic critique of learning assumptions,
though even here the new 'comprehensive' teachers are
apt to question the routine skill-training view of
education for working-class students.

In more socially-mixed comprehensive schools, or in
schools where students from non-manual backgrounds
predominate, there is less challenge to social relations by students. Here it is the teachers who are
disorientated. They are faced with attempting to unify
what is, in fact, not unifiable - social relations
of education relevant to routine workers with those
relevant to managerial/technological workers. What
brings the contradiction out most clearly is the
irreconcilability of the two styles of social control
appropriate to the two modes of social relations -
coercive authority and moral, 'academic' authority.
The consequent confusion of relations in education
is intensified by the fact that, at the school stage,
in the academic sector of socially organized learning
in Britain, many aspects of pre-rational 'moral' or
'ideological' authority are preserved from pre-capital-
ist social relations. In fact, at all levels, strong
elements of Sartre's (1974) 'guardianship of ideology'
are preserved in British academia, particularly in the
'arts' subjects. Important in the social relations of
this conservative tradition is the notion of the coincidence of personal and academic authority and, therefore, of the pastoral, tutorial role of the teacher.
The preservation of this aspect of feudal authority in
'arts' knowledge has conflicted with the requirements

of practical knowledge to the extent that its preval-
ence in British academic schools - including the most
prestigious independent public schools - has been at
the expense of the status of technology. On the other
hand, practical knowledge is typically developed at
post-school level, and the academic schools have
functioned well as agents of ideological control for
the more routine managerial workers, precisely because
of their conservative tendencies as preservers of
'values' and 'standards'.

Socially mixed comprehensive schools, therefore, do
not merely represent a confrontation between coercive
and manipulative relations, which to a certain extent
can be accommodated by preserving the dualism in academic and non-academic courses; they also represent
a confrontation between coercive and neo-feudal styles
of dominance. Such styles of dominance are not a
matter of different relations in learning, as is the
case with coercion versus manipulation: they involve
basically different modes in the social relations of
learning, modes which directly represent the different
modes of the social relations of production in the whole
society. The conflict between these disciplinary
styles reveals, in fact, the contradiction of the
comprehensive school: the contradiction of a unitary
social organization of learning within a class-divided
society. The resolution of such a basic contradiction
involves a fundamental questioning of the social
relations of education, a making problematic what has
hitherto been thought of as unproblematic. Since
neither neo-feudal 'moral' authority, nor simple
coercion, can serve the needs of schools,(including
students destined for both routine labour and various
forms of management, the social organization of learning has to be changed autonomously at the level of
the individual school. The social organization model
shown in Figure 1 is, in effect, upended. It is now
the students who determine the social relations by
forcing the school to attempt changes which, if
effected, will produce a mismatch between the needs
of capital and the consciousness produced in state
schools. A second diagram may perhaps clarify the
point (see Figure 2).

The upper part of Figure 2 describes the extent of
autonomous institutional change already under way. Of
course, as a model it does not entirely correspond to
the concrete historical process - much of which is not
yet clear. What is certain is the fact of conflict -
before and after formal reorganization - and the new

SOCIAL RELATIONS OF BRITISH EDUCATION

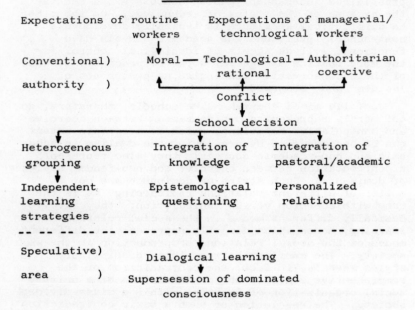

imperative for school-level decisions. It is also
clear, as I have argued elsewhere (see Holly, 1973),
that the needs of schools are being institutionalized
in such institutions as the Schools Council, originally
set up to meet the needs of capital for technological-
rational reform in the curriculum. This contradictory
development accords well with the general dialectic of
historical development in State organizations.

On the level of school decision, though, there is
considerable ambiguity. In the case of team-teaching,
for instance, it is possible to see an attempt to
generalize technological rationality, heavily reinforced
ideologically by the aura of technical fetishism generated by reliance on mechanical 'aids' to basically
didactic teaching. Alternatively, it is possible to
see the introduction of criticism into teacher-
consciousness by the need for team-planning and,
consequently, pedagogical argumentation. For the purposes of the model, I have selected the types of autonomous innovation which are relatively unambiguous in
their consequences.

The speculative area concerns a development which does not appear to have taken place yet in any concrete instance, but which appears predictable as a possible consequence of the coincidence of student independence, teacher questioning and mutually personalized relations. This is what Freire (1974) calls 'dialogical relations' in learning, in which organized learning is returned to a non-alienated state, a subjective-social project which derives directly from material conditions and the situation of the learner, together with his/her fellows and teachers, in respect of the general social relations of the society. Such a posture is, of course, revolutionary. And revolution waits upon the conscious determination of history by men and women.

NOTES

1. K. Marx, Capital Vol. 1, p.157 quoted in B. Simon (1971) Karl Marx and Education in Intelligence, Psychology and Education Lawrence & Wishart p.182.

2. K. Marx Grundrisse Penguin edition, 1973, p.611.

3. K. Marx, Capital Volume 1, Moscow 1961, pp.177-178.

4. M. F. D. Young Curricula and the social organization of Knowledge B.S.A. Conference Paper 1970, published in R. Brown (Ed) Knowledge, Education and Cultural Change (a modified version of the same paper appears as An approach to the study of curricula as socially organized knowledge in M. F. D. Young (Ed) Knowledge and Control).

5. See K. Marx, Capital, Volume 1, Moscow 1961, p.354.

6. See K. Marx, Capital, Volume 1, Moscow 1961, p.361.

REFERENCES

BERNSTEIN, B. B. (1971) 'On the classification and framing of educational knowledge' in M. F. D. Young (Ed) Knowledge and Control London: Collier-Macmillan.

BROWN, R. (Ed) (1973) Knowledge, Education and Cultural Change London: Tavistock.

Central Advisory Council for Education (England) (1960)

(Crowther Report) Fifteen to Eighteen London: H.M.S.O.

FLOUD, J. et al (1956) Social Class and Educational
Opportunity London: Heinemann.

FREIRE, P. (1974) Education for Critical Consciousness
New York: Sheed and Ward.

HIRST, P. H. (1965) 'Liberal education and the nature
of knowledge' in R. D. Archambault (Ed) Philosophical
Analyses and Education London: Routledge and Kegan
Paul.

HOLLY, D. (1971) Society, Schools and Humanity London:
McGibbon and Kee.

HOLLY, D. (1973) Beyond Curriculum London: Hart-Davis
McGibbon.

ILLICH, I. (1971) Deschooling Society New York: Harper
and Row.

KEDDIE, N. (1971) Classroom knowledge in M. F. D. Young
(Ed) Knowledge and Control London: Collier-Macmillan.

MARCUSE, H. (1964) One Dimensional Man London:
Routledge and Kegan Paul.

MARSDEN, D. (1969) Which comprehensive principle?
Comprehensive Education No. 12, Autumn 1969.

MARX, K. (1973) Grundrisse Harmondsworth: Penguin
Books.

ROBBINS Report (1963) Higher Education: Report of the
Prime Minister's Committee on Higher Education London:
H.M.S.O.

SARTRE, J - P. (1960) Critique de la raison dialectique
English commentary by R. D. Laing (1964) Reason and
Violence London: Tavistock.

SARTRE, J-P. (1974) Between Existentialism and Marxism
London: New Left Books.

VYGOTSKY, L. S. (1934) Myshleniye i rech translated
by E. Hanfrmann and G. Vakar (1962) as Thought and
Language Boston: M.I.T. Press and Wiley.

YOUNG, M. F.D. (Ed) (1971) Knowledge and Control

London: Collier-Macmillan.

YOUNG, M. F. D. (1973) 'Curricula and the social organization of knowledge' in R. Brown (Ed) Knowledge,
Education and Cultural Change London: Tavistock.

2.4
Capitalism and Education in the United States

Samuel Bowles and Herbert Gintis

In the last two decades the educational system in the United States has been the site of many of the most intense political and social struggles that have occurred in the society. These struggles have concerned almost all aspects of the internal structure of the educational system and its relation to other institutions. In the recent past the educational system has often seemed to be on the verge of total breakdown.

There have been previous periods in which the educational system faltered, and then recovered. The present crisis of the educational system provides opportunites and imposes responsibilities on the Left; an understanding of the dynamics of the history of education in the United States, particularly of the complex relations between educational structure and economic forces, is important to developing a Left practice in the educational system. This article is concerned with advancing a general view of the history of education in the United States. We will begin with a brief sketch of that history, and of the present major interpretations of it. We will then advance our own view. And finally, we will treat one crucial period, the Progressive period, in more detail[1].

Much of the Marxist analysis of education has dealt with the ways that the schools work to legitimate class divisions and to produce a labour force shaped by the requirements of profitable employment in the capitalist system. The correspondence between the organization of schooling and that of work is an essential structural characteristic of American education. However, we need to know more than the main economic functions of

* First published in Socialist Revolution No. 25.

schooling and the ways that these functions are performed - we need to know how the school system changes.
The history of the school system in the United States is
a conflict-ridden course of struggle and accommodation,
rather than a smooth adjustment of educational structure
to the evolution of economic life. For substantial periods, the school system has been organized along lines
which, far from corresponding to the structure of economic life, appear bizarre or anachronistic. The process
of change, as revealed in the history of educational
reform movements, has significantly affected the impact
of schooling on ideology and class structure. The discrepancy between the rhetoric and reality of educational
reform has been particularly important. The popular
slogans and perspectives of reform movements have often
imparted an egalitarian and humanistic ideology to the
educational system, while the highly selective implementation of reforms has tended to preserve the role of
schooling in the perpetuation of economic order.

Two centuries ago the structure and scope of American
education bore little resemblance to the current system.
Looking backwards one might - and many educational historians do - see an inexorable march along a single line
of ascent. But to educators, politicians, and others
living in each period the way forward did not seem so
clear;   education has reached and passed many cross-
roads.

We are struck first by the sheer magnitude of educational change since the American War of Independence.
Until quite recently, in no society did more than a tiny
minority of children spend more than a small part of
their youth in formal educational institutions. Even
today there are relatively few countries in which the
majority of young people spend most of their youth in
schools. In most societies throughout recorded history,
schools have not played a major role in preparing children for adulthood. American colonial society was no
exception. Prior to the nineteenth century, the main
job of training young people was done by the family,
occasionally supplemented by apprenticeship or the
church (Bailyn, 1960 and Cremin, 1970). The school was
marginal to the process of child-rearing.

In colonial America, the basic productive unit was
the family. Most families owned the tools of their
trade and worked their own land. Transmitting the necessary productive skills to children was simple, not
because the work was devoid of skill, but because the

substantial skills required were virtually unchanging
from generation to generation, and because the transition to the work world did not require that the child
adapt to a wholly new set of social relationships.
Children both learned the concrete skills and adapted
to the social relations of production within the family;
production and reproduction were unified in a single
institution. While the nuclear family rather than the
extended family was the norm, people did not move
around much (Gordon, 1973). Relatives tended to live
fairly close to one another; children had ample opportunity to learn to deal with complex relationships
among adults other than their parents and with children
other than their brothers and sisters.

Children were not required to learn a complex set of
political principles or ideologies, as political participation was limited. The major cultural institution
outside the family was the church, which sought to in-
culcate the accepted values and attitudes. Elementary
schools focused on literacy training to facilitate
familiarity with the Scriptures. Above this level, education tended to be narrowly vocational, restricted to
preparation of children for a career in the church, the
'learned professions', or the state bureaucracy. The
curriculum of the few universities reflected an aristocratic penchant for conspicuous intellectual consumption.

Rapid economic change in the half-century following
the War of Independence set into motion forces that
radically altered the relation between the family and
the system of production. Commerce expanded dramatically; in the decade and a half prior to 1807, the value
of foreign trade increased fourfold (US Bureau of the
Census, 1960). Larger commercial interests amassed
substantial concentrations of capital and sought new
arenas for profitable investment. Increasingly, capital
was used for the direct employment of labour in production rather than remaining confined to commercial
activities. The expansion of capitalist production,
particularly the factory system, undermined the role of
the family as the major unit of both child-rearing and
production. Cottage industry and artisan production
were gradually destroyed. Small shopkeepers and farmers
were often forced out of business. Ownership of the
means of production became heavily concentrated. Faced
with declining opportunities for an independent live-
lihood, workers were forced to relinquish control over
their labour in return for wages or piece-rates. The
pay workers received increasingly took the form of a

'wage' rather than a 'price'(Ware, 1964).

The statistics for New York City for the years 1795
to 1855 illustrate these trends: a fourfold increase
in the relative numbers of wage workers and a reduction
by two-thirds in the relative numbers of independent
merchants and proprietors (Kaestle, 1973). In the country as a whole, agricultural pursuits - the stronghold
of independent production - lost ground to manufacturing. In 1820, for every person working in manufacturing
and distribution there were six people engaged in agriculture; by 1860, this figure had fallen to three. By
the Civil War, the family no longer constituted the
dominant unit of production; production was carried on
in large organizations in which an employer directed
the activities of the work force and owned the products
of their labour. The social relations of production
became increasingly distinct from the social relations
of reproduction.

The emerging class structure evolved in accord with
these new social relations of production: an ascendant
and self-conscious capitalist class came to dominate
the political, legal, and cultural superstructure of
society. This class attempted to shape the evolution
of the educational system.

The expansion and continuing transformation of the
system of capitalist production led to unprecedented
shifts in the occupational distribution of the labour
force and constant changes in the skills requirement
for jobs. Training within the family was not sufficient; the productive skills of the parents were no
longer adequate for the needs of the children during
their lifetime. The apprentice system of training,
which by custom committed masters for a period of as
much as seven years to supply apprentices with room and
board as well as (sometimes) minimal levels of training
in return for labour services, became a costly liability
as the growing severity of depressions made the demand
for the products of the apprentices' labour more uncer-
tain. The further expansion of capital increasingly
required a system of labour training that would transfer
the costs of training to the public. Equally important,
the dynamism of the capitalist growth process required
a training system that would facilitate a more rapid
adjustment of employment to the business cycle and allow
the constantly changing dictates of profitability to
govern the allocation of labour.

At the same time, workers were thrown together in
large factories, and the isolation which had helped to

maintain quiescence in earlier, widely dispersed farming
populations was broken down. With an increasing number
of families uprooted from the land, the workers' search
for a living resulted in large-scale labour migrations.
Labour scarcity induced by an abundance of land and
rapid capital accumulation led employers in the expanding sectors of the economy to rely increasingly on an
influx of foreigners to staff the lowest paying jobs.
In the ten-year period beginning in 1846, the United
States absorbed 3.1 million immigrants - a number equal
to an eighth of the entire population at that date.
(The better known massive immigration of the pre-World
War I decade constituted a somewhat lesser fraction of
the total population.) Most immigrants arrived with
few resources other than their labour power and became
part of the growing urban proletariat. Others, less
fortunate, swelled the ranks of the 'reserve army' of
the unemployed, ready to take jobs at near subsistence
wages. Transient - often foreign - elements came to
constitute a major segment of the urban population and
posed seemingly insurmountable problems of assimilation,
integration, and control (see Thernstrom, 1973).
Cultural diversity came to be seen as a social problem.
Ethnic conflicts threatened the political stability of
many towns.

Inequalities in wealth increased with the rapid expansion of both industrial and commercial capital.
Using data from New York City, Brooklyn, and Boston, we
estimate that early in the nineteenth century the wealthiest one per cent of urban residents in the Northeast
owned a quarter of all tangible wealth. By mid-century
the figure had risen to about two-fifths. Moreover,
fragmentary evidence suggests a drastic reduction in
general mobility into the ranks of the very wealthy.
Significantly, only the economically stagnant towns
appear to be exceptions to this trend[2].

Inequality was difficult to justify. The broadening
of the electorate and of political participation generally - first sought by the propertied and commercial
classes in their struggle against the British Crown -
threatened to become a powerful instrument in the hands
of farmers and workers. Working people did not limit
their political efforts to the ballot box alone; after
the close of the War of Independence, the Dorr War, the
Whiskey Rebellion, Shays' Rebellion, and a host of minor
insurrections were supported by thousands of poor and
debt-ridden farmers and workers. The expansion of
capitalist production greatly enhanced the power of the
capitalist class and created political conditions that

challenged their continued domination. Economic leaders
urgently sought means to ensure political stability and
the continued profitability of their enterprises.

Confronted with novel and rapidly changing economic
conditions, working people sought new solutions to the
problems of security, independence, and material welfare. As farmers and artisans became wage workers, they
sought a means by which they, or their children, might
regain their lost status. Some - a small minority -
proposed to attack the wage-labour system. Many saved
what they could in hopes of eventually getting back into
business on their own. Others followed the lure of
independence and cheap land and moved West. But for
many, education seemed to promise the respectability and
security that they wanted.

The importance that working people often attached to
education has led many educational historians to see
the history of education as the triumph of the 'little
people' over the powerful. Ellwood Cubberley (1934)
writes:

> The second quarter of the nineteenth century may be
> said to have witnessed the battle for tax-supported,
> publicly controlled and directed, and non-sectarian
> common schools. Excepting the battle for the aboli-
> tion of slavery, perhaps no question has ever been
> before the American people for settlement which
> caused so much feeling or aroused such bitter anta-
> gonism.[3]

Naturally such bitter discussion of a public question
forced a division of the people for or against publicly
supported and controlled schools. This 'alignment of
interests', according to Cubberley, saw 'philanthrop-
ists, humanists, public men of large vision, New England
men and intelligent working men in the cities' pitted
against the forces of reaction - 'politicians of small
vision, the ignorant, narrow-minded and penurious, the
old aristocratic class and the non-English-speaking
classes' - in a battle for progress.

Frank Tracy Carleton (1911), a historian, stressed
the role of labour in the struggle:

> Practically every workingmen's meeting ... took up
> the cry. Horace Mann, Henry Barnard, James G. Carter,
> Robert Dale Owen, George H. Evans, and others dir-
> ected the movement, but the potent push came from the

firm demand of an aroused and insistent wage earning
class armed with the ballot.
The rural districts, employers, and men of wealth
were rarely favourable to the tax-supported schools;
and often their voices were raised against it in
bitter protest or stinging invective. A careful
study of the development of a free school system in
the different states - and the utter lack of a free
school system in the slaveholding South, confirms
these general statements.

We refer to Cubberley and Carleton's view (recently
espoused by S. M. Lipset as the 'democratic class struggle' theory) as the 'popular demand for education'
interpretation. Others have put forward a 'technological' interpretation of American educational history,
according to which the growth and structure of education
have responded to the labour training needs generated
by the growth and structure of skill requirements in
the economy. Martin Trow (1966), writes:

The mass public secondary school system as we know it
has its roots in the transformation of the economy
and society that took place after the Civil War ...
The growth of the secondary school system after 1870
was in large part a response to the pull of the economy for a mass of white collar employees with more
than an elementary school education.

Neither the 'popular demand' nor the 'technological'
interpretation is adequate. The 'technological' perspective finds little support in the history of mass
elementary education. There is no evidence of a growth
of skill requirements in the nineteenth-century economy
(Field, 1973). Nor did the proponents of mass education
embrace the notion that schools would teach occupation-
ally relevant skills. Educated workers may have been
better behaved in the eyes of employers, but they were
not more productive than unschooled workers (Luft,
1971). It is particularly difficult to make the case
that the objective of early school reform movements
was mass literacy, because literacy was already high
(about ninety per cent of adult whites) prior to the
'common school revival'[4]. For secondary and higher
education, the occupational skills perspective explains
the need for an educational system to foster cognitive
development, but leaves untouched the crucial issue as
to why the school system took the form that it did.
For the social relations of today's schools cannot be
deduced from the technical requisites of imparting

cognitive skills. Moreover, the cognitive skills imparted do not account for the association between educational attainment and economic success (Bowles and
Gintis, 1976).

The evidence for the 'popular demand' interpretation
is at first glance convincing. Workers' organizations
and citizens' groups often demanded more schooling, and
the school system expanded. A closer look reveals a
number of difficulties with this view. First, working
people's organizations made a number of demands throughout the periods we have studied. Educational reform
and expansion tended to be minor concerns compared to
more direct economic demands for land reform, co-ops,
job security, and the like. What explains the ability
of working people to achieve a larger school system when
their other demands were not met with such conspicuous
success? The answer, we believe, is that the expansion
of public education was supported by employers and other
powerful groups as well as by organized labour. Where
the educational demands of organized labour diverged
from those of business elites - as in the turn-of-the-
century struggle for control of vocational education -
labour generally lost. (But not always, as the successful battle against vocational tracking by the Chicago
Federation of Labour reveals.)

A second problem with this interpretation is that
the evidence of working-class support for educational
expansion is not unambiguous. Educational demands by
working people's organizations do not necessarily indicate the views of the majority of workers. In the
nineteenth and twentieth centuries, only a small minority of workers have been in unions. The educational
demands of unorganized farmers and workers are very
difficult to discover, but the available evidence is
hardly supportive of the popular demand approach.
Substantial opposition to educational consolidation and
expansion in the nineteenth century is evident both in
the rural small farmers' opposition to the demise of
the district school, and in the widespread non-attend-
ance, and later truancy, of Irish children. The
evidence from the turn of this century is similarly
ambiguous. Opposition to the school reformers came
primarily from popular urban machines and to some extent from teachers. Educational reform in rural areas
was almost always imposed from the outside (Tyack,
1974).

Third, did working people get what they wanted from
education? The available evidence on the timing and
content of educational change does not support an

affirmative answer. The periods of pre-Civil War educational ferment in New England and New York were prompted largely by the growing militancy of workers and the poor. Workers spoke out for universal education and local control. What they got was a different matter: taking New England as a whole, the percentage of all children attending school fell slightly from 1840 to 1860 (Vanovskis and Bernard, 1973). Local control was gradually undermined by the formation of centralized school systems, by professionalization of teaching and the gradual assertion of State government authority over education. In New York City, neither the level of enrolment nor class composition changed much between 1795 and 1860 (Kaestle, 1973). Other regions - the upper Midwest, in particular - witnessed substantial educational expansion. But these were not areas of strong working-class organization. The antebellum period in the Northeast was one of educational reorganization, not expansion, though enrolments did expand in New England, New York, and throughout the country after the Civil War.

We find little support for the view that our educational system took its shape from popular demands. Working people have managed over the years to get more education, but they have managed to get the kind of education they demanded only when their needs coincided with those of economic elites. Not even the most generous treatment of evidence can invoke 'popular pressure' as an explanation of the structure of control - from the classroom to the school board to the private foundation - of American education. Nor can the popular pressure argument deal effectively with the extensive need for truancy officers, nor the nearly universal tracking and labelling of working-class and minority youth.

A 'revisionist' viewpoint of educational history has challenged the importance of working-class pressure as an agent in educational change. In less than a decade the work of Michael Katz (1971), Clarence Karier et al (1973), Marvin Lazerson (1971), Carl Kaestle (1973), David Tyack (1974), Colin Greer (1973) and others has offered a dramatically different picture of educational history. These authors have gone back to the early school committee reports, the personal letters of the major reformers, and the relevant business and foundation reports, and have used statistical treatments of empirical data, to put forward a new view coherent enough to summarize. The expansion of mass education and the evolution of its structural forms, they have argued, was sparked by demographic changes associated

with the industrialization and urbanization of economic
and social activity. The main impetus for educational
change was not, however, the occupational skills demanded by the increasingly complex and growing industrial
sector, nor was it primarily the desire for the elimina-
tion of urban squallor. Rather, schools were promoted
first and foremost as agents for the social control of
an increasingly culturally heterogeneous and poverty-
stricken urban population in an increasingly unstable
and threatening economic and political system. Katz
(1971) has argued that schools, far from being won by
workers over the opposition of capitalists and other
entrenched interests, were imposed upon the workers.
We have learned much from the revisionist historians.
Yet our reading of the history of American education has
led to an alternative interpretation, which differs in
essential respects from the 'revisionist' view.

CAPITAL ACCUMULATION, CLASS CONFLICT, AND EDUCATIONAL CHANGES

Capital accumulation has been the driving force behind
the transformation and growth of the American economy.
Labour is combined in production with increasing amounts
of machinery and other capital goods. At the same time,
labour is itself augmented by schooling and training[5].
Two important aspects of the process of capital accumulation may be identified. The first is the expansion
of the technical forces with a consequent rapid and
sustained increase in the output of goods and services
per worker[6]. The second is an equally dramatic transformation of the social relations of production.
Capitalist control over production is widened through
the integration of ever-increasing segments of the population into wage labour, and deepened through the
extension and refinement of the hierarchical division of
labour.

The accumulation of capital and the extension of the
wage-labour system are essential to the expanded reproduction of the capitalist system. The capitalist
economy and bicycle riding have this in common: forward
motion is essential to stability. Yet the accumulation
of capital and the widening of capitalist control over
production also undermine the reproduction of the capitalist order, because of the increased potential for
working-class action against capital afforded by the
agglomeration of workers into large enterprises and
urban areas. We refer to this tension between growth
and stability as the contradiction between the

accumulation of capital and the reproduction of the
capitalist relations of production[7]. This contradiction
has been basic to American history for the past
century and a half.

At times the contradiction between accumulation and
reproduction has been expressed in militant class struggle: the mass strikes which paralysed the economy in
the last quarter of the nineteenth century and again
following World War I, the Populist Revolt of the 1880s
and 1890s, the sitdown strikes and mass labour organizing drives of the late 1930s, and the urban uprisings
of the 1960s. However, through much of American history,
class conflict has been confined to the isolated daily
struggles of workers in the factories, offices, and
shops. The ever-present contradiction between accumulation and reproduction has been temporarily resolved or
suppressed in a variety of ways: through social reforms,
through the force of the state, through racist, sexist,
and credentialist strategies used by employers to divide
and rule, and through ideologies that hide the sources
of exploitation and alienation. The expansion of mass
education, embodying each of the above means, has been
a central element in resolving - at least temporarily -
the contradiction between accumulation and reproduction.

Many of the manifestations of this contradiction in
the American economy have appeared in the state sector,
and particularly in the educational system. Reformers
have consistently believed that our most pressing social
problems could be solved, or at least significantly
attenuated, through the state. Yet the types of social
distress that excite reformers' conscience result from
the most basic workings of the capitalist economy, and
are not readily alleviated through reforms that leave
capitalist property and market institutions untouched.
For example, the intervention of the state in the income
distribution process - through welfare assistance,
social security, unemployment insurance, and progressive
taxation - has probably helped to limit the extent of
open class conflict in the economic sphere. Yet inequality remains, though its form is changed, and we observe
a welfare crisis, or a conflict over taxes, or a conflict in the school system over resource transfers.
Inequality remains. Increasingly, the classroom and
the admissions office as well as the factory floor are
the arenas in which the basic social conflicts are
fought out.

But the reform strategy can hardly be considered a
failure from the standpoint of the capitalist class.
The displacement of social problems into the school

system and other parts of the state sector plays a
central role in the reproduction of the capitalist order.
Conflicts within the state sector, even if bitter and
enduring, seem to be less threatening to capital and
less disruptive to profits than those that take place
on the shop floor or in the office. The class nature
of social problems is often obscured when the manifestations of the underlying contradictions appear in the
state sector.

The main periods of educational reform coincided
with, or immediately followed, periods of deep social
unrest and political conflict. The major reform periods
have been preceded by the development of significant
divergences between the ever-changing social organization of production and the structure of education.
Each major reform period has been associated with the
integration into the wage-labour system of new groups
of workers emerging from the relatively stagnant sectors
of the economy or from abroad. The uneven expansion of
the school system has played the role either of recruiter
or of gatekeeper for the dynamic sectors, depending on
the level of labour needs. Schools supply labour to the
dominant sectors, and reinforce the racial, ethnic,
sexual, and class segmentation of the labour force.

The evolving social relations of the classroom and
school, too, responded primarily to the form of capitalist development in the changing organization of work in
enterprises of the dynamic sectors of the economy. The
system of class, race, and sex relations, shaped and
reshaped by the evolving structure of production, has
for the past century been reflected in the segmented,
hierarchical, racist, sexist, and nativist structure
of American education. The educational system developed
out of the political and economic conflicts arising from
increasing capitalist control over production, and the
contradictions inherent in this process.

The three main turning points in American educational
history correspond to intense periods of struggle around
the expansion of capitalist production relations. Thus
the decades prior to the Civil War - the era of the
common school reform - were a period of labour militancy associated with the rise of the factory system,
growing economic inequality, and the creation and vast
expansion of a permanent wage labour force. The progressive education movement - beginning at the turn of
the present century - grew out of class conflict associated with the rise of organized labour and corporate
capital, and was a response to the social unrest and
dislocation stemming from the integration of rural

labour - both immigrant and native - into the burgeoning
corporate wage-labour system. The particular concerns
of the progressives - efficiency, cooperation, internalization of bureaucratic norms and preparation for
variegated adult roles - reflect the changing organization of production in the giant corporate enterprises.
The progressive reforms represented in their implementation little more than an echo of the corporate managers'
growing commitment to a 'scientific management' of
production and personnel. The recent period of educational change and ferment - covering the sixties to the
present - is in large measure a response to the post-
World War II integration of three major groups into the
wage-labour system: uprooted Southern blacks, women,
and the 'solid' members of the pre-corporate capitalist
community - the small business people, independent
professionals, and white-collar employees.

THE PROCESS OF EDUCATIONAL REFORM:
CONFLICT AND ACCOMMODATION

   The moving force behind educational change is the
contradictory nature of capital accumulation and the
reproduction of the capitalist order. Thus analysis
of the process of educational reform must consider the
shifting arenas of class conflict and the mechanisms
that the capitalist class has developed to mediate and
deflect class conflict. A thorough treatment would
require - as a bare minimum - an extended investigation
of the bureaucratization and professionalization of
education, the role of the major private foundations and
quasi-public institutions, the composition of major
public decision-making bodies, the crucial process of
educational finance and resource allocation, the impact
of parental and student opinion, and the role of teachers' associations. Research into these areas is at
best rudimentary; our interpretation is necessarily
tentative.

   The economic and educational systems possess fairly
distinct and independent internal dynamics of reproduction and development. Incessant change within the
economic system is basic to capitalism. The educational
system is less dynamic: schools and colleges, foundations and schools of education tend to sustain cultural
values and to support an educational elite that stabil-
izes these institutions through time.

   The independent internal dynamics of the two systems
raise the possibility of a significant mismatch arising

between economy and education. The relatively static educational system can periodically fail to correspond to the social relations of production, and thus retard capitalist development. This conflict between an economic dynamic that extends the wage-labour system and incessantly alters the organization of work and the class structure, and an educational system that tends to stabilize the existing class relations, is essential to the process of educational change.

The accommodation of the educational system to new economic conditions proceeds by two distinct but parallel processes. One operates through the relatively uncoordinated pursuit of interests by millions of individuals and groups - through local school boards, the market for private educational services, and other decentralized decision-making arenas. This process, which we shall call 'pluralist accommodation', involves a more or less automatic reorientation of educational perspectives in the face of a changing economic reality. In periods of economic change, educators tend to alter their educational values and goals in 'progressive' directions - directions conforming to the new 'economic rationality' emerging in the social relations of production[8]. Parents who want a secure economic future for their children often support moves toward a more 'vocationally relevant education'[9]. The different governmental inputs into the educational decision-making process seek to tailor education to the perceived needs of their political constituencies. These elements of 'pluralist accommodation' in education provide a strong latent force for re-establishing a 'natural' correspondence between the social relations of education and production. Periodic financial crises can play an important role in this process of educational rationalization. When budgets are ample and the demand by employers for the products of the school system is high, educators have a relatively independent hand in developing new programmes and approaches to instruction. Students, also, are freer to pursue their own interests. This was certainly the case for higher education during the late 1960s. But a budget squeeze and the threat of unemployment serve to weed out both the opportunity and the student demand for educational experiences that do not contribute directly to employability.

The day-to-day operations of these 'pluralist' forces - the 'free market' choices of students, the school bond issue referenda, the deliberations of elected school boards, and the like - reinforce the image of an educational system whose open and decentralized structure

defies control or even significant influence by an elite.
Indeed, it is absolutely essential for the school system
to appear to be democratically controlled if it is
successfully to contribute to the legitimation and reproduction of the capitalist order.

But the accommodation by the educational system to a
changing economic reality, however pluralistic, is in
essence led by a changing structure of production, and
thus operates within an economic framework determined
almost entirely outside of the formally democratic political arena. During the crisis periods - which appear
in retrospect as the major turning points in American
educational history - control over the relevant decision-
making institutions makes a major difference. It is
here that our second process of adjustment - concrete
political struggle along the lines of class interest -
comes to the fore. Particularly in periods of serious
disjuncture between the school system and the economy -
the 1840s and the 1850s, the first two decades of the
present century, and the 1960s and early 1970s - the
school system appears as an arena for struggle among
major social groups. The response of forward-looking
capitalists to popular unrest is typically dual:
material amelioration and educational expansion or
reform. Thus the response to the strikes of the 1840s
was higher wages for organized workers and the consolidation of the common school. The fruits of populism
as a political movement were somewhat higher farm incomes and the development of agricultural extension and
education. The response to the civil rights movement
and black urban rebellions of the 1960s was an attempt
to ameliorate the economic condition of blacks and a
massive programme in so-called compensatory education.

In each case, the capitalist class - through the
police power of the state in suppressing anti-capitalist
alternatives, through general political power accompany-
ing its control over economic resources, and through its
control over the financial resources for educational research, innovation, and training - has been able to define a feasible model of educational change from which
the relatively unorganized popular forces had no recourse
save chaos. Forces for educational reform can coalesce
only around a common social philosophy and programme of
action. Yet the ideological framework for educational
reform is determined in what is called, with embarrass-
ing accuracy, the 'free market place in ideas'. In a
relatively decentralized decision-making framework the
preponderant control over information, educational
values, and programmatic ideas exercised by the capitalist class in large measure through its foundations

has been crucial in adapting the process of educational accommodation to economic change.

In the absence of any clearly spelled out alternative to the evolving capitalist system, and lacking a political vehicle for the transformation of social life, those who have proposed school reforms that would have significantly undermined the profitability or stability of the economy have been more or less easily swept aside as utopians. The only feasible counterforce to the capitalist domination of the educational reform process would have been - indeed is today - a united mass party forcefully articulating both concrete educational reforms and a general ideological and programmatic alternative to capitalism. Only the Socialist Party during the second decade of this century came remotely close to providing such a real alternative. In general, then, popular forces have had no recourse from the capitalist-dominated strategy of educational reforms save chaos.

Partly as a result, the accommodation of working people's educational objectives to changing economic conditions has tended to betray a partially regressive character. Groups have struggled against a change in economic status - for instance, proletarianization - that they are more or less powerless to prevent, rather than against the system imposing the change. Thus struggle has frequently taken the form of attempts to restore the irretrievable past. Such has been the case with farmers in the 1840s, workers' organizations in the mid-nineteenth century, craft unions in the early twentieth century, and the student movement of the 1960s.

The development of mass education - now extending up through the college level - was in many respects genuinely progressive. A larger fraction of American youth is now enrolled in college than was enrolled in elementary school 135 years ago. Illiteracy has been virtually eliminated: in 1870, one tenth of whites and four-fifths of blacks could not read or write[10]. This massive expansion of schooling and the structural forms it assumed were not simply an imposition on the working class, though workers and their children did sometimes resist attendance. Less still was it a victory for the working class, though the benefits of literacy, access to more advanced learning, custodial care of children, and the like are real enough. The spread of mass education can best be seen as an outcome of class conflict, not class domination. The impetus for educational reform and expansion was provided by the growing class consciousness and political militancy of working people.

While working people's groups have, at least for the past hundred and fifty years, demanded more and better education for their children, demands for economic reform and material betterment have been both more urgent and more strongly pressed. Progressive elements in the capitalist class have yielded what would minimize the erosion of their power and privilege within the structure of production: educational change has been a substitute for economic reform, not its complement.

The evolution of American education over the last century and a half represents an unequal compromise between the capitalist class and subordinate social classes. Though the capitalist class did not always prevail, they were highly successful in maintaining ultimate control over the administration of educational reform. Working people got more schooling, but the form and content of schooling was usually out of their hands.

The liberal professionals and 'enlightened' school reformers - from Horace Mann and Henry Barnard to John Dewey and Ellwood Cubberley, to Clark Kerr and Charles Silberman - were essential mediators of this compromise. They developed its ideological rationale, articulated its objectives, and helped shape its programmes, but were ultimately dependent on the capitalist class and could not mount an independent and sustained movement for overall reform.

The major actors with independent power in the educational arena were, and continue to be, labour and capital. The structure of the modern American educational system cannot be explained without reference both to the demands of working people - for literacy, for occupational mobility, for financial security, for personal growth, for social respect - and to the efforts of the capitalist class to construct an institution that would simultaneously enhance the labour power of working people and help to reproduce the conditions for its exploitation. To a major extent, the schools did successfully weld together the functions of accumulation and reproduction. By helping to contain the contradiction between accumulation and reproduction, the school system has been important in preserving the capitalist order; within that order, it has brought tangible, if limited, benefits to the working people of the United States.

The expansion of schooling, like the expansion of the wage-labour system, has had unanticipated and undesired consequences for the capitalist class and

professional elites. The schools have been used to
smother discontent, yet the basis for conflict continues
in the underlying contradictions of the capitalist economy. When educational reformers have partially suc-
ceeded in displacing these conflicts out of the workplace
and into the classroom, they have frequently surfaced as
contradictions within the educational system. This observation, and our general approach to the dynamics of
historical change in education, are best illustrated
through a concrete example. We shall focus on the
progressive movement in educational reform.

CORPORATE CAPITAL AND PROGRESSIVE EDUCATION

The period 1890-1930, from the Progressive Era to the
Great Depression, was a turning point in the history of
American education. Like the reform movement of the
mid-nineteenth century, progressive education arose
amidst labour strife and social unrest. Like the earlier movement, progressivism coincided with a dramatic
shift in the structure of the economy and the integration of masses of new workers into the wage labour
system. The progressive movement, like the 'common
school revival', gave birth to a radically new educational philosophy. It stressed diversity, unity of the
school with the community, and what is now called 'child-
centred' instruction. Articulated by John Dewey and
others, the precepts of progressive education were
selectively implemented by Ellwood Cubberley and the
small army of 'education executives' trained and de-
ployed across the country. The familiar coalition of
liberal professionals and business leaders, often working through philanthropic foundations, pressed the cause
of educational reforms. The progressive movement lacked
the ideological unity and the fusion of educational
theory and practice of the common school revival. It
embraced such proclaimed socialists as Dewey, business-
men, major capitalist foundations, upper-crust 'good
government' groups, and even a few trade unionists.
From the ideological and political cross-currents of
this movement emerged a radically transformed school
system.

During these years, the public high school became a
mass institution: in 1890 high school graduates constituted less than four per cent of all seventeen-year-
olds; by 1930, twenty-nine per cent of seventeen-year-
olds were graduates of high school. In 1890 public
high school students represented one per cent of all
children enrolled in elementary and secondary education

(eighty-six per cent were in public primary schools and
the rest were in private schools); by 1930 this figure
had risen to fifteen per cent. Between 1890 and 1930
the percentage of all fourteen- to seventeen-year-olds
attending public high schools rose from four to forty-
seven. By 1930 private secondary schools enrolled only
seven per cent of all secondary school students (US
Office of Education, 1974).

The educational practice of progressivism brought us
the comprehensive high school, tracking, educational
testing, home economics, the junior high school, the
student council, the daily flag pledge, high school
athletics, the school assembly, vocational education and
guidance, clubs, school newspapers, and monopolization
of executive authority by superintendents and other
professionals[11].

The objectives of social equality and full human
development, central to the thinking of John Dewey and
his followers, were pursued within the constraints set
by the imperative of producing a labour force for corporate enterprises. Indeed, Dewey seems to have been
aware of these constraints and, true to his pragmatism,
to have operated consciously within them (Feinberg,
1972). In the end, the role of education in capitalist
expansion and the integration of new workers into the
wage-labour system dominated the potential role of
schooling as 'the great equalizer' and the instrument of
'full human development'. Here we will outline the main
economic and social trends, and offer a more detailed
treatment of two important cases: the vocational
education movement, and the emergence of educational
testing.

EXPANSION OF CORPORATE CAPITAL

By 1890 almost two-thirds of all economically active
people were employees (US Bureau of the Census, 1974).
Family farming continued to lose ground to large-scale
capitalist agriculture and to manufacturing; simple
manufacturing gave way to production involving complex
interrelated processes; an increasing fraction of the
labour force was employed in producing services rather
than goods. Domestic, craft, and entrepreneurial production were giving way to the corporate capitalist
sector. In a few critical industries - steel, for example - a handful of giant firms came to be predominant.

Millions of Europeans, many of them peasants driven

out of business by cheap American grain imports, came
to the United States in search of a living wage. In
1910, sixteen per cent of the country's population was
foreign-born; another forty per cent had foreign-born
parents. Until immigration was effectively cut off in
1924, the increasing numbers of foreign-born workers
played a major role in keeping wages low and profits
high. The integration of farmers into the world market
and the attendant fluctuations in farm incomes as well
as the growing monopolization of agricultural trade and
transportation were challenged in the 1880s and 1890s
by the Populist movement. The growth of wage employment, the increasing similarity among workers in the
conditions of employment, and the hardship of three
major depressions in the course of two decades spurred
the development of organized resistance. Opposition to
the evolving capitalist relations of production broke
out during the latter part of the nineteenth century.
The Populist farmer, at odds with the railroads and 'the
trusts', and the industrial worker, struggling for
collective bargaining rights, had much in common. A
series of major strikes - Homestead in 1892, Pullman in
1894, and others - signalled a growing militancy among
workers. Membership in labour unions grew fourfold
between 1897 and 1904.

Like those of the earlier radicals of the 1840s,
however, the objectives of the labour movement were in
many respects backward-looking. The labour historian
Gerald Grob (1969) has noted that to the extent that
working people's organizations challenged the social
relations of production, they tended to take as their
norm 'the vision of a past society (perhaps one that
existed only in their own minds) where the independent
artisan combined in his own person both employer and
employee functions'. With the significant exceptions
of the Socialist Party and the International Workers of
the World, most workers' organizations lacked a political perspective consistent with the forces of production
under corporate capitalism. They did not espouse any
comprehensive and viable alternative to capitalism. The
potentially radical thrust of these movements was deflected and their force eventually either crushed or
harnessed to the pursuit of more manageable objectives
such as higher wages: 'In return for labour non-support
of revolutionary theories, industry promised the worker
a rising standard of living and a respected, though
subordinate, position in the community.'[12] Yet from the
late 1870s to World War I, the perpetuation and extension of the capitalist system was problematic.

Capitalists faced the problem of controlling labour
within their own enterprises as well as in the social
system as a whole (Edwards, 1974). With the increased
centralization and concentration of capital, the direct
control mechanisms that had extracted the maximum work
at the lowest price became inadequate. The personalized
authority and direct overseeing of the boss was no
longer sufficient to control even the supervisory personnel, much less production workers.

Corporate employers responded by encouraging the
growth of a complicated vertical segmentation of the
labour force. In the new division of labour, power was
bureaucratically - not personally - sanctioned within
a hierarchical job structure. A large middle group of employees was created, including clerical, sales, book-
keeping, and low-level supervisory workers, who maintained some control over their work and at times directed
the work of others, while falling under the direction
of higher management. The division of labour within the
enterprises was dominated by a small group with control
over work processes and a high degree of personal autonomy in their work activities; the division of labour
proceeded by stages down the chain of bureaucratic
command to those who worked under close supervision.
The bureaucratic hierarchy of the corporation replaced
the simple boss-worker hierarchy of older entrepreneurial firms; ethnic, racial, and sexual divisions and
differences in educational credentials were used to pit
workers against one another.

The structure of jobs, as much as the size of the
work force, made the control of labour increasingly
difficult. There were fewer jobs like self-employed
craft work, farming, and piece-rate work in manufacturing in which material reward was tied directly to effort.
As work became more complicated and interrelated and
as the output shifted towards intangible services rather
than material goods, the evaluation of an individual
worker's performance became more difficult. Employers
in the dynamic sectors of the economy began to require
more than obedience and punctuality from their workers;
they began to look for workers who had internalized the
production-related values of the firm's managers.

Frederick Winslow Taylor's school of 'scientific
management' captured the attention of employers
(Braverman, 1974). Central to Taylor's approach was the
concentration of the relevant production knowledge and
skills in the hands of management, and the reduction of
most jobs to carrying out simple, explicit directives.
The position of foreman came to occupy a central role

in the corporate strategy of deepening control over the
work force and taking power away from skilled workers.

In response to the strains induced by the continuing
integration of once-independent workers into wage labour,
the state began to take a larger positive role in the
regulation of social and economic activity (Kolko, 1963
and Weinstein, 1968). Changes in the structure of employment reflected the growth of the corporate sector,
and corporate strategies for social control. Clerical
and sales workers, only five per cent of the labour
force in 1900, accounted for a quarter of the increase
in total employment over the next three decades. The
number of manufacturing and construction foremen grew
from 90,000 to 336,000 between 1890 and 1930. In 1900,
employers hired on the average one foreman for every
eighty-nine workers; by 1930 they were hiring one foreman for every thirty-four workers. Between 1890 and
1930, government employment (excluding education) grew
fivefold, well over twice the rate of total employment.
(US Bureau of the Census, 1960)

The changing division of labour within the corporation, the conflict between capital and labour both
within the enterprise and in the larger society, and the
changing occupational structure were at the root of the
expansion of schooling and the implementation of progressive educational reforms. The expansion of education
was also pressed by elites alarmed by growing labour
militancy. Schooling was seen as a means of producing
the motivation required in the emerging corporate order,
a way of disciplining the new proletariat. Schooling
would 'Americanize' immigrant groups with a dangerous
tendency towards European radicalism and socialism. The
expansion of education was also pressed by progressives
who hoped it would prove an effective antidote to urban
poverty. Finally, with the closing of the frontier and
the declining prospects for workers going into small
businesses or cooperative trades, labour often supported
educational expansion as the only remaining path towards
mobility, security, and social 'respectability'.

VOCATIONAL EDUCATION AND THE
DEMISE OF THE 'COMMON SCHOOL'

As large numbers of working-class and immigrant children began attending high schools, educational reformers
proposed a system of stratification within secondary

education. The older ideology of the common school –
the same curriculum should be offered to all children –
increasingly came under attack. The uniform curriculum
symbolized to liberal reformers an elitist and anachronistic hold-over from the nineteenth century. The high
school could not remain a minority institution designed,
in the words of an 1893 Declaration of the National
Education Association Committee of Ten[13]:

> To prepare for the duties of life that small propor-
> tion of all the children in the country ... who show
> themselves able to profit by an education prolonged
> to the eighteenth year, and whose parents are able
> to support them while they remain so long in school.

In its place appeared the 'progressive' insistence that
education should be tailored to the 'needs of the child'.

The uniform curriculum, in a situation where high
school attendance was skewed in favour of the upper
economic strata[14], tended to ignore the needs of the
majority. The demand for flexible programmes to handle
ethnic diversity in language skills was progressive, as
was the demand for curricula sensitive to the later life
and family surroundings of the students. The expansion
of public secondary education, and its transformation
from an upper-class preserve to a mass institution, was
eminently consistent with the democratic and egalitarian
tradition. In the context of a rapidly developing corporate division of labour, however, such demands spelled
not equality and democracy, but stratification and
bureaucracy.

Special curricula were developed for the children of
working families. The academic curriculum was preserved
for those who might later have the opportunity to make
use of book learning, either in college or in white-
collar employment. A superintendent of schools of
Cleveland argued[15]:

> It is obvious that the educational needs of children
> in a district where the streets are well paved and
> clean, where the homes are spacious and surrounded
> by lawns and trees, where the language of the child's
> playfellows is pure, and where life in general is
> permeated with the spirit and ideals of America – it
> is obvious that the educational needs of such a child
> are radically different from those of the child who
> lives in a foreign and tenement section.

The arguments for and against educational stratification

were clearly exhibited in the course of the vocational
education movement[16] which during the 1890s gathered the
political support of major educators and the financial
backing of a number of leading capitalists - J. P.
Morgan and John D. Rockefeller among them[17]. From the
late 1890s until World War I virtually every national
conference of the National Association of Manufacturers
passed resolutions advocating vocational education. The
reasons for this widespread support among employers were
simple enough. As late as the 1890s, skilled workers
exercised considerable power within the enterprise. In
many industries they collectively retained control of
the shop floor, often hired their own assistants, and
substantially influenced the recruitment of new skilled
workers through their control over the apprenticeship
system (Stone, 1974). The employers' strategy to break
the power of the skilled workers centred on a largely
successful attempt to destroy their unions. The ideological rationale for limiting the power of the skilled
workers was propagated by the school of 'scientific
management', which held that the behaviour of workers,
down to the movements involved in a mechanical operation,
must be controlled and dictated by technicians and managers according to 'scientific principle'. Employers
seized upon vocational education as a means of breaking
the workers' control over skills training, and as a
means of training and labelling the growing stratum of
foremen so as to set them above and apart from other
production workers.

Until the turn of the century organized labour took
little part in the discussions of vocational education.
Opposition, while a minority position, was vociferous.
The secretary of the Twist and Warp Lace Makers Association warned that vocational education 'would be rather
a curse than a blessing by placing at the disposal of
every capitalist bent on grinding down wages to the
lowest point an unlimited number of skilled out of work,
to supersede those who might resist his tyranny' (Cremin,
1964). The flagrantly anti-union advocacy of vocational
education by the NAM increased labour's opposition and
by the turn of the century the AFL had taken a firm
position against the movement. The final legislation
was not all that some employers had hoped for. Federal
aid was to be restricted to those over fourteen years
old, thus dampening the hopes of some advocates that the
newly formed junior high school could become 'the vocational preparatory school of the future'.

However, with the growing momentum of the vocational
education movement, labour's position shifted. Faced

with the virtual certainty of a federally funded vocational education programme, organized labour sought by
joining the movement to gain some influence over its
direction. By World War I there was virtually no organized opposition to federal aid to vocational education.
The movement culminated in 1917 with the successful
passage of the Smith-Hughes Act, providing federal support for vocational education, and in most respects
reflecting the views of the NAM.

Labour was successful in preventing the development
of dual school systems. In Massachusetts, a partially
implemented plan for the housing of vocational education
in separate trade schools incurred substantial opposition from educators as well as organized labour, and was
ultimately rejected. In Chicago, a similar proposal
arrayed the Chicago Federation of Labour, supported by
most of the city's teachers and its most renowned educator - John Dewey - against a coalition built around the
Chicago Association of Commerce and including virtually
every major business organization in the state of
Illinois (Grubb and Lazerson, 1974). At issue was the
Cooley Bill, which would have provided a dual vocational
and academic secondary education system for the state.
Introduced in 1913 and in subsequent years, the bill was
defeated. As the 1920s progressed it became clear that
the impact of the vocational education movement would
not be - as many of its early business backers had
hoped - separate school systems, but rather the development of vocationally oriented tracking within the comprehensive high school.

The Chicago Federation of Labour's opposition to the
Cooley Bill and other mechanisms of early selection and
educational stratification was based on the understanding that vocationalism would channel working-class,
immigrant, and black children into manual jobs. In fact,
the vocational education movement was less a response to
specific job training needs of the rapidly expanding
corporate sector than an accommodation of a previously
elite educational institution - the high school - to the
changing needs of reproducing the class structure. The
ideology of vocationalism could justify a tracking system that would separate and stratify young people
loosely according to race, ethnic origins, and class
backgrounds[18].

The history of the vocational education movement
illustrates well the contradictions of progressive education. While Dewey and other progressive educators
sought to replicate the community in the school and to
build a sense of unity and common experience among

students, the stratification of the high school -
pressed by those more concerned with processing future
workers - advanced apace. Those who opposed stratification gained important concessions, but yet they could
not resist tracking within the high school. Attempts
to bring students together and to forestall differentiation were limited to the more or less peripheral
sphere of extracurricular activities, but no amount of
school-wide assemblies, clubs, or athletics - all of
which were institutionalized during this period - could
bridge the racial, ethnic, and class divisions reinforced by curriculum tracking.

TESTING AND TRACKING: STREAMLINING THE 'MERITOCRACY'

The frankness with which students were channelled
into curriculum tracks on the basis of their ethnic,
racial, and economic background in the early twentieth
century raised serious doubts about the 'openness' of
the social class structure. By the end of the 1920s,
the relation between social background and a child's
tracking assignments would be disguised - though not
mitigated much - by another reform: 'objective' educational testing[19]. Particularly after World War I, the
capitulation of the schools to business values and concepts of efficiency led to the increased use of intelligence and scholastic achievement testing as an osten-
sibly unbiased means of measuring the product of
schooling and classifying students[20]. The complementary
growth of the vocational guidance profession allowed
much of the channelling to proceed from the student's
own well-counselled choices, thus adding a welcome
element of voluntarism to the system[21].

If the rhetoric of the educational response to the
economic changes after the turn of the century was
'progressive', much of its content and consciousness
was supplied by the new science of 'evolutionary
genetics'. Its grounding in Mendel's Law, Darwinism and
the sophisticated statistical methodologies of Pearson,
Terman, and Thorndike lent testing an apparent scientific rigour. IQ tests captured the imagination of
high-level policy makers and were seized upon by school
administrators. By 1939, no fewer than 4,279 mental
tests were in circulation; a survey of 150 school systems in 1932 revealed that three-quarters were using
intelligence tests to assign students to curriculum
tracks (Cohen and Lazerson, 1972).

An essential theme of the testing movement was the

unified character of human excellence; moral character,
intelligence, and social worth were inextricably connected and biologically rooted. In the words of the
psychologist Edward L. Thorndike (1911), 'to him that
has a superior intellect is given also on the average a
superior character'. Study after study exhibited the
'low intelligence' of 'wards of the state' and social
deviants: in Albany, New York, it was reported that
eighty-eight per cent of the city's prostitutes were
feebleminded; sixty-nine per cent of the white inmates
and ninety per cent of the black inmates in a Kansas
prison were found to be morons; a study revealed that
ninety-eight per cent of unmarried mothers were feebleminded (Marks, 1974). Immigrants, tests showed, were
particularly prone to 'low intelligence'. Professor
Henry Goddard's 1912 study, sponsored by the United
States Immigration Service, found that eighty-three per
cent of Jews, eighty per cent of Hungarians, seventy-
nine per cent of Italians, and eighty-seven per cent of
Russians were 'feebleminded' based on 'culture-free'
tests (Kamin, 1974).

Alfred Binet's original 'intelligence' test had been
developed for use in the French school system. The
translation of his 1905 test and its early growth in
popularity in this country is to be explained largely
by interest in military classification and immigration
restriction. Many of the early American testers were
quick to perceive the potential use of the tests for
achieving a more efficient and rationally ordered society. The major capitalist foundations concurred; much
of the early work on testing was financed by the Carnegie
Corporation of New York (Marks, 1974) and both Thorndike
and Terman received substantial foundation grants.
Terman argued for the application of IQ tests as clearly
as any of their early proponents : (quoted by Karier,
1974):

At every step in the child's progress the school
should take account of his vocational possibilities.
Preliminary investigations indicate that an IQ below
70 rarely permits anything better than unskilled
labour; that the range from 70 to 80 is pre-
eminently that of semi-skilled labour, from 80 to 100
that of the skilled or ordinary clerical labour, from
100 to 110 or 115 that of the semi-professional pursuits; and that above all these are the grades of
intelligence which permit one to enter the professions
or the larger fields of business ... This information
will be a great value in planning the education of a

particular child and also in planning the differentiated curriculum here recommended.

Proponents of the use of tests for educational tracking
found support in John Dewey's writings. In 1900 he had
written, 'In the great majority of human beings the
distinctively intellectual interest is not dominant.
They have the so-called practical impulse and disposition.' (Dewey, 1915).

IQ test results could be used to justify tracking by
race, ethnic origin, and class background. While IQ
tests were standardized to produce equal results for
boys and girls, the testers provided an equally scientific justification for sexual channelling in the
schools. This is how Thorndike (1914) put it:

> The most striking difference in instinctive equipment
> consists in the strength of the fighting instinct
> in the male and of the nursing instinct in the female
> ... And probably no serious student of human nature
> will doubt that these are matters of original nature.
> The out-and-out physical fighting for the sake of
> combat is pre-eminently a male instinct and the
> resentment at mastery, the zeal to surpass and the
> general joy at activity in mental as well as physical
> matters seem to be closely correlated with it. It
> has been common talk of women's 'dependence'. This
> is, I am sure, only an awkward name for less resent
> ment at mastery. The actual nursing of the young
> seems likewise to involve equally unreasoning tender
> ness to pet, coddle, and 'do for' others.

Boys and girls, Thorndike (1911) concluded, should not
share an identical curriculum: boys should be subjected
to educational environments that by evoking their competitive and fighting instincts would prepare them for
adult positions of 'mastery'; girls should be encouraged to develop their 'unreasoning' instinct to 'pet,
coddle, and "do for" others'.

The last stage in the implementation of testing as
the basis of tracking was the institutionalization of
the testing system. Carl Brigham developed the
Scholastic Aptitude Test in his capacity as the secretary of the newly formed College Entrance Examination
Board. In 1930 Rockefeller's General Education Board
gave half a million dollars for the founding of the
Cooperative Test Service to the American Council of
Education (itself established in 1918 by Rockefeller and
Carnegie money). In addition to the Cooperative Test

Service, Carnegie and Rockefeller supported the
Educational Records Bureau, the Graduate Records Office,
the National Committee on Teachers Examinations, and the
College Entrance Examination Board. Prodding and a
substantial grant from the Carnegie Foundation achieved
the consolidation of these testing units under the aegis
of the Educational Testing Service in 1948. In the
first half of the twentieth century these organizations
alone received over $7 million from the Rockefeller and
Carnegie Foundations (Marks, 1974).

CONCLUSION

   Major periods of educational change are responses to
changes in the structure of economic life associated
with the process of capital accumulation. The common
school movement of the nineteenth century developed to
complement a factory system that increasingly rendered
the family inadequate to the task of reproducing the
capitalist division of labour. The Progressive Era
accompanied the transition to corporate capitalism, for
which the small decentralized common school was mani-
festly unsuited.

   The legacy of the urban school reform movement in
this period reflects both its class basis and its commitment to social control as the overriding objective
of schooling. Social amelioration, open education, and
equalization of opportunity could have been pursued only
insofar as they contributed to - or at least did not
contradict - the role of the school in reproducing the
class system and extending the capitalist mode of production. The essence of progressivism in education was
the rationalization of the process of reproducing the
social classes of modern industrial capitalism. The
progressives viewed the growing corporatization of economic activity as desirable and forward-looking - indeed,
the best antidote to the provincialism and elitism of
American culture. For some, Taylorism in the schools
was, in turn, seen as an ideal. For others, the unified
and centralized high school with the differentiated
curriculum represented the most efficient accommodation
to the new exigencies of economic life.

   As a force for qualitatively new types of social
stability, the progressive movement must be judged an
eminent success. As a force for equality and human
development, however, it went little beyond the progressive elements in the organizational revolution of
turn-of-the-century economic life. The counterpoint of

success and failure in this period of change highlights
the general contradictions of liberal educational reform: the incompatibility of the egalitarian, develop-
mental, and integrative functions of education within
the context of capitalist relations of production.

That a school system geared towards 'moral development'
and towards domesticating a labour force for the rising
corporate order might readily embrace standardization
and testing - to the benefit of the leaders as well as
the led - seems in retrospect to have been almost inevitable.   Lacking any strong grass-roots support, and
self-consciously eschewing any systemic critique of
the evolving economic order, it is not surprising that
the idealistic progressives worked in vain for a humanistic and egalitarian education.   More in tune with
immediate economic realities, the bureaucratization,
tracking, and test-orientation of the school system
proceeded smoothly, promoted by seed money from large
private foundations, articulated by social scientists
at prestigious schools of education, and enthusiastic-
ally implemented by business-controlled local school
boards (Cremin, 1964).   Only a mass-based organization
of working people powerfully articulating a clear alternative to corporate capitalism as the basis for a progressive educational system could have prevented this
outcome.

NOTES

1.   Our treatment here is necessarily brief.   We present our case in greater detail and historical scope
in our forthcoming book BOWLES, S. and GINTIS, H.
(1976) Schooling in Capitalist America: Educational
Reform and the Contradictions of Economic Life
London: Routledge and Kegan Paul.

2.   PESSEN, E. (1971) The egalitarian myth and the
American social reality American Historical Review,
Vol. 76, No. 4 (October 1971).   Boston's wealthiest one
per cent owned sixteen per cent of all tangible wealth
in 1821 and thirty-seven per cent in 1845.   The figures
for New York City are twenty-nine per cent in 1828 and
forty-nine per cent in 1845.

3.   Cubberley's writings on educational history are
hard to categorize.   Though clearly influenced by the
conflict theory originally proposed by Carleton,
Cubberley also expressed an evolutionary idealism, and

at times appears to express the 'technological' perspective which we discuss.

4.   FISHLOW, A. (1966) 'The American common school revival: fact or fancy?' in H. Rosovsky (ed) Industrialization in Two Systems New York: John Wiley & Sons; and VANOVSKIS, M. and BERNARD, R. (1973) Women in Education in the Ante-Bellum Period   Madison: University of Wisconsin Centre for Demography and Ecology, Working Paper 73-7.

5.   Considering only the increase in schooling and conventionally measuring capital per worker, the amount of past labour per present worker - the organic composition of capital in Marx's terminology - is today probably three or four times what it was at the turn of the century.   See DENNISON, E. (1972) Sources of Economic Growth   New York.

6.   By the forces of production, we mean the technological, organizational, and labouring capacities of the population and the stock of machinery and other equipment which makes up the society's productive capacity.

7.   James O'Connor develops a related but not identical concept - the contradiction between accumulation and legitimation - in his Fiscal Crisis of the State   New York: St. Martin's Press, 1973.

8.   See Raymond Callahan, Education and the Cult of Efficiency Chicago: University of Chicago Press, 1962; Joel H. Spring, Education and the Rise of the Corporate State Boston: Beacon Press, 1972;   Clarence Karier Ideology and Evaluation: In Quest of Meritocracy for the Wisconsin Conference on Education and Evaluation at Madison, April 1973;   Katz (1968) Irony of Early School Reform Cambridge: Harvard University Press.

9.   BINSTOCK, JEANNE (1975) Survival in the American College Industry; ROSENTHAL, BURTON E. Educational Investments in Human Capital: The Significance of Stratification in the Labour Market unpublished thesis for Harvard University, 1972.

10.   U.S. Bureau of the Census (1960) Historical Statistics of the US.

11.   For surveys of this period, see CREMIN, LAWRENCE (1964) The Transformation of the School New York: Alfred A. Knopf;   SPRING Education and the Rise of the Corporate State; and COHEN, DAVID L. and LAZERSON, MARVIN (March 1972), Education and the corporate order Socialist Revolution 8.

12.   See GROB, G. (1969) Workers and Utopia Chicago:

Quadrangle Books. Also see the excellent treatment by
Herbert Gurman (1973), Work, culture and society in
industrializing America 1815-1919 American Historical
Review June 1973.

13. See TYACK, D. (1974) The One Best System: A History
of American Urban Education Cambridge: Harvard
University Press.

14. See TROEN, S. (1973) Popular education in 19th
century St. Louis History of Education Quarterly 13,
(Spring 1973).

15. Elson and Backman as quoted in Sol Cohen, The
industrial education movement, 1906-1917, American
Quarterly 20, (Spring 1968);   see also CREMIN,
Transformation of the School;   COHEN and LAZERSON,
Education and the Corporate Order; and GRUBB, W. NORTON
The Impact of the Vocational Education Movement after
1910, unpublished thesis for Harvard University, 1971.

16. We have relied heavily on the work of GRUBB and
LAZERSON American Education and Vocationalism New York:
Teacher's College, Columbia University 1974;   CREMIN,
Transformation of the School, and COHEN Industrial
Education Movement.

17. CREMIN, Transformation of the School, McCONNELL,
GRANT The Decline of Agrarian Democracy New York:
Harper & Row, 1969;   CLEAVER, HARRY The Southern
Colony: The Attempt to Transform Southern Agriculture
and Make It Safe for Democracy and Profits unpublished
paper for Sherbrooke University, 1974.

18. See GRUBB, B. and LAZERSON, M. (1974) American
Education and Vocationalism New York: Teacher's
College, Columbia University, for a more complete
presentation of this view.

19. In this section we have made extensive use of the
research of KARIER, CLARENCE Ideology and Evaluation:
In Quest of Meritocracy and Testing for order and
control in the corporate liberal State, from KARIER,
SPRING and VIOLAS Roots of Crisis;   and MARKS, RUSSELL
Trackers, Testers, and Trustees unpublished doctoral
dissertation for Harvard University, 1974.

20. Callahan Education and the Cult of Efficiency;
Cohen and LazersonEducation and the Corporate Order
and Cremin Transformation of the School.

21. On the role of IQ testing and reproducing and
legitimizing the class structure of corporate capitalism see Karier's essays in Karier, Spring, and Violas,
Roots of Crisis.

REFERENCES

BAILYN, B. (1960) Education in the Framing of American Society Chapel Hill: University of North Carolina Press.

BENDIX, R. and LIPSET, S. (Eds) (1966) Class, Status and Power New York: Free Press.

BOWLES, S. and GINTIS, H. (1976) Schooling in Capitalist America: Educational Reform and the Contradictions of Economic Life London: Routledge and Kegan Paul.

BRAVERMAN, H. (1974) Labour and Monopoly Capital New York: Monthly Review Press.

CALLAHAN, R. (1962) Education and the Cult of Efficiency Chicago: University of Chicago Press.

CARLETON, F. T. (1911) Economic Influences upon Educational Progress in the U.S. 1820-1850 Madison: University of Wisconsin Press.

COHEN, D. L. and LAZERSON, M. (1972) Education and the corporate order Socialist Revolution 8 (March 1972).

CREMIN, L. (1964) The Transformation of the School New York: Alfred A. Knopf.

CREMIN, L. (1970) American Education: The Colonial Experience 1607-1783 New York: Harper and Row.

CUBBERLEY, E. P. (1934) Public Education in the U.S. Boston: Houghton Mifflin.

DEWEY, J. (1915) Education vs. trade-training New Republic Vol. 3, No. 15 (May 1915).

EDWARDS, R.C. (1974) Capital Accumulation and Corporate Power in the Transition to Monopoly Capitalism Unpublished manuscript for the University of Massachusetts, Amherst.

FEINBERG, W. (1972) Progressive education and social planning Teachers' College Record May 1972.

FIELD, A. J. (1973) Skill Requirements in Early Industrialization: The Case of Massachusetts; Working paper in Economics: University of California at Berkeley, December 1973.

FISHLOW, A. (1966) 'The American common school revival: fact or fancy' in H. Rosovsky Industrialization in Two Systems New York: John Wiley and Sons.

GORDON, M. (1973) The American Family in Social Historical Perspective New York: St. Martin's Press.

GREER, C. (1973) The Great School Legend New York: Viking Press.

GROB, G. (1969) Workers and Utopia Chicago: Quadrangle Books.

GRUBB, B. and LAZERSON, M. (1974) American Education and Vocationalism New York: Teachers' College, Columbia University.

GURMAN, H. (1973) Work, culture and society in industrializing America 1815-1919; American Historical Review June, 1973.

KAESTLE, C. (1973) The Evolution of an Urban School System: New York City 1750-1850 Cambridge: Harvard University Press.

KAMIN, L. (1974) The Science and Politics of IQ Potomas: Erlbaum Associates.

KARIER, C., SPRING, J. and VIOLAS, P.C. (1973) Roots of Crisis Chicago: University of Illinois Press.

KARIER, C. (1974) 'Ideology and evaluation - in quest of meritocracy' in M. W. Apple and M. J. Subkoviak (Eds) Educational Evaluation - Analysis and Responsibility Berkeley: McCutchan.

KATZ, M. (1968) The Irony of Early School Reform Cambridge: Harvard University Press.

KATZ, M. (1971) Class, Bureaucracy and Schools New York: Praeger.

KOLKO, G. (1963) The Triumph of Conservatism Chicago: Quadrangle Books.

LAZERSON, M. (1971) Origin of Urban Schools: Public Education in Massachusetts Cambridge: Harvard University Press.

LUFT, H. (1971) New England Textile Labour in the

1840s: From Yankee Farmgirl to Irish Immigrant mimeograph, January 1971.

MARKS, R. (1974) Trackers, Testers and Trustees Unpublished doctoral dissertation for Harvard University.

McCONNELL, G. (1969) The Decline of Agrarian Democracy New York: Harper and Row.

O'CONNOR, J. (1973) Fiscal Crisis of the State New York: St. Martins Press.

ROSOVSKY, H. (Ed) (1966) Industrialization in Two Systems New York: John Wiley and Sons.

SPRING, J. H. (1972) Education and the Rise of the Corporate State Boston: Beacon Press.

STONE, K. (1974) The origin of job structures in the steel industry Review of Radical Political Economics Summer 1974.

THERNSTROM, S. (1973) The Other Bostonians Cambridge: Harvard University Press.

THORNDIKE, E. (1911) Individuality Boston: Houghton Mifflin.

THORNDIKE, E. (1914) Educational Psychology, Briefer Course New York: Teachers' College, Columbia University.

TROEN, S. (1973) Popular education in 19th century St. Louis History of Education Quarterly 13 (Spring, 1973).

TROW, M. (1966) in R. Bendix and S. Lipset (Eds) Class, Status, and Power New York: Free Press.

TYACK, D. (1974) The One Best System: A History of American Urban Education Cambridge: Harvard University Press.

US Bureau of Census (1960) Historical Statistics of the United States - Colonial Times to 1857.

US Bureau of Census (1974) Statistical Abstract of the US.

US Office of Education (1974) Digest of Educational
Statistics.

VANOVSKIS, M. and BERNARD, R. (1973) Women in Education
in the Ante-Bellum Period Madison: University of
Wisconsin Centre for Demography and Ecology, Working
paper 73-7.

WARE, N. J. (1964) The Industrial Workers 1840-1860
Chicago: Quadrangle Books.

WEINSTEIN, J. (1968) The Corporate Ideal in the Liberal
State 1900-1918 Boston: Beacon Press.

3.0
Beyond Critiques:

Introduction

The 'new' sociology of education was in part a conscious attempt to make the sociological analysis of
education more directly relevant to the everyday world
of teachers and pupils than work in earlier traditions
had been. The recognition that definitions of education
were social constructs and hence potentially changeable
was seen to offer teachers the possibility of transforming the contexts in which they and their pupils
worked. However, Young's paper in this final part shows
how the 'new' sociology's critique of the curriculum as
'fact', and its proposed alternative conception of
curriculum as 'practice', failed to address the concrete
historical context of schooling in which there are limits
as well as possibilities. If the 'new' sociology of
education went some way towards explaining 'the sources
and nature of discontent experienced by the social
actors' (and we have argued earlier that its contribution
was limited even in this respect), it failed to meet
Fay's (1975) other criteria for a critical social
science. It failed to demonstrate how such discontent
could be 'eliminated by removing ... the structural
contradictions which underlie it'. It did not help
actors to 'understand themselves in their situation as
the product of certain inherent contradictions in their
social order' which could be removed by 'taking an
appropriate course of action to change this social
order'. Insofar as it did seem to propose courses of
action at all, they tended (as Whitty's paper in section
one implied) to be somewhat inappropriate. Even if it
did assist social actors in the school to 'see themselves and their social situation in a new way', the
analysis offered also implied that individualistic and
localised strategies of change could 'alter the conditions which they (found) repressive'. Its contribution to the transformation of consciousness thus tended
to be limited and its strategies for educational change

ineffective. In the real world of schooling, the result could often be disillusion.

Young's paper is therefore less 'education-bound' than much of the earlier work in the 'new directions' tradition. Like the contributions to section two, it attempts to develop the sort of critical theory which can overcome the limitations of the earlier work without denying the possibility and the importance of practical action for change within the school arena. It stresses that action to change that which is the outcome of the collective actions of men must itself necessarily be collective, and that the development of educational experiences which offer a realistic possibility for human liberation will 'involve many others who have no direct involvement with the school'. Within the article, however, the nature of these 'others' is not specified, and rhetorical appeal for 'making more explicit the political character of education' fails to make explicit the nature of the linkages which are to be developed between the classroom practice of radical teachers and that which is conventionally regarded as 'political' practice.

This is the issue which is explored in the paper by Frith and Corrigan, who locate the politics of education firmly in the wider politics of the struggle for socialism. Much of their paper is concerned with the pervasive state of confusion and contradiction in the educational theory and practice of the Left. They also point to the difficulty of separating the various aspects of education, and re-emphasize the importance of an analysis of the ideology of state education for the attempt to formulate and implement alternatives. They stress the need to focus on the content and control of education, and argue that classroom struggles have to be articulated by socialist teachers in the context of working-class politics if they are to be more than easily-crushed diversions. Parallel with this, in a way neglected by most Marxist writers on education, they argue that as our schools are among the institutions of capitalism, they cannot avoid being among the sites of the struggles between social classes. From this point of view, the analysis and transformation of curricular and pedagogic practices become a central element in any socialist strategy. As they themselves indicate, slogans like 'bring politics into the classroom' can easily remain at the level of rhetoric and be no less empty than the appeals referred to earlier in Young's paper. What is absent, and is crucial to their case, as well as ours in arguing for the need to transform critiques of education into political practice, is the beginnings of

an analysis of the social position of teachers. The elements of such an analysis can only be hinted at here,
but would need to recognize that there is common ground
between teachers and other workers who sell their labour.
It would also be concerned with the particular circumstances teachers share with other employees of the state.
At the same time, teachers are intellectual workers who
can either identify themselves subordinately with academic or other professional communities or, in Gramsci's
term, develop 'organic' links with the working-class
movement (Hoare and Nowell-Smith, 1971). The history of
the training and professionalizing of elementary, and
later primary and secondary teachers (Tropp, 1957), can
be read as a strategic attempt to minimize the likeli-
hood of the second of these two possibilities. The
relations between teachers and working-class pupils thus
parallel, in some respects, the relations between technical and production workers discussed by Gorz in his
paper in section two. We therefore face a considerable
theoretical and political task in developing a concrete
understanding of the class position of teachers, even
in the kind of monopoly capitalist society in which,
as Braverman (1974) puts it, 'almost all of the
population has been transformed into the employees
of capital'. This does not mean finding a simplistic
definition of teachers as, for instance, 'the new
proletariat' or a 'fraction of the petit-bourgeoisie',
for such definitions forget that, to a certain extent,
'classes ... are not fixed entities, but rather ongoing
processes, rich in change ... and incapable of being
encapsulated in formulae, no matter how analytically
proper such formulas may be'. It is probably in historical studies that Braverman's point is most easily
grasped, and it is Thompson (1968) who reminds us that
class, in Marx's own historical writing, is a relationship not a thing. In the context of developing a
strategy for change in education, this means we need
to focus not just on the class position of teachers as
state employees, but also in relation to pupils who
are legally compelled by the state to attend school
until the age of sixteen. With the new phenomenon of
teacher unemployment and the various other ways in
which teaching is beginning to take on the character
of other mass labour markets, it will be tempting to
develop a class analysis purely in terms of a straightforward 'proletarianization' of teachers. But this
alone would miss the distinctive character of teachers
as 'reproducers of labour'. Just as factory workers
can begin to transform their experience of alienation
in the workplace through collective action and political struggle by challenging the relations of production, so too can teachers collectively help to

challenge the relations of reproduction in the classrooms and the schools. It is for this reason that
questions of curriculum and teaching methods remain
crucial, but only, as we argued in section two, if they
are linked to the broader strategy for change that
expresses the interdependence of factory and school in
an overall political programme.

Despite the differences between them on particular
issues, the contributors to this book all point to the
necessity of overcoming the Left's traditional fear
of bringing politics into education and education into
politics. This, for us, is perhaps the central conclusion towards which the sort of practical theory developed in this book points. The analysis of education
cannot be isolated from the analysis of capitalist
society, so neither can the struggle to change it be
isolated from broader struggles against oppression and
exploitation. Work within the field of education can
be linked to these broader struggles in a number of
ways. Trade union activity of teachers on economistic
issues is as important as trade union activity amongst
any employees of the state, but the struggles of radical
teachers within the school on issues of curriculum and
control are also significant in ways which Apple discussed in his paper in section one. Further concrete
examples of the significance of the struggle for change
in schools are discussed in Explorations in the Politics
of School Knowledge (Whitty and Young, 1976). On the
other hand, a great deal of the rhetoric about teachers
as agents of change remains empty because it fails to
address the sort of problems which teachers attempting
to introduce truly 'oppositional' change into schools
would face (see Williams, 1973). The analysis of state
education in terms of content and control reveals the
strength of the interests with which prevailing definitions of education are linked and any conception of
alternative practice which challenges them is likely
(as historical studies of education demonstrate) to
be co-opted by those interests unless it is linked to
other oppositional struggles within and beyond education. The fear of political 'movements' among liberal
and progressive educators (see, for example, Stenhouse,
1975) is likely to make their proposals for school-
based transformation of education ineffective -
particularly when they look outside the school only to
existing and narrowly 'educational' agencies of support. It is crucial that those concerned to introduce
radical changes in schools find support and solidarity
amongst those movements which are concerned to change
society, rather than from agencies whose primary

purpose is (in the long term) to adapt the curriculum
to the changing needs of capitalist society.

This alone will not, of course, lead to the victory
of socialist values in school or society, but it will
politicize the struggle which is already immanent in
schools because schools are in society. Clearly, most
of the examples which are generally quoted to show how
schools can help change the direction of society are
ones in which there has already been a change in the
political orientation of the country, for example, Cuba
and Tanzania. In such countries the schools were seen
to serve the interests of the deposed colonialist system and hence they were changed to serve the social
purposes of the new regime. Furthermore, in these
countries, and to a greater extent in China, North
Korea and Vietnam, political change has not just been
a change of orientation but an explicit attempt to
change the division of labour, and thus break down the
separations between work and school, town and country,
and mental and manual labour. Thus the struggle in
education cannot be conceived as primary or isolated
from struggles towards economic and political transformation. The necessity of seeing these struggles as
linked is captured in the following passage from
Bowles and Gintis (1976):

> A proper organization of educational and economic
> life, we believe, can unleash a people's creative
> powers without recreating the oppressive poles of
> domination and subordinacy, self-esteem and self-
> hatred, affluence and deprivation.
>
> A revolutionary transformation of social life will
> not simply happen through piecemeal change. Rather,
> we believe it will occur only as the result of a
> prolonged struggle based on hope and a total vision
> of a qualitatively new society, waged by those
> social classes and groups who stand to benefit from
> the new era.

However, the prolonged struggle for economic change
will itself have been in vain unless the necessity for
it to be accompanied by a politicized struggle within
institutions of education and culture is also recognized. The struggle within schools is, for Bowles and
Gintis, part of the strategy for economic transformation (producing workers 'unwilling to submit to the
fragmented relationships of dominance and subordinacy'),
but it is also, we would argue, a process of cultural
prefigurement (albeit an unsatisfactory one) for an

alternative future. This future would be empty if the struggle for cultural hegemony were to be postponed until economic transformation had been achieved.

The case for attempting to see the struggle for change in education in terms of the social relations in education as well as the social relations of education, and to go beyond the narrow conceptions of change adopted by various particular factions on the Left, must therefore be seen in terms of the cultural features which we envisage as central to any alternative society. It is thus fitting to end with a long quotation from a recent declaration of faith by Raymond Williams (1975) which we believe resonates with the message of this book:

> So if I am asked finally to define my own position, I would say this. I believe in the necessary economic struggle of the organized working class. I believe that this is still the most creative activity in our society, as I indicated years ago in calling the great working-class institutions creative cultural achievements, as well as the indispensable first means of political struggle. I believe that it is not necessary to abandon a parliamentary perspective as a matter of principle, but as a matter of practice I am quite sure that we have to begin to look beyond it. For reasons that I described in The Long Revolution and again in The Mayday Manifesto I think that no forseeable parliamentary majority will inaugurate socialism unless there is quite a different kind of political activity supporting it, activity which is quite outside the scope or perspective of the British Labour Party or any other likely candidate for that kind of office. Such activity involves the most active elements of community politics, local campaigning, specialized interest campaigning: all the things that were the real achievements of the politics of the sixties and that are still notably active. But finally, for it is the sphere in which I am most closely involved, I know that there is a profoundly necessary job to do in relation to the processes of the cultural hegemony itself. I believe that the system of meanings and values which a capitalist society has generated has to be defeated in general and in detail by the most sustained kinds of intellectual and education work. This is a cultural process which I called 'the long revolution' and in calling it 'the long revolution' I meant that it was a genuine struggle which was part of the

necessary battles of democracy and of economic victory for the organized working-class. People change,
it is true, in struggle and by action. Anything as
deep as a dominant structure is only changed by
active new experience. But this does not mean that
change can be remitted to action otherwise conceived.
On the contrary, the task of a successful socialist
movement will be one of feeling and imagination
quite as much as one of fact and organization. Not
imagination or feeling in their weak senses:
'imagining the future' (which is a waste of time) or
'the emotional side of things'. On the contrary, we
have to learn and teach each other the connections
between a political and economic formation, a cultural and educational formation and, perhaps hardest
of all, the formations of feeling and relationship
which are our immediate resources in any struggle.
Contemporary Marxism, extending its scope to this
wider area, learning again the real meanings of
totality, is then a movement to which I find myself
belonging and to which I am glad to belong.

We embrace the central sentiments of this passage, and
hope that the contributions to this book will play some
small part in persuading educational reformers to
recognize their membership of the broader struggle of
the working classes against oppression, and in convincing other participants in that struggle that
radicals working within the field of education are not
irrelevant to it.

REFERENCES

BOWLES, S. and GINTIS, H. (1976) Schooling in Capitalist
America London: Routledge and Kegan Paul.

BRAVERMAN, H. (1974) Labour and Monopoly Capital - the
degradation of work in the twentieth century New York:
Monthly Review Press.

FAY, B. (1975) Social Theory and Political Practice
London: Allen and Unwin.

HOARE, Q. and NOWELL-SMITH, G. (1971) Selections from
the Prison Notebooks of Antonio Gramsci London:
Lawrence and Wishart.

STENHOUSE, L. (1975) An Introduction to Curriculum
Research and Development London: Heinemann.

THOMPSON, E. P. (1968) The Making of the English Working Class, Harmondsworth: Penguin Books.

TROPP, A. (1957) The School Teachers London: Heinemann.

WHITTY, G. and YOUNG, M. (1976) Explorations in the Politics of School Knowledge Driffield: Nafferton Books.

WILLIAMS, R. (1973) 'Base and Superstructure in Marxist Cultural Theory', New Left Review, 82.

WILLIAMS, R. (1975) 'You're a Marxist, Aren't You?' in Parekh, B. The Concept of Socialism London: Croom Helm.

3.1
Curriculum Change: Limits and Possibilities

Michael Young

I am concerned with the problem of change in education; with developing a theory or theories that may
enable those involved in education to become aware of
ways of changing their or their pupils' or students'
educational experience, even if this leads us to conceive of teachers struggles as not independent from
other struggles in the work places and communities where
people live[1]. I want to do this through a critical
examination of two contrasting conceptions of the curriculum. These are well expressed by Maxine Greene (1971),
where she describes the dominant view of the curriculum
of educational philosophers, such as Hirst and Peters[2],
in terms of 'a structure of socially prescribed knowledge, external to the knower, there to be mastered';
which she compares with her own phenomenological view of
the curriculum as 'a possibility for the learner as an
existing person mainly concerned with making sense of
his own life-world'[3]. For the present purposes, I shall
call these two views 'curriculum as fact' and 'curriculum as practice'[4]. The 'curriculum as fact', or
commodity-view[5] of knowledge, has been rightly criticized as both dehumanizing and mystifying education,
mostly by Marxist and phenomenologically-inspired sociologists and philosophers - Paulo Freire and Maxine Greene
are but two. These critiques, as expressed in the view
of 'curriculum as practice', do not start from the
structure of knowledge but the intentions and actions

* This paper was first delivered as a Doris Lee Memorial
Lecture on 20th February, 1975. It was originally given
without references and can still, I hope, be read in
that way. I have added the notes and bibliography in
case readers wish to follow up some of the work that I
drew on and found valuable in preparing the Lecture. In
its present form it was first published in Educational
Studies 1(2), June 1975.

of men. I shall want to argue, that such a view, as a
kind of over-reaction to the pervasiveness of subjects,
forms of knowledge and objectives, can itself be a form
of mystification. I shall suggest that 'curriculum as
fact' needs to be seen as more than mere illusion, a
superficial veneer on teachers' and pupils' classroom
practice, but as a historically specific social reality
expressing particular production relations among men[6].
It is mystifying in the way it presents the curriculum
as having a life of its own, and obscures the human
relations in which it, as any conception of knowledge,
is embedded, leaving education as neither understandable
nor controllable by men. The alternative conception of
'curriculum as practice' can equally mystify to the
extent that it reduces the social reality of 'curriculum'
to the subjective intentions and actions of teachers
and pupils. This limits us from understanding the
historical emergence and persistence of particular conceptions of knowledge and particular conventions
(school subjects for example). In that we are limited
from being able to situate the problems of contemporary
education historically, we are again limited from understanding and control.

Before exploring these contrasting views in more
detail, I should like to take an example, mathematics,
as an unlikely case to illustrate the distinction between theories of knowledge that I wish to make. To do
this, I shall draw on a discussion by David Bloor
(1973), who begins by quoting from G. H. Hardy's A
Mathematician's Apology:

> 317 is a prime, not because we think so, or because
> our minds are shaped in one way rather than another,
> but because it is so because mathematical reality is
> built that way.

Hardy exemplifies the kind of realist theory of knowledge which posits a realm of truth independent of man;
such a theory underlies what I have referred to as the
view of 'curriculum as fact'. Bloor contrasts Hardy
with Wittgenstein who, in discussing logical inferences
involved in simple number sequences, writes as follows:
'with endless practice, with merciless exactitude; that
is why it is inexorably insisted that we shall all say
"two" after "one", "three" after "two" and so on'. For
Wittgenstein, it is we, not mathematics, who are inexorable, Bloor remarks. 'Our children' Wittgenstein
writes, 'are not only given practice in calculation, but
are also trained to adopt a particular attitude towards
a mistake in calculating' - the feeling, Bloor suggests,

that the calculation goes its own way, even if we as
calculators may lapse. This seems to me a profound
insight into how our concepts of knowledge are related
to our ideas about teaching and learning. This, as
Bloor points out, is not a theory which denies the
social reality of mathematics. It recognizes that
mathematics is an invention, not a discovery, but that
it, like all inventions, can come to have a life of its
own, to be reified, and therefore experienced as external to men. The question which I shall return to, of
how particular forms of reification emerge and persist,
is not adequately dealt with, either by dismissing the
problem as theories such as Hardy's do, nor by treating
the rules of mathematics, or any forms of knowing, as
mere convention or usage, as Wittgenstein might be
interpreted as doing.

Let us now return to the first of my two views of
curriculum, 'curriculum as fact'. Most writing and
research concerned with curriculum unavoidably treats
it as in some way a topic, thus affirming rather than
explaining it as a social reality. It becomes something
to be preserved or brought up-to-date, as in grammar
schools, modified or made more relevant for the so-
called less-able, broadened or integrated for those who
specialize too soon, and so on. We can also trace a
range of administrative practices, which though doubt-
less starting with a concern about what should be hap-
pening to pupils and students, in effect sustain the
idea of the curriculum as something to be studied,
reorganized and analysed. We find deputy-headteachers
and vice-principals for curriculum, professors, journals,
degrees and departments, and of course the final academic accolade of all otherwise unrecognized activity,
attempts to develop curriculum 'theory'. Parallel to
this, we find new special interests like the sociology
and psychology of the curriculum in which the two
disciplines apply their respective vocabularies - for
sociology it has been stratification and integration,
and, for psychology, mental development and stages of
learning. I would suggest that in each case problems
are created, such as the separation and hierarchies
between different areas of enquiry in sociology, which
our methods do not enable us to solve, for our starting
points have been knowledge and curricula rather than
their production in teachers' and pupils' practice.
Academic theorists, often in search of a spurious scientism, can be far more naive than teachers. They present
curriculum as a reality to which the language of cause
and effect, resistance and change is appropriate, and
we discover articles with absurd titles like 'How does

the curriculum change?'. This is not so different from
politicians' talk of 'the National Interest', or 'the
Economy', in which an ideology is mistaken for the set
of social relations it seeks to legitimate. These
social relations between teachers and taught, and the
assumptions about knowledge and curriculum embedded in
them become masked, or even subsumed, by the language
of curriculum theory. A parallel might be drawn with
classical economics which took prices and wages as its
topics, thus masking the production relations between
owners and employees. This conception of 'curriculum
as fact', with its underlying theory of knowledge as
external to the knower, both teacher and student,
embodied in syllabuses and text-books, is widely held,
and has profound implications for our conceptions of
teaching and learning. To say 'I teach history' or
'physics' implies a body of knowledge to be transferred
from the teacher who has it to the pupil who has not,
whether by rote and test, or enquiry and project.
Though this applies most obviously to secondary schools,
the notion of a body of knowledge, though not formal-
ized as a set of 'subjects', is no less involved in
saying 'I teach fourth-year juniors'. This is the
framework that has been taken as given by most of those
who have theorized about educational or curriculum
change. It is teachers as well as philosophers who see
teaching as initiating children into 'worthwhile'
activities, and so long as the idea of initiation, with
the knowledge and the worthwhile presupposed, and with
its unavoidably hierarchical relations, is not questioned, educational philosophy merely confirms what
every teacher and pupil knows, and the only possible
explanations of pupil failure are either 'bad teaching'
or in terms of social or psychological characteristics
of the pupil. Nell Keddie (1971) suggests what is
involved in such a conception of curriculum and teaching - she argues that becoming initiated into the
teachers' form of knowledge, or, as we more normally
describe it, becoming an educational success, is
premised precisely on pupils not questioning the grounds
of teachers' knowledge. I would like to illustrate the
way in which I see notions of teaching as 'knowledge to
be transmitted' involved in teacher pupil interaction,
by referring to a transcript I made from a first-year
science class in a large East London comprehensive
school. I think it also illustrates how, with such a
conception of knowledge prevailing, passivity is almost
forced on, in this case, a remarkably reluctant pupil:

(Teacher and pupils have a worm in front of them)

T   Have you ever seen examples of when it (soil)
      is produced?

P   No.

T   Earth on the grass.

P   No, I just seen holes on the grass.

T   Have you ever seen anything else that might tell
      you there was a worm on the grass?

P   Yeah, they're what's called again, the holes
      they make are called ...

T   Have you seen those little piles?

P   Piles?

T   Have you seen those little heaps of ...?

P   Leaves.

T   On the grass, little ...

P   Holes.

T   Em?

P   Dots.

T   Have you seen ...?   Have you ever come ...?

P   I've seen holes.

T   Do you know something called a cast?

If you should see this as just an example of 'bad
teaching', I would suggest you might ask similar questions about any example of what you would consider
'good teaching'. I would want to argue that the assumptions about knowledge as external, to-be-transmitted,
are no less a feature of 'good' teaching than 'bad',
and that they are integral for both teachers and pupils
in creating a sense of pupils as 'not knowing', at least
till his 'knowledge' is confirmed by the teacher.

If we turn specifically to what Banks has called
'mainstream' or 'traditional' sociology of education[7],
we find a conception of 'curriculum as fact' as no less
pervasive. Most writers, from Durkheim to Parsons and
Banks, conceive of education as cultural transmission,
or socialization into skills and values. Thus, the
teacher's problem, which he hardly needed the sociologist to tell him, is already defined, how is he or
she to devise more effective ways of transmitting these
skills, whatever they are, to as many pupils as possible? All such sociological theory can do is to offer
a range of explanations, from cultural inadequacy or

lack of innate ability of the pupils to some reference
to 'the structure of our society', to account to
teachers why, according to conventional academic standards, they are so often unsuccessful.

The school curriculum becomes presented as a set of
gateways to a world of adult competence, though educationalists are inclined to find all kinds of justification for the very tenuous relationships between school
defined 'competence' and what any one needs to survive
in or understand, let alone change, the world they are
supposedly being prepared for. It is, predominantly,
a subject-ordered world - even when presented as
integrated studies - on what grounds, one might ask,
can we distinguish the new 'integrations' from the old
'subjects'? Take geography and chemistry for example;
they are undoubtedly ways of producing, anyway for
teachers, a sense of integration of a very disparate
set of themes and topics, so that as with Nuffield
Secondary Science, it is possible to say 'it's a bit
short on chemistry'. However, this sense of integration
is also produced by, say, those who teach environmental
studies or material science, and it would be extremely
difficult to claim, except in terms of custom and
tradition, any distinctiveness about the second examples
of integration. There is a more important point:
integration in both cases produces an ordering of the
world through which the learner has to find his way,
rather than involving the learner in the process of
integration himself. Where pupils reject the discon-
tinuity between their knowledge of the world and what
they experience as school orderings, subjects, topics,
etc., they invariably become described as less-able or
non-academic. Such descriptions depend for their
plausibility on a view of 'curriculum as fact', which
tells us what 'able' and 'academic' refer to. That
this view of curriculum is also presupposed by the
proposals for 'curricula for the less-able' is illustrated for example by the Schools Council's project
'Mathematics for the Majority'. The difference is that
while knowledge is still seen as external to both
teacher and pupils, it involves not only ideas about
what counts as mathematics, but about the supposed
relevance of certain mathematical practices for pupils'
lives outside of school.

More generally then, I would suggest that the prevailing notions of curriculum to which I have referred,
express a power relation between teacher and learner,
and a relatively passive model of the teacher as reproducing the knowledge produced elsewhere by others.

One way in which this passivity is displayed is the way outside bodies such as University Examination Boards are able, almost without question, to define what counts as knowledge in the schools. Even bodies such as the CSE Boards and the Schools Council are, more often than not, felt as external constraints on the work of classroom teachers. You have only to talk to teachers who have tried to obtain Schools Council support for local development projects, or in many areas, to develop Mode 3 schemes with minimal formal examinations, to be aware that 'teacher control' of these organizations is more of a constitutional rhetoric than a reality.

To sum up this section: I have suggested that a view of 'curriculum as fact' expresses many of the prevailing assumptions or theories of practitioners, both teachers and pupils. In that most of what passes for curriculum theory, whether of that name or derived from philosophy, psychology or sociology, confirms such assumptions, it can do little more than re-describe a world that teachers and pupils already know. Paradoxically, it confirms for teachers both the irrelevance of theory for practical change in schools, and their own insignificance as theorists; teachers have theories of knowledge, teaching and curriculum which, I shall argue later, are crucially important for the possibilities of change, but they lack the abstract elegance and empty clarity of philosophy, the conceptual obscurity of sociology, and the mindless banalities of the curriculum taxonomies. As a theory therefore, 'curriculum as fact' fails according to the criteria I started with, in 'not enabling people to become aware of ways of changing their world', for that would be about enabling teachers and pupils to theorize, rather than to learn that others theorize about their practice. 'Curriculum as fact' presents education as a thing, hiding the social relations between human beings who collectively produce it. What then of the view of 'curriculum as practice', the theory which informs the critique of prevailing ideas such as those I have referred to?

The basic premise of a view of 'curriculum as practice'[8] is not a structure of knowledge, but how men collectively attempt to order their world and in the process produce knowledge. In education, the focus has been on teachers' and pupils' classroom practices, and how educational realities such as subjects, curriculum and ability, are not external or attributes of pupils, but products of these practices and the

assumptions about knowledge, learning and teaching which
are embedded in them[9]. From this view, teachers' practices are seen as crucial in sustaining or challenging
prevailing views of knowledge and curriculum which thus
ceases to be treated as distinct from the variety of
ranking activities through which teachers produce marks,
discipline, and children of differing abilities[10]. The
implication that follows is that a critical examination
of assumptions underlying teachers' activities will
enable them to implement change almost at will. Such
a theory, while valuable in challenging the view of
'curriculum as fact' and teachers as passive reproducers,
is misleading both theoretically and practically in
locating the possibilities of change in education
solely within teachers' practices. Teachers are thereby
given a kind of spurious autonomy and independence from
the wider contexts of which their activity is a part,
and thus have no way of understanding their own failures
except in terms of personal inadequacy.

A view of 'curriculum as practice' involves a radically different view of knowledge to that referred to in
Hardy's mathematics, for no longer can knowledge be
viewed almost as private property handed down from the
academic 'discoverers' for the teacher to distribute
or 'transmit'. Knowledge becomes that which is accomplished in the collaborative work of teachers and
pupils. Theoretically, this has profound implications
for existing school hierarchies and for how we organize
educational practice. What might be involved for example in seeing education as the collaborative production
of history or science when we normally think of teaching as the transmission of knowledge, however we dress
it up as enquiry or projects? The problem is not just
that such possibilities may seem exciting to some but
threatening to others, but that they remain possibilities 'in theory', generated as they are from a view of
curriculum as teachers' practice. In other words, such
a view of curriculum can itself be seen as an ideology
in treating teachers' practices as some independent
reality. Radical changes based on a theory of 'curriculum as practice' are likely to face very quickly the
practical experience that curriculum is not just
teachers' and pupils' practice, but that it involves
also the views of parents, employers, administrators
and so on, about what education should be. If there
was a situation in a school or group of schools where
teachers began a critical examination and reformulation
of current practice with pupils, then I would suggest
that in their attempts to implement alternatives they
would practically be taken far outside the context of

the classroom, and theoretically they would be forced
to develop a theory more adequate for understanding
their situation than that of 'curriculum as practice'.

I would like to illustrate these general points by
two specific examples from science education, which I
would argue have a more general relevance to the problems of a view of curriculum as practice. Innovation
in science education has been virtually synonomous with
the Nuffield/Schools Council projects, which have tended
without exception to sustain rather than challenge
existing conceptions of school science, and to perpetuate its stratification into 'pure' and 'applied' (Hardy,
1975). The attempts to introduce Project Technology
largely through craft departments in schools is a case
in point; as is in a different context the remark of
a head of chemistry in a North of England comprehensive
school that he thought he could get his environmental
science syllabus through for CSE 'if the highest grade
he asked for was Grade 3'.

At a meeting of the British Association in September
1974, Professor Jevons was quoted as saying that in
science education 'we are up against something in the
cognitive structure of science itself', and that therefore science was not appropriate 'to meet the more
radical ideals of education'; a very clear example of
the mode of reasoning underlying the view of 'curriculum
as fact' and the kind of teaching that it implies. If,
however, we go back a century, we can see how our conceptions of school science, as a body of knowledge
enshrined in textbooks, syllabuses and laboratories,
gradually gained ascendancy over quite different possibilities. A recent study (Layton, 1973) brings this
out well by describing the fate of a movement during
the early days of school science called by its founder,
Richard Dawes, the 'Science of Common Things'. In the
work of this movement, pupils' experiences of the natural world, in their work, their homes and their daily
lives, formed the basis of the development of their
enquiries in school science. A particular example
Layton cites is the 'radical curriculum' of Arthur Rigg,
Principal of Chester Training College, in which a major
emphasis was placed on the kind of science and workshop
skills relevant to an area where most people were employed in the cotton industry. This project was short
lived, Layton suggests, because it undermined the
separation of teachers from those they were to teach,
and it was feared by the Inspectorate that those studying their own work context might come to see it too
critically. Furthermore, it was felt that teachers

emerging from such a course might become as one
Inspector put it 'active emissaries of misrule'. Both
Dawes and Rigg can be seen as working with notions of
curriculum as practice, in which school and college
science is the emergent product of teacher and student
collaborative activities. In the particular context,
their proposals were perceived by their opponents anyway
as raising questions of significance far outside the
classroom or the laboratory; the powerlessness and
ultimate demise of the movement can be seen in part as
reflecting the limitations of a theory that restricts
itself to what happens in the school. Though it is not
possible to draw any direct parallels with science
education today, what is emphasized is the historical
emergence and political character of the most basic
assumptions of what is now taken to be school science.

My second example illustrates the limits of a view
of curriculum as practice, and suggests how examiners
outside the school context are involved in sustaining
particular notions of school knowledge. It is taken
from the Nuffield Science 'A' Level in which the typical
practical test is replaced by a project to be devised
and written up by the candidate, and is allocated 15 per
cent of the marks. In one case a girl chose to investigate problems of streamlining a boat, and, in doing so,
she drew on and learnt a considerable amount about
viscosity - a standard school science topic at 'A'
level. In the context of her project, viscosity was
not an external body of knowledge to be learnt because
it was on the syllabus, but a way of understanding and
transforming an aspect of her environment which was
important to her outside school[11]. The teacher and
pupil activity, both theoretical and practical became,
in this instance, the reality of science education.
However this practice, as a part of teachers' and pupils'
activity on a physical science course, was crammed into
one afternoon a week, while the rest of the time was
used in the 'real' work of reproducing knowledge for
the formal examinations which count for 85 per cent of the
marks. It may be, therefore, that such liberalization
tends to sustain rather than challenge, both for teachers and pupils, a view that knowledge of viscosity,
like all real knowledge, is something to be learnt and
reproduced rather than a way of understanding the world
we are part of. Thus a view of curriculum as fact
rather than as practice is confirmed.

To summarize this section: I have argued that a
view of curriculum as practice does challenge attempts
to legitimate particular educational practice in terms

of structures of knowledge, but that in replacing a
notion of reality located in such structures by one
located in teachers' classroom practice, it has serious
weaknesses. Attempts by teachers to develop strategies
in terms of such a theory will not only confront them
with the limits on their possibilities of action, but
also with the limits of a theory that cannot enable them
to comprehend the character of such limits.

I would like to conclude by drawing together the
themes of the two critiques in relation to my original
problem - developing a theory or theories that may enable those of us involved in education to be aware of
ways of transforming educational practice. Curriculum
as fact, with its concepts of teaching, knowledge and
ability, takes for granted just that which its task as
a theory should be to explain. How did education
formulated in terms of curricula originate and why does
it prevail or persist? By failing to ask these questions
such a theory must be assuming, at least for advanced
industrial societies, that the kind of educational practices which prevail are in a sense necessary. This is
a kind of end-of-history argument, in which the past, as
a dynamic of action and interests which produced the
present, is forgotten, and the future is viewed as some
kind of universal present. The significance of this
view of curriculum is the extent to which it is not
just a theory produced by academics, but rather that
it represents the way those involved in ordering our
educational institutions, administrators, headmasters
and teachers, actually conceive of education. In this
way, it represents part of the circumstances within
which anyone concerned to change educational practice
has to work. If it is a characteristic of any critical
theory[12] that the starting point of its argument must
be people's everyday views of the world, and, if as I
have suggested, the concept of education expressed in
the idea of 'curriculum as fact' is such a view, then
any theory concerned with the possibilities of change
cannot treat such a view as mere illusion, the irrelevant product of ivory tower academics. This then is the
major weakness of the view of curriculum as practice.
Though challenging prevailing conceptions of education
in treating them as conventions arbitrarily imposed on
the real practices of men, it can mislead as to the
possibilities of change by locating them primarily in
teachers' practices. In doing so it directly contradicts the lived experience of those about whom it
theorizes, contributing, paradoxically to the division
between theory and practice, which its critique of

structures of knowledge would seem to question[13]. In
emphasizing the conventionality of prevailing hierarchies of knowledge - academic and non-academic,
theoretical and practical, abstract and concrete, for
example - it limits the possibility of understanding
how these particular educational hierarchies - the
separation of science from technology is but one - are
embedded in historically specific sets of social relations both in and of education[14].

Convention implies that things could be otherwise
(which is like equating the ordering of knowledge with
customs of eating or greetings) - that school subjects
like mathematics only persist through habit or custom,
or because that is how those in power define what is
conventional. What starts as a critique of the separation of knowledge from the knower, ends up in a contradiction by having to invoke the crudest of mechanistic
relations between knowledge and social position, which
in effect explains nothing, and not surprisingly offers
no strategies for change.

A theory that can provide for possibilities of change
in education does not emerge either from the dominant
view of 'curriculum as fact' or from a critique of such
a view expressed in the idea of curriculum as practice.
The first, by starting from a view of knowledge abstracted from men in history and from the teachers and
pupils to whom it is addressed, denies them possibilities except within its framework and definitions. The
second, in its concern to recognize teachers and pupils
as conscious agents of change, as theorists in their own
right, and to emphasize the human possibilities in
all situations, has also become abstracted from the
constraints of teachers' lived experience. Possibilities may be recognized in theory, but their practical
implementation is experienced as something quite remote.
A theoretical critique of the necessity of hierarchies
of knowledge and ability may be exciting in a seminar,
but is not any good to those who experience such necess-
ities as real in practice. The problem then is not to
deny or accept these hierarchies as necessary, but to
try and reformulate them as not in the order of things
but as the outcomes of the collective actions of men -
and thus understandable and potentially changeable.
This takes me to the three directions in which I see a
critical theory which transcends the dichotomy of 'fact'
and practice will need to develop.

1. The prescription to start from teachers' and pupils'
   practice, the theories that they evolve in their day

to day practice, can itself remain mere theory. This
will be so without a practical change in the relations between those who are currently labelled
theorists and those about whom they theorize. This is
not an anti-theory argument, for this could lead to an
uncritical acceptance of any tradition and custom
currently found in school. It is a recognition that
the testing ground of a theory is not its conceptual
clarity nor its ability to predict outcomes (criteria
we have inherited from a narrow conception of philoso-
phizing and a dubious scientism), but how such ideas
are transformed into action in the practice of teachers and pupils that make up our schools.

. Educational practice is often experienced and thought
about as if it was either isolated or separate (see
Chapter 2.2). I would want to emphasize that
theories and innovations in education rarely challenge
existing hierarchies within schools let alone without,
and thus our own activity tends to create its own
sense of autonomy. However, if questions about our
assumptions about curriculum are to be more than just
questions, political problems will inevitably be
raised for teachers and anyone involved in education.
This suggests that prevailing notions about curricula,
though sustained by those in formal education, are not
sustained by them alone. A more adequate theory of
curriculum as practice would not restrict practice
to that of teachers, nor of teachers' practice to
their activities in the school and classroom. If the
educational experience of both teachers and pupils
is to become a realistic possibility of human liberation, then this is going to involve many others who
have no direct involvement with the school, and much
action by teachers and pupils that would not be seen
as either confined to school or, in conventional
terms, necessarily educational at all.

3. Both views of curriculum I have referred to tend to
obscure the political and economic character of education; which as I have argued sets limits on their
possibilities as a theory of change. They also have
in common with much educational writing, a lack of
any sense of history or of linking the present to the
past, a fault also of much of what passes for 'history
of education'. The nearest one gets is some kind of
inevitable tradition or evolution. One crucial way
of reformulating, and so potentially understanding
and transcending the limits within which we work, is
to see, as in Layton's example referred to earlier,
how such limits are not given or fixed, but produced

through the conflicting actions and interests of men
in history (Stead, 1974). The recent historical
studies of the origins of psychological testing, and
the way compulsory education was used to impose central control on grassroots popular education movements (Karier, 1972) are an important example. They
offer much more to a theory of the possibilities of
change in education than the static analyses of the
deschoolers and the critics of behavioural psychology.
Similarly, studies of Trades Councils and Local
School Boards at the turn of the century present a
very different picture of working-class parental
involvement when compared with the current Plowden-
type dogmas, and also, a very different strategy to
the well-intentioned paternalism of the E.P.A.
Projects (Lynch, 1974).

These suggestions are no more than tentative directions as to how limits can become transformed into
possibilities and possibilities made real in practice.
They do argue for making more explicit the political
character of education, and to argue for a shift of
responsibility to define education from colleges and
offices to classrooms and communities. In doing so, I
see this as recognizing that much of what we hope can
be realized in education will not take place in school,
and as part of an attempt to enable all involved in
education to learn about the world we live in, and that
it is our world to make.

NOTES

1. A discussion of the limits and possibilities of
community action is given by Dearlove (1974) and others
in the symposium Community Work One.

2. Also of course most sociology, psychology and so-
called curriculum 'theory'.

3. Some of the possibilities for theory of educational
change Maxine Greene develops in a more recent paper
(1974).

4. This distinction is developed from ideas worked out
with Geoff Whitty (Whitty and Young, 1975). Of course,
if treated as a kind of mechanistic dichotomy it can
become as misleading an oversimplification as Marx's
famous 'base' and 'superstructure' (Williams, 1973).

The intention of this paper is to suggest that a
critical theory needs to see 'fact' and 'practice' as
both theoretically and practically related.

5. The theoretical and practical importance of a critique of a commodity-view of knowledge for educational
change is pointed out in Whitty's paper in section one
Sociology and the problem of radical educational change.

6. I do not use the term 'production' in any narrow
'economistic' sense. Economic relations are as Ollman
(1972) argues, even for Marx, but one aspect, albeit a
critical one, of men's productive activity at any
particular time.

7. See Olive Banks' (1974) article in Forum and my
reply in the same journal (Young, 1975).

8. Two books which trace this idea of man as an active
sense-maker in what are in other ways, very diverse
philosophical traditions are Roche (1973) and
R. J. Bernstein (1971).

9. A recent example of a study which shows how the
assigning of a quality like academic ability to a child
can be viewed as the practical accomplishment of teachers is the work of Cicourel et al (1974).

10. Very different and potentially exciting possibilities for conceiving of teachers' ranking practices are
suggested by Hextall and Sarup in their paper in this
book.

11. This example taken from an unpublished paper by
Mr. B. J. Hine of Queen Elizabeth's Girls' School,
Barnet.

12. The clearest and most explicit formulation of
the distinction between critical and traditional theory
is to be found in Horkheimer (1972).

13. Bartholomew (1975) points out the necessity of seeing the problem of theory and practice as a problem of
the division of labour between theorists and practitioners.

14. This distinction is explored by Holly in his
paper in section two.

REFERENCES

BANKS, O. (1974) The 'new' sociology of education Forum
Autumn, 1974.

BARTHOLOMEW, J. C. (1975) Theory and practice: an as
yet unaddressed issue?   Education for Teaching May,
1975.

BERNSTEIN, R. J. (1971) Praxis and Action London:
Duckworth.

BLOOR, D. (1973) Wittgenstein and Mannheim on the
sociology of mathematics Studies in the History and
Philosophy of Science No. 4 1973.

CICOUREL, A. V. et al (1974) Language Use and School
Performance New York: Academic Press.

DEARLOVE, J. (1974) The control of change and the regulation of community action in D. Jones and M. Mayo (Eds)
Community Work 1 London: Routledge and Kegan Paul.

GREENE, M.   (1971) Curriculum and consciousness The
Record Vol. F3, No. 2.

GREENE, M.   (1974) Countering privatism Educational
Theory Vol. 24, No. 3.

HARDY, J. (1975) Ideology and Natural Science; Possib-
ilities for Science Educators?   Paper presented to
British Sociological Association - Sociology of Science
Study Group - February 1975.

HORKHEIMER, M. (1972) Critical Theory New York: Herder
and Herder.

KARIER, C. (1972) Testing for order and control in the
liberal corporate state Educational Theory 22, No. 2.

KEDDIE, N. (1971) 'Classroom knowledge' in M. F. D.
Yound (Ed) Knowledge and Control London: Collier-
Macmillan.

LAYTON, D. (1973) Science for the People London: Allen
and Unwin.

LYNCH, G. (1974) MA dissertation - University of London
Institute of Education.

OLLMAN, B. (1972) Alienation - Marx's concept of Man in Capitalist Society London: Cambridge University Press.

ROCHE, M. (1973) Phenomenology, Language and Social Science London: Routledge and Kegan Paul.

STEED, D. (1974) MA dissertation, University of London Institute of Education.

WHITTY, G. and YOUNG, M. F. D. (1975) Sociology and the Politics of School Knowledge unpublished paper.

WILLIAMS, R. (1973) Base and superstructure in Marxist cultural theory New Left Review 82.

YOUNG, M. F. D. (1975) Sociologists and the politics of comprehensive education Forum Summer.

3.2
The Politics of Education

Simon Frith and Paul Corrigan

INTRODUCTION

William Tyndale School will, without a doubt, become
a symbol for a variety of assertions about the state
of education in Britain in the mid-1970s. For us, the
situation there reflects very clearly the muddles in
the Left's educational theory and practice. Whatever
else a complicated dispute between working-class parents, radical teachers, Labour-appointed managers and
a Labour-controlled education authority may mean, it
certainly reveals the lack of any consensus on the
political Left as to what state education should be
about.

Such a consensus has never existed, but its lack is
especially serious now when there are a number of
reasons for believing that education is becoming an
increasingly important arena for political struggle.
After decades of expansion, education is having to bear
its burden of the cuts in national and local state
expenditure. The immediate response to cuts may be
united 'fight the cuts' campaigns, but their effect
will be divisions as different groups compete for state
resources, and demoralization for the losers. Everyone
is going to have to make decisions about priorities,
and if the Left is going to play an effective role in
the 'politics of economy' it must be clear about what
is valuable in education, and it must be organized to
achieve it. The educational arguments that will be
involved are likely, paradoxically, to be more intense
if the comprehensive school issue is finally solved by
legislation - future disputes are going to focus on
the practice (rather than organization) of secondary
schooling, and, again, the Left must be organized
theoretically and politically to win these disputes.

The Right is already mobilized. The Black Paper may
originally have been a response to what was seen as the

unopposed forward push of progressive education, but
the 'Black Paper' ideologues are now taking the political initiative. This is most clearly seen in the end-
ing of the moderate Tory tradition of education,
symbolized by Sir Edward Boyle. The new spokesmen,
Norman St. John Stevas and Rhodes Boyson, provide
political muscle and legitimation for an aggressive
Right wing educational ideology, and the Left should
not underestimate the Right's power[1]. Ten years ago,
for example, the 'voucher scheme' could be laughed at
as an eccentric idea, today educational authorities are
discussing how it might be implemented.

In the next few years there are likely to be an
increasing number of incidents in which children, teachers, parents and politicians find themselves engaged
in conflicts which have no clear solutions. The Right
will be on hand to provide them, and it is vitally
important that the Left understands the politics of
State education and is organized to intervene in it.
The point of this paper is to contribute to such an
understanding. Our approach is explicitly Marxist but
we are not attempting to suggest the 'correct line' for
future practice. We want to open a discussion. Its
closure will only be possible when all people involved
in education - parents, teachers and children - have
taken part, and when the politics of education have
become an integral part of the overall political struggle for a socialist society.

I

Critical educational theorists of all types (from
Althusser to Illich) are agreed that state education is
one of the most important (if not the most important)
institutions by which the bourgeoisie establish and
maintain their hegemony and reproduce the conditions of
capitalist production. Althusser (1971), for example,
in emphasizing education's ideological functions, concludes that education is the key 'Ideological State
Apparatus' for capitalism, as the church was for
feudalism, and Joel Spring (1972)cites Ivan Illich to
make the same point: 'As Ivan Illich has suggested,
the modern school is the new Church, and like the
Church of the Middle Ages is pervasive and dominating'.
There may be many different accounts of the nature of
state education's function (ideological? technological?
political?), but there is general agreement that State
schooling is essential for the reproduction of capitalism. In so stressing the significance of education,

these theorists are doing no more than trying to make
sense of obvious facts of capitalist life: in all
capitalist societies (if at different speeds) the state
has taken over from 'private' institutions (bourgeois
and proletarian, secular and religious) the responsibility for education;   in all capitalist societies the
proportion of the state's resources invested in education has steadily grown (until in Britain, for example,
education now commands a bigger proportion of the
state's resources than any other state activity, including defence). The importance of education for capitalism is clearly revealed by the state's action in taking
control of educational institutions and expanding them;
the question for Marxist theory is why. We can take as
given that education does fulfil a basic function for
capitalism, the task is to understand this function.

But there is a further task for Marxists: to relate
this theoretical understanding to day-to-day educational practice. In England there are significant
divergences between the theory of education developed
by Marxist intellectuals, and the theory of education
that underlies the practice of Left (including Marxist)
educational activists. This is not just a theoretical
problem but also an organizational one;   it reflects
the lack of political solidarity between educational
thinkers and practitioners. The Marxist theorists
whose work has been most influential intellectually in
the last few years, Gramsci and Althusser, both wrote
as Communist Party members, but in reaching England
their theories have been abstracted from their original
political contexts;   they have not been reworked in the
context of English political practice.

Historically, the organized British working-class has
been at the forefront of the struggle for state education - ever since the Knowledge Chartists argued that
education could be an important counter to the raw
exploitation of working-class children by an unre-
strained labour market[2]. The Labour Party, the Trade
Union Movement, the Communist Party have all regarded
State education as a weapon to be used by the working-
class against exploitation - as long as the necessary
resources can be squeezed out of the state, as long as
education is organized to ensure equality of opportunity. It can be argued that the 'Left', as theorists
and ideologues and political activists, has set the
pace in the history of British education. None of the
major changes - compulsory schooling, secondary education for all, the expansion of higher education,
comprehensive schools, the raising of the school leaving

age to sixteen - can be adequately explained without
reference to the demands of the organized (and even, on
occasion, unorganized) working-class[3]. It can be argued, in short, that the history of British education
is the history of a reluctant bourgeoisie slowly
yielding to socialist and working-class demands. This
argument obviously raises questions about the theory of
State education as an instrument of bourgeois hegemony.

We can best illustrate this point by citing the
Coventry Trade Council's recent report on education in
Coventry[4]. Their 'central demand is for a substantial
increase in the total expenditure per pupil', which
would enable a variety of improvements in the quality
of existing education (better equipment and buildings,
more teachers, smaller class sizes, etc.) and allow the
expansion of state education - to cover nursery schools
and 'compulsory day release for all sixteen to nineteen
year olds' ('to widen educational opportunity and choice
for people of all ages'). At no point are questions
raised about the content or control of these improved
facilities. This document is interesting because of
the composition of the Coventry Trades Council. It is
an organization of trade unionists which also brings
together representatives of the whole range of Left
political groups in Coventry, Marxist and non-Marxist.
Its ideology cannot simply be classified as 'social
democratic' - many of the participants in the discussion
that led to the educational document regard themselves
as revolutionaries and argued from a Marxist position.

II

If 'pro-State education' arguments do not only
reflect the politics of the Labour Party, so 'anti-
state education' arguments have emerged from a variety
of groups and practices.

Libertarianism The libertarian critique of state
education (by libertarian we mean a critique based on
the analysis of education's repressive effects on the
individual) has developed during the last ten years in
a variety of situations. The student movement of the
late 1960s had a significant libertarian element (the
'counter culture'); among teachers and educationalists
'radical' education has often meant the Free School
movement and Summerhillian principles of liberation;
the 'new' sociology of education is based on an account
of the autonomy of the working-class pupil and their
repression by the classroom situation[5]. Libertarians

in all these spheres are engaged in a genuine attempt
to change educational institutions; the problem is to
decide how their struggles relate to the politics of
class struggle. It is noticeable that opposition to
the libertarian approach (at least in Britain) has come
not just from bourgeois authorities but also from the
'Old Left' (so that, for example, the Communist Party
is still engaged in heated debate about the significance, if any, of the counter-culture); the National
Union of Teachers has been the most vociferous critic
of Free and Deschooling, even withdrawing its support
from the National Council of Civil Liberties in the
face of the latter's support of 'children's rights';
and the most solid criticism of the 'new' sociology has
come from academics like Brian Simon, a communist, and
the leading advocate of comprehensive schools for the
last thirty years)[6]. In general terms, the 'Old Left'
argues that the individualism of the libertarian
approach makes it positively inimical to the needs of
the working-class, anti-socialist, and akin to the
Right wing, laissez-faire approach of the 'educational
voucher' Tories[7].

The Student Movement Some of the above issues were
debated in the late 1960s when the student movement
seemed to be a lasting political force but as the movement lost its significance, so this debate lost its
impetus. There has not yet been a full Marxist analysis
of what happened in the 1960s and why. There is a
generation of activists which got most of its initial
political education in those student struggles, but
there is little agreement about what lessons were
actually learned.

Radical Teachers A large number of radical students
remained within the education system as school, college
and university teachers. This choice of career has
rarely been a positive political one made with a clear
notion of the political possibilities and problems
involved. Rather, having become teachers for a variety
of individual reasons, radicals have had to 'politicize'
their role in the ad hoc context of immediate issues.
The result has been a variety of activities of which
the most organized have been in the area of trade
unionism. The National Union of Teachers is affiliated
to the TUC and has taken an increasingly militant
stance on wage demands and wage policy in the last ten
years. Left wing teachers are organized within the
NUT, both in the Trotskyist Rank and File group, and
in a looser Broad Left. But such 'economistic' politics have, for the most part, remained separate from the

other aspects of teaching that are problematic - in the areas of content and control. Partly, this is because such problems are experienced individually, with relationship to particular schools and departments and policies (hence the appeal of libertarianism even to Marxist teachers), but we can illustrate the difficulties involved by reference to a general issue, syllabus reform.

Most Left groups in education are suspicious of proposals for syllabus reform that emerge from the educational establishment. The most recent issue for debate has been 'relevant education', the notion, given an early airing in the Newsom Report (1963) and its most explicit content in some CSE mode 3 courses, that working-class children should be given an education that is deliberately relevant to their present and future situation as working-class children. For some Left teachers this means a legitimation of a new sort of second class education, one that re-establishes the old secondary modern/grammar school distinctions within the comprehensive schools, and is designed to fit working-class children for their future subordinate position in society[8]. For other Left teachers, 'relevant' education opens a space in the orthodox syllabus in which working-class children can be given a politically relevant education, one which can fit them for their future as a potentially dominant class[9]. Both groups face difficulties. The former, in rejecting syllabus change, appear to be in favour of orthodox practices and so sacrifice their radical credibility; the latter, in trying explicitly to politicize education confront the power of the establishment and rarely have the political organization or support to withstand it. The overall result is that teachers, from both positions, become demoralized and discredited and divided against each other - hence, for example, the teachers at William Tyndale School and their relationship to their local NUT branch.

Pupils There's an increasing number (or at least an increasingly noticed number) of working-class children who are responding to their schooling with apathy, vandalism, indiscipline and truancy. There is no doubt that this is seen as a problem by state authorities (we could cite numerous reports and speeches concerned with 'the collapse of authority in the school', with the 'recalcitrant pupil'), but it is equally a problem for socialists - what is the political meaning of this 'resistance'? Can classroom struggle contribute to class struggle? This is precisely the problem of the

(Communist Party-organized) National Union of School
Students. The NUSS organize round a platform which
combines an 'Old Left' line (increase the State's
resources of education, smaller class sizes, more money
for teachers, etc.), with some aspects of libertarianism
(give the pupil more freedom at school, abolish uniforms
and corporal punishment, etc.), but they have found it
difficult to attract support from school 'failures'.
Their members have a commitment to education which
makes the NUSS a useful organization; the children
who smash windows and smoke in the bogs haven't. This
does not make the latter correct, class-conscious or
revolutionary, but it does mean that the NUSS has got
to work out how to recruit them. Without the 'failures'
the union is not even creating union consciousness -
these stroppy pupils leave school untouched by any
organized form of politics, and the NUSS is left in an
elitist position.

III

The confusions that we have been describing with
reference to a number of contemporary issues have a
long history. In the mid-nineteenth century, before
State education was established in Britain, Thomas
Hodgskin argued that:

It would be better for men to be deprived of education than to receive their education from their
masters; for education, in that sense, is no better
than the training of cattle that are broken to the
yoke[10].

Twenty years after state education was introduced, Karl
Marx commented ironically on similar statements by
workers (and in the light of some statements by radicals
in the 1970s it is important to stress the heavy
irony):

It is better that working men and working women
should not be able to read and write or do sums than
that they should receive education from a teacher
in a school run by the state. It is far better that
ignorance should debase the working classes than
that eternal principles should be violated ...[11]

The difficulty of the politics of education is summed
up then: state education is a good thing as a source
of the skills necessary for the working-class to resist
the brutalizing effects of the market; state education

is a bad thing as an instrument of bourgeois domination.
It is our argument that these contradictions reflect
the contradictions within capitalism itself. It is not
surprising that the politics of education are, in their
daily practice, confused. In the long run, the contradictions will only be solved by the transformation of
capitalist relations in general, but the immediate
problem of educational politics is a tactical one: how
can educational struggle become a part of the struggle
for socialism. The answer to this question must rest
on a clear understanding of the functions of education
for capitalism.

The economic functions of education - the reproduction
of a labour force

This function has two aspects: (a) to provide for
capitalism a labour force with the necessary skills
and values to be 'good workers'. Initially, education
meant giving workers a rational work discipline and
the elementary skills of literacy, but the technological
dynamism of capitalism has meant that education has
continuously had to adapt to new needs (this is the
argument of technological determinism[12]) - secondary
and higher education have been developed to teach more
advanced skills (whether specific knowledge or simply
the general ability to learn and adapt). With these
new skills have gone new values (e.g. with respect to
mobility, careers, advancement, change, etc.); and
(b) to provide for capitalism a structured, differentiated, labour force. State education has been used to
ensure that the supply of labour matches the demand in
terms of a distribution of skills; the job structure
has been supported by a qualification structure (hence
the importance of the mechanisms of selection).

This analysis underlies what we have called the 'Old
Left' theory of education. State education is seen as
the necessary source of skills and qualifications for
working-class children (there are no alternative
institutions). The Left's goal has been to use this
resource for the benefit of its children while trying
both to improve the chances of selection within it
(through the various means of equalizing opportunity),
and to minimize the impact of bourgeois values (for
example by opposing single sex schools, streaming and
anything which leads to premature 'failure'). The
problems of this approach to education from a socialist
point of view are obvious: the notion of 'equality of
opportunity' rests on a basic premise of the bourgeois
ideology of education - that an individual can use

educational qualifications to 'escape' from the working-
class - and this conception of education as competition
contradicts any attempts a school might make to counter
bourgeois values, and fails to confront the problem of
what the mass of working-class children are being educated for. In short, the 'Old Left' attempted to
separate skills from values; their politics rested on
an inadequate analysis of the ideology of state education.

The ideological functions of education - the
reproduction of the relations of production

   The argument here is that education's function is to
reproduce the labour force in its relationship to a
capitalist class; that is a labour force with ideas
and values and practices which are consistent with, and
in acceptance of, existing power relations. This involves values concerning society and not just concerning work. In British schools, what is involved are the
principles around which schools are organized -
authority and hierarchy, uniform, discipline, assembly,
games, etc.

   This argument raises a number of points for discussion: (a) For many working-class children the ideological aspects of education are what schooling means and
what are resisted through truancy, etc. (such 'anti-
school' children will often complain that school is
useless because it doesn't teach them anything, only
bosses them around)[13]. (b) These aspects of education
are also exactly what the libertarian critiques of
education are about[14]. The problem with these critiques is that they interpret ideological domination
not as a class relation but as a classroom relation, as
something individual and accidental (i.e. alterable by
good will). This criticism could also be made of the
'new' sociology, which tends to blame middle-class teachers for working-class educational experience, and to
treat the 'hidden curriculum' as if it were somehow un-
intentional[15]; (c) It is worth stressing that the key
organizing principle of state schools is selection
(grading, streaming, examining), and this process is
the key to education's ideological effect (as well as
to its economic function) of individualizing what
happens[16]; (d) The problem of this approach is that
(like other functionalisms) it tends to be static (at
least the technological determinists are concerned with
the dynamism of capitalism), and to assume a lack of
conflict. Althusser, for example, sometimes gives the
impression that education fills an otherwise gaping

hole in working-class experience. But the working-class
has experiences outside education which have an independent effect on the reproduction of class values.
State education is an intervention[17]; it meets
opposition and doesn't always work. The problem is
that this opposition is rarely organized or consciously
political; (e) Ideological institutions are anyway not
'pure' - there are remnants of previous social values
(cf universities, especially), and education has the
basic problem of having to provide an ideology which
can in itself be a source of changing values as new
conditions demand[18].

Why State education?

    We conclude from the previous arguments that educa-
tion in a capitalist society has to fulfil both functions (economic and ideological), and it's precisely
because these functions must be combined in order to
reproduce the conditions of capitalism that the state
has to take charge. This follows from Marx's theory of
the state as the means by which the bourgeoisie protect
their long-term interests (rather than immediate needs)
as a class (and not just as competitive profit makers).
There are several reasons, then, why the state must
take charge (individual, 'private' capitalists could
not be so efficient at producing a planned labour
market, at creating a national qualification system,
even if they were convinced that their 'private' interests made the expense necessary), but we want to
emphasize two points: (a) the skills that are needed
in the reproduction of the labour force are also the
skills necessary for the creation of an organized
working-class (which is the point of the 'Old Left'
argument). The means and relations of production are
contradictory and it is therefore in the bourgeois'
long-term interest to counter and control the use of
these skills - hence the ideological functions of
education. (Historical note: in England schools developed first as ideological institutions, as means
by which individual bourgeois - through the Church -
sought to control the new industrial work force morally;
job skills and values were developed on the job. It
was only when the needed skills began to have political
implications and require national organization that the
State first took over education and then began to
integrate it into the labour training process); and
(b) private ideological education (as by the Church,
for example) tends to be conservative and rigid;
ideology must move in response to the dynamic needs of

capitalism; only the state can ensure this[19].

The form which state education must adopt (i.e. the
types of institution involved - organized around selection) is determined by its functions, and in establishing its hegemony through this form the bourgeoisie
have to impose a definition of education - of what is
involved in educating (having certain skills and
qualifications - one of the earliest tasks for the
State in English education was establishing what was
meant by being a 'qualified teacher'), and of what is
involved in being educated (having the right bits of
paper, examination passes, degree, etc.). In imposing
these definitions, the bourgeoisie have to destroy
alternative educational forms and institutions; such
imposition needs the state because only the state has
the necessary power (cf, the 1870 and subsequent
Education Acts in Britain, legally compulsory schooling,
etc.). The effect of the state's monopoly of educational resources is that in practical terms even
proletarian education (in the sense of giving people
skills and knowledge that they don't otherwise have,
but in the context of working-class values) is only
available in state institutions. There have been
occasional attempts to create alternative, proletarian
means of education [20] but they have failed and, as we
suggested in the first section of this paper, organized
working-class groups have usually sought to work through
the state rather than against or even parallel to it.
But if education is, as we have argued, a form of class
power, then the political problem is not how to use it,
or even how to resist it (the libertarians' problem),
but how to wrest it away. And this is where the tactical questions reappear. Does the politics of education mean gaining control of existing institutions
(pupil power? parent power? teacher power?). Or does
it mean creating independent, socialist institutions?
These questions can't be answered without reference to
the general strategy of a political organization seeking
state power.

IV

Behind many of the educational differences that we
discussed in section II lies a basic disagreement about
the correct place of education in working-class politics. On the one hand is the assertion that the fight
for state power must take precedence over the fight
for educational change, on the other hand is the belief
that educational change is a necessary precondition for

a truly socialist politics. The first argument derives
from the analysis of education as a state apparatus:
in a capitalist society the state is a capitalist state,
state institutions are capitalist institutions; there
is therefore no way that capitalist state education can
operate in favour of the working-class; 'reform' is
a dangerous delusion, what is necessary is the smashing
of the educational machine and its ideologies; the
precondition for such destruction is control of the
state - it is to that that our energies should be
directed. But the conclusion of this argument, that
education can be removed from the immediate political
agenda, is false. It is precisely because state education is capitalist education that it is a setting for
contradictions and class struggle, and it is precisely
because class struggle continues in education (as in
every other capitalist institution) that we go on
believing in a socialist future. Educational conflicts
may be fought without political consciousness but they
do, nonetheless, reflect aspects of working-class
politics. (Schools, for example, are crucial institutions for the development of 'trade union consciousness' - the collective techniques pupils learn to deal
with teachers and school situations are equally useful
in the subsequent situation of bosses and work). The
correct socialist position is to politicize these
struggles (with theory and organization) not to ignore
them.

The second argument is that of the 'reformist'
approach to education, and our critique of this was
implicit in our comments on the English Left's traditional educational practice. The point is simply that
just as Marxist theorists are in danger of keeping
education out of their political practice, so reformists
have made the mistake of keeping politics out of their
educational practice. The error of both approaches is
the separation of education and politics. 'The fight
for state power' and 'educational change' are not
mutually exclusive acts, the one to be preceded or
followed by the other; they are mutually necessary
aspects of the same political process. The problem
for a socialist party (the organizational link between
educational and other struggles) is to make all class
struggle political. Our slogans should be: 'Bring
Politics into the Classroom!' 'Bring the Classroom
into Politics!'

These slogans are easy to write (or chant) but difficult to act on. By politics we mean organized politics and we mean organized working-class politics. To

be effective, socialist parents and teachers and children must work with and through and in organized
socialist parties. That is what the politics of education means both practically (the only source of the
power necessary to change education is the political
muscle of the working-class), and theoretically (it is
only through constant discussion of the general strategies of socialism that we can develop a specific
educational policy). Bringing politics into education
in this concrete, organized, sense will arouse not just
the opposition of anti-socialist forces, but also doubts
among socialist parties themselves. There has always
been a strange reluctance on the Left in Britain (none
such on the Right) to get stuck into the details of
what schooling should involve. The idea that children
are 'innocent' and should not be 'corrupted' or
'prejudiced' by an explicitly political education dies
hard - despite our knowledge of the implicit anti-
socialist political effects of current state education.
Our final two points relate to this issue.

First, with regard to the struggles within state
schools. Political activists, in placing education in
the wider context of political struggle, must focus on
the questions of education content and control. The
point is this: the State does monopolize educational
resources, and these resources must (as Marx pointed
out) be used by the working-class. If, then, schools
are to be used in the context of political struggle,
an explicit link has to be made between education and
the future - the content of education has to be given
socialist (and not just capitalist) relevance (it is
not enough simply to press for an expansion of educational resources or to call for 'relevant' education -
relevant for the working-class within capitalism). It
is necessary to make education relevant in a new way
and for an alternative future (and this would help
clarify the arguments that socialists must make against
truancy and vandalism). Such an open attempt to subvert bourgeois schools will make central the question
of control of educational power - a socialist party
must use what power it can get, both through the
'democratization' of the school internally (pupil and
teacher power), and through an assault on educational
administrators (parent and community power, the
reassertion of the political direction of bureaucrats).
We shouldn't underestimate the difficulties of the
struggle here. For example, a prior propaganda task
is to attack the deeply held notion, particularly among
working-class parents, that the only point of schooling
is job qualifications. Nor should we forget the

permanent dangers of bourgeois co-option (cf the present lip service paid to concepts like 'pupil power' and
'community schools'). One important task for a socialist party is to ensure that educational means are never
isolated from political ends[21].

Secondly, there is the problem of creating an alternative education, outside the state system. Again,
the point of such alternatives must be political.
There is no point in setting up echoes of state schools,
more efficient or more sympathetic but with the same
ultimate purposes (cf Free Schools) - the purpose of
alternative socialist education must be revolutionary,
revolutionary both in challenging bourgeois norms and
in creating new, socialist, institutions. There are
some lessons to be learned here from the deschoolers
(and from educational history): the form of bourgeois
schooling is a bourgeois form, socialist education must
break down the differentiations of age and sex and
ability, must integrate work and culture and action (in
the present situation such alternatives would seem more
appropriate for adult education - children will continue
to be dependent on the state). Too many 'progressive'
educational ideas are progressive only by reference to
bourgeois values; education can only be progressive
when we know where we're progressing to, when it is, in
a revolutionary sense, political. We must take educational debates out of their exclusively educational
contexts (where the bourgeoisie still set the limits
of discussion), and place them in the context of organized socialist politics. It is only there that a truly
radical educational practice can be constructed.

NOTES

1. See also the new offensive in higher education:
Caroline Cox et al The Rape of Reason and Paul Johnson's
recent series on Universities in The Times Higher
Educational Supplement.

2. For the best history of British education from this
perspective see Brian Simon Studies in the History of
Education (3 volumes); and D. Rubinstein and B. Simon
The Evolution of the Comprehensive School, 1926-72.

3. cf Simon op cit and M. Parkinson The Labour Party
and the Organization of Secondary Education.

4. We chose this example as it was immediately to hand

(the document was circulated in November, 1974), and its very availability makes it a good example of the sorts of demands that the Left is actually making.

5. By the 'new' sociology we mean the approach represented in M. F. D. Young (Ed) Knowledge and Control which, through its use in Open University education courses, has become very influential in teacher training colleges.

6. For the Communist Party debate on youth and counter-cultures see the most recent issues of Marxism Today. For the critique of the 'new' sociology, see Brian Simon and others in recent issues of Forum for the Discussion or New Trends in Education.

7. See Guy Neave 'The "Free Schoolers"' (in D. Holly (Ed) Education of Domination).

8. cf The recent Communist Party resolution in the 34th Congress.

9. cf The work of Chris Searle. Note the response in the Times Educational Supplement.

10. Quoted in B. Simon Studies in the History of Education vol. 1, p.215.

11. See K. Marx 'Political Indifferentism' (1873).

12. See for example Gero Lenhardt's position paper for Kapitalistate.

13. See Paul Corrigan Smash Street Kids.

14. See for example, the work of John Holt or Paul Goodman.

15. See Joan Simon's piece on the 'new' sociology in Forum November 1974.

16. A good illustration of how the process works is C. Lacey Hightown Grammar.

17. See N. Poulantzas Political Power and Social Classes.

18. cf S. Bowles and H. Gintis 'The Origins of Mass Public Education' and 'Corporate Capital and Progressive Education' (chapters in their forthcoming Nightmares and Visions).

19. Ibid.

20. For examples see J. F. C. Harrison Learning and Living, 1790-1960; F. Reid 'Socialist Sunday Schools in Britain, 1892-1939' International Review of Social History, 1966.

21. cf The School of Barbiana Letter to a Teacher.

REFERENCES

ALTHUSSER, L. (1971) 'Ideology and Ideological State Apparatuses' in L. Althusser (Translation B. Brewster) Lenin and Philosophy and Other Essays London: New Left Books.

CORRIGAN, P. (forthcoming) Smash Street Kids London: Macmillan.

COX, C. et al (1975) The Rape of Reason London: Churchill Press.

LACEY, C. (1970) Hightown Grammar Manchester: Manchester University Press.

NEAVE, G. (1974) The 'Free Schoolers' in D. Holly (Ed) Education or Domination? London: Arrow

PARKINSON, M. (1970) The Labour Party and the Organization of Secondary Education London: Routledge & Kegan Paul.

POULANTZAS, N. (1973) Political Power and Social Classes London: New Left Books.

RUBINSTEIN, D. and SIMON, B. (1969) The Evolution of the Comprehensive School 1926-72 London: Routledge and Kegan Paul.

SIMON, B.(1960-74)Studies in the History of Education Vols. I-III London: Lawrence and Wishart.

SPRING, J. (1972) Education and the Rise of the Corporate State Boston: Beacon Press.

YOUNG, M. F. D. (Ed) (1971) Knowledge and Control London: Collier-Macmillan.

4.0
Postscript

Michael Young and Geoff Whitty

One of the major arguments of this book has been
that any realistic strategy for radical educational
change would involve linking the 'politics of the
classroom' to the 'politics of the class struggle'.
Even since the paper by Frith and Corrigan was written
in January, 1976, the interdependence of the crisis in
education and the crisis in capitalism has been brought
into still sharper focus. In particular, the role of
the state in education and the ideological character of
schooling have become more clearly apparent. Teachers
have been made dramatically aware that it is not just
reactionary or incompetent heads, or the conservatism
of examination boards, which constrain their activities,
but the material effects of decisions about priorities
for expenditure in a capitalist society in crisis. At
the same time, the D.E.S. 'Yellow Paper' and the Prime
Minister's Ruskin College speech have heralded a
greater degree of direct state involvement in controlling the content of the curriculum. Thus, while this
book has been in preparation, many of the issues discussed here have emerged into the arena of public
debate and are no longer the restricted concern of
academic educational theorists. Since, during the same
period, the terms of both educational and political
debate have shifted markedly to the Right, the theoretical and practical tasks facing the Left have become
all the more urgent.

The Prime Minister's speech and its subsequent articulation by Shirley Williams seem to contradict one
of our criticisms of traditional Labour policy on education - that it neglected content. It is, of course,
ironical (though probably predictable) that, when leading Labour Party politicians do attempt to intervene
directly in what have conventionally been regarded as
'professional matters', their views seem barely distinguishable from those of the Conservative Right. Two
themes seem to underlie their pronouncements (couched,

of course, in terms of 'opening up the great debate').
First, the emphasis is on greater control over content
and methods - expressed through the possibility of a
'common' national curriculum, regular monitoring of
standards, and giving increased powers to the Inspectorate. The second and related theme (for this is what
gives control its purpose) is the importance of respon-
siveness to the 'needs of industry'. This is expressed
variously in an emphasis on 'vocational preparation', an
increase in the funding of courses sponsored via the
Training Services Agency, a greater technological emphasis in school science, and the priority placed upon
instilling in pupils the importance of industry to our
'national survival'. This whole emphasis is also reflected in the recent decision to fund a joint Schools
Council/CBI/TUC project on industry which, in many of
its underlying assumptions, seems to differ little from
other projects financed directly by the CBI or by industrial corporations such as IBM and Rio Tinto Zinc.
The crucial point is that all these proposals accept the
existing relations of production in industry and the
needs they express - particularly for sophisticated
technologically-minded managers with a background in
production engineering, competent technical personnel,
and a large number of people willing to remain part of
the 'reserve army' of unemployed or accept that the
most they can expect is the tedium of routine jobs
which demand virtually no skill at all.

In one sense, therefore, the intimate connection
between the profitability and survival of British capitalism and the content and control of our education
system has never been clearer. Similarly, the role of
a reformist Labour government in managing British
capitalism in a period of crisis has become as evident
in the field of education as it is in the fields of
wages policy and industrial investment. Nevertheless,
the current debate also illustrates the limitations of
a view of education as in any straightforward sense
'reproducing the relations of production'. Thus, while,
as Bowles and Gintis argue, the prevailing nature of
education is largely determined by the nature of capitalist production, it is also being depicted as not
sufficiently responsive to capital's needs, either in
providing an appropriately skilled labour force or in
adequately reproducing the relations of production. As
increasing emphasis is placed on how the state, and in
particular state education, can 'assist in our economic
recovery', it becomes even more vital to analyse the
role of education in serving (or resisting) the needs
of capital, and its potential significance for any

socialist strategy for change.

On the Left we are now beginning to see the emergence
of that new critique of education for which Frith and
Corrigan were calling, as well as the beginning of a new
politics of educational practice. This in no sense
plays down the importance of struggles on more narrowly
economistic issues such as the campaigns against the
cuts, but recognizes that those campaigns can only be
part of the much wider struggle to transform capitalism,
which, though its basis is economic, is also sustained
(and challenged) by the social relations of classroom
and school. This new awareness and re-alignment on the
Left was evident, for example, at a Radical Education
Conference in November, 1976, where speaker after
speaker spoke of the importance of not separating conventional trade union issues from ideological issues.
Likewise it was expressed in the decision of the
Socialist Teachers' Alliance to break with the narrow
economism which has come to dominate the Rank and File
Group within the NUT.

In our introduction we pointed out that the limitations of traditional Left analyses of education were not
restricted to the Labour Party, but had also characterized dominant strands of thinking within the British
Communist Party. In particular, we referred to the
writings of Maurice Levitas and the much publicized
speeches of Max Morris, a leading member of the NUT
executive. In recently announcing his resignation from
the party after forty years as a member, Morris is
reported as having said that 'there were now considerable differences between his views and those of the
party on problems facing the teaching profession today
and the role of the schools' (The Times Educational
Supplement 19th November 1976). We can only surmise
that there are now those within the Communist Party who
have begun to raise questions about the ideological
character of education in this country, which for Morris
anyway had previously been restricted to those he refers
to as 'trendy sociologists' and the 'ultra Left'.

It may therefore be suggested that although recent
events have on the surface been almost wholly regressive
for socialists in education, they have also served to
hasten the end of the deeply-embedded notion that education can be kept out of politics and politics kept out
of education. The William Tyndale Affair, the Tameside
Judgment, the education cuts and government's attempts
to control assessment and curriculum content have high-
lighted the inescapably political nature of all aspects
of educational practice. We can perhaps take hope that

a more adequate analysis of the relations between
society, state and schooling will emerge from this
situation and that socialists working within education
and elsewhere will begin to develop more realistic
strategies for change.

Contributors

GEOFF WHITTY lectures in Education at the University of Bath.

JOHN AHIER is Senior Lecturer in Education at Homerton College, Cambridge.

MICHAEL ERBEN is Senior Lecturer in Sociology at Garnett College, London.

DENIS GLEESON is Lecturer in the Sociology of Education at the University of Keele.

MICHAEL APPLE is Associate Professor in Curriculum and Instruction at the University of Wisconsin - Madison.

ANDRE GORZ is a journalist and has written widely on Marxist theory.

IAN HEXTALL lectures in Education at Goldsmiths' College, London.

MADAN SARUP lectures in Education at Goldsmiths' College, London.

DOUGLAS HOLLY lectures in Education at the University of Leicester.

SAMUEL BOWLES is Professor of Economics at the University of Massachusetts.

HERBERT GINTIS is Associate Professor of Economics at the University of Massachusetts.

MICHAEL YOUNG is Senior Lecturer in the Sociology of Education at London University Institute of Education.

SIMON FRITH   lectures in Sociology at the University
of Warwick.

PAUL CORRIGAN   lectures in Sociology at the University
of Warwick.

INDEX
Author Index